Ricoeur and Lacan

Continuum Studies in Continental Philosophy Series Editor: James Fieser
University of Tennessee at Martin

Deconstruction and Democracy, Alex Thomson
Deleuze and Guattari's Philosophy of History, Jay Lampart
Deleuze and the Meaning of Life, Claire Colebrook
Derrida and Disinterest, Sean Gaston
Husserl's Phenomenology, Kevin Hermberg
The New Heidegger, Miguel de Beistegui
Sartre's Ethics of Engagement, T. Storm Heter
Wittgenstein and Gadamer, Chris Lawn
Deleuze and the Unconscious, Christian Kerslake
Sartre's Phenomenology, David Reisman

Ricoeur and Lacan

Karl Simms

continuum

Continuum International Publishing Group
The Tower Building
11 York Road
London
SE1 7NX

80 Maiden Lane
Suite 704
New York
NY 10038

www.continuumbooks.com

British Library Cataloguing-in-Publication Data
A catalogue record for this book is available from the British Library

ISBN-10: HB: 0-8264-7796-8
ISBN-13: HB: 978-0-8264-7796-5

Library of Congress Cataloging-in-Publication Data
Simms, Karl.
Ricoeur and Lacan / by Karl Simms.
p. cm.
Includes bibliographical references and index.
ISBN-13: 978-0-8264-7796-5
ISBN-10: 0-8264-7796-8
1. Ricoeur, Paul. 2. Lacan, Jacques, 1901-1981. I. Title.

B2430.R554S57 2007
194–dc22

2006038869

Typeset by YHT Ltd, London
Printed and bound in Great Britain by Biddles Ltd, King's Lynn, Norfolk

Dedicated with love to

Miles Lucas Simms

Born at the same time as this book

Contents

Acknowledgements

This book was researched during a semester's study leave from the University of Liverpool. I am grateful to Philip Davis for facilitating this (he'll hate the word 'facilitate').

My thanks are due to my long-suffering editor at Continuum, Sarah Douglas, and to my long-suffering wife, Tracy Simms, both of whom have shown patience beyond the call of duty towards my delays in finishing the manuscript.

1

Introduction

A comparison between Ricoeur and Lacan might on the face of it lead one to expect a simple contrast. After all, it is hard to imagine two thinkers more different in terms of style or of general intellectual predisposition. This is reflected, for example, in their respective public personae. As a speaker, Ricoeur was prone to deliver what might be called an 'anti-performance', making little attempt to address the audience directly, and speaking in a quiet, unprojected voice in disregard of the size of the lecture hall. (Of course, this would have the effect of holding the audience's attention just as effectively as would a highly rhetoricised performance.) Lacan, meanwhile, was a hyperbolic performer, as reflected in the films he made for French television (broadcast in the UK by Channel 4 in 1989). There were the theatrical props (water jug, bent cigar), there was the hierarchical arrangement of the audience (the privileged inner circle of the 'seminar' and the outer circle of the general public), there were the slightly stage-managed audience interventions, and there was the Socratic arrangement of material into strophe and antistrophe, punctuated by dramatic pregnant pauses.[1]

These differing public personae were indicative of broader and deeper differences of personality. In one of her two biographies of Lacan, Elisabeth Roudinesco (1997: 376) reports that 'convinced that he was world famous, [Lacan] wanted to be allowed to make a private visit to the [New York] Metropolitan Opera House. "Tell them I'm Lacan", he bade his three bemused companions', and further, in conversation with the painter François Rouan, he once randomly remarked, 'I'm very famous, you know' (Roudinesco 1997: 381). Ricoeur, meanwhile, was seemingly content to be photographed in front of student graffiti reading 'Ricoeur vieux clown', chalked up during his ill-starred Nanterre days (Reagan 1996: 118–19). These differences in personality translated readily into the political sphere. During the *événements* of 1968 (or, more precisely, during their aftermath in 1969), Lacan revelled in being a hero of the revolution (whether the revolutionaries repaid the compliment by acknowledging him as such is another matter), a role which suited his outsider status, having being excluded from the International Psychoanalytic Association and later losing his seminar room at the Hôpital Saint Anne (cf. Lacan

1987b). Ricoeur, meanwhile, as *doyen* of Nanterre, tried to act as mediator between the political establishment and the students but was forced into an impossible position, caught between intractable far-left students (and faculty) and an out-of-control local police force, and within a political system whereby the power to hire and fire faculty lay with the minister for education, rather than with the *doyen.*[2]

As in life, so in his work: Ricoeur's philosophy, from beginning to end, always seeks to find a 'secret communion' between apparently opposing positions. In this his philosophy is more successful than his tenure at Nanterre, which was to lead (unjustly, in the view of most commentators and biographers) successively to illness, resignation, depression and voluntary exile. Closely allied to this philosophical negotiationism is Ricoeur's love of argument (in the philosophical sense), which leads him to admire Anglo-American philosophy and to quote it extensively in his later works, sometimes to the consternation of his French public. Again, this places Ricoeur in opposition to Lacan who, notwithstanding his fondness for alluding to the likes of Frege and Russell (often inaccurately), had a tendency to assert a position rather than argue a case. This was the source of another disquiet on the part of Ricoeur, not least because his son Jean-Paul was to become a psychiatrist influenced by Lacanian psychoanalysis:

> Paul waited patiently for his son to finish and then said that the problem is, anyone can say anything he wants. There is no careful argumentation, only invective and polemic. Paul contrasted this with the Anglo-American habits of careful philosophical argumentation, with its legalistic refutations, rejoinders, rebuttals, all focused on the philosophical claims themselves (Reagan 1996: 60–1).

The present book is caught in something of a double bind, since it also, to some extent, seeks to mediate between Ricoeur and Lacan, but by so doing is automatically placed on the side of Ricoeur. Moreover, it seeks to demonstrate the points of contact between Ricoeur and Lacan through argument rather than through mere assertion, and again this is a mode of discourse closer to Ricoeur's than it is to Lacan's. And who would attempt to replicate Lacan's style?

If, then, there is a default bias in favour of Ricoeur in the present work, nevertheless it is hoped that the points of similarity between Ricoeur and Lacan are demonstrated to be real, while the points of irreconcilability are not glossed over. The most striking point of intellectual contact between Ricoeur and Lacan is in their relation to the Cartesian *cogito.* In the 'Introduction' to his *Oneself as Another,* Ricoeur (1992: 4) remarks that

> the quarrel over the cogito, in which the "I" is by turns in a position of strength and of weakness, seems to me the best way to bring out the problematic of the self, under the condition that any subsequent investigations confirm the claim that I formulate here, namely that the hermeneutics of the self is placed at an equal distance from the apology of the cogito and from its overthrow.

This 'placing at an equal distance' between defence and apology for the *cogito* can be traced in Ricoeur's work as far back as his earliest writings on Husserl (which were in part composed during his internment in a German POW camp), and well before the development of Ricoeur's philosophy into a 'hermeneutics' towards the end of *The Symbolism of Evil.* In *Oneself as Another* it manifests itself as a critique of Descartes' *Meditations* and *Discourse on Method,* but this critique traces the path already forged by Husserl in his *Cartesian Meditations,* as Ricoeur tacitly acknowledges. Ricoeur had already trodden the path of a critique of the *cogito* in the essays collected in *Husserl: An Analysis of His Phenomenology* (especially 'Husserl: Fifth Cartesian Meditation'), where he writes that '"explication" . . . is held midway between a philosophy of construction and a philosophy of description' (Ricoeur 1967a: 140), which surely anticipates the hermeneutic project which is to follow. Moreover, in the earlier essay Ricoeur (1967a: 141) notes that 'the Husserlian cogito is not a truth to be followed by other truths in an "order of reasons"'; the 'Introduction' to *Oneself as Another* works out what happens in Descartes when such an order of reasons is followed. In short, following Gabriel Marcel and Karl Jaspers, who were to provide the subject matter for Ricoeur's earliest books, when it comes to the *cogito,* Ricoeur situates himself more on the side of the *I am* than of the *I think.*

Lacan, too, has a certain preoccupation with the Cartesian *cogito,* although in his case it is motivated by his interpretation of Freud's famous reworking of it at the end of 'The Dissection of the Psychical Personality' (Lecture 31 of the *New Introductory Lectures*), '*Wo Es war, soll Ich werden*'. This reworking, in its conception of the *Es* (dating back to Freud's essay *The Ego and the Id*), is somewhat indebted to Nietzsche, who, in *Beyond Good and Evil* (Nietzsche 1966: 23) and elsewhere, is dismissive of the 'immediate certainty' of the knowledge presented by the *cogito.* Lacan's attitude towards the *cogito* shares what Ricoeur calls the 'philosophy of suspicion' with regard to the *cogito* of Nietzsche and Freud: the *cogito,* he says in 'The Instance of the Letter in the Unconscious', 'limits me to being there in my being only insofar as I think that I am in my thought; to what extent I really think this concerns me alone and, if I say it, interests no-one' (Lacan 2006: 420). Lacan's solution to the problem of the limitation of the *cogito* is not merely to accept Freud's formula, *Wo Es war, soll Ich werden*, but to translate it radically: 'Where (it) was itself, it is my duty to come into being' (Lacan 2006: 347–8).

Another point of contact between Ricoeur and Lacan is in their respective attitudes to Freud. Lacan, of course, is consistent in his overall view of Freud: his entire career can be seen as an attempt to establish himself as the heir to Freud in France and, ultimately, the world, in contradistinction to the 'legitimate' reading of Freud promulgated by the seven analysts to whom Freud gave each a symbolic ring, designating them as heirs, shortly before his death. Ricoeur's view of Freud, meanwhile, develops and alters over time. In the 1950s, heavily influenced by the phenomenology of Husserl, he is predominantly hostile. In *The Voluntary and the Involuntary* (the first volume of his *Philosophy of the Will*, published in 1950 but containing ideas developed during the war), Ricoeur attacks Freud on two fronts: his realism of the unconscious, and his idealism of the unconscious (that Freud is held to be both realist and idealist demonstrates, also, how, for Ricoeur, Freud is led into philosophical contradiction). In addressing the realism of the Freudian unconscious (the notion that the unconscious is a something, and, moreover, a something that itself thinks), Ricoeur agrees with Lacan and with Freud himself, that this represents a 'Copernican revolution' in the conception of humanity: 'the centre of human being is displaced from *consciousness and freedom* as they give themselves to the unconscious and the absolute involuntary of which we are ignorant' (Ricoeur 1966: 385). The point of irreconcilable difference here between Ricoeur and Lacan is, however, that Ricoeur cannot accept this 'realism', and this remains the case even when Ricoeur becomes more sympathetic to Freud in the 1960s. For Ricoeur (1966: 386), 'the refusal to conceive of the unconscious as thinking is a foregone conclusion of freedom itself'; that (in Lacan's phrase) 'it thinks' flies in the face of what Ricoeur calls 'Cartesian generosity'. This generosity is nothing other than the intentionality that Ricoeur, following Husserl, perceives as being entailed by the *cogito*: any intentional assertion such as 'I believe', 'I wish', 'I know', etc., presupposes the 'I think', and reciprocally 'I think' entails all possible intentional modes. By 'idealism' of the unconscious, meanwhile, Ricoeur means the notion that the unconscious is hidden, or that it has a hidden meaning. Again following Husserl, for Ricoeur all thought is thought *of* something; a hidden thought could not be a thought of something, and so could not be a thought. Likewise with meaning: meaning is by definition 'transparent' in the sense of accessible: I may not understand what something means, but I can always work out a meaning based on the evidence presented before me: that evidence is not hidden. Moreover, when it comes to my 'ownmost' consciousness, I can always do this myself: I do not need the intercession of a psychoanalyst to provide a meaning that I am incapable of discovering for myself.

Ricoeur becomes more sympathetic towards Freudian psychoanalysis at about the time of the publication of *The Symbolism of Evil* (the second volume of the second part of *Philosophy of the Will*), a time when Ricoeur discovers hermeneutics and reorientates his phenomenological philosophy in a hermeneutic direction. This also roughly coincides with Ricoeur's first direct encounter with Lacan, at the Bonneval Colloquium organised by Lacan's old mentor Henri Ey. The Bonneval Colloquium is of historical interest regarding the development of Lacanianism, in that it marked the first theoretical split between Lacan and some of his students, namely Leclaire, Laplanche and Pontalis. For our purposes, though, we may agree with S. H. Clark (1990: 81), who writes that 'the subsequent fiercely contested polemics hinge on a single relatively minor point'. More importantly for our present purposes, Bonneval was also the occasion at which Ricoeur (1989: 99–120) presented his paper, 'Consciousness and the Unconscious'. The first part of this paper reprises the critique of the realism of the unconscious elaborated in *The Voluntary and the Involuntary*. But Ricoeur very soon moves the analysis in a hermeneutic direction, claiming that 'the unconscious is an object in the sense that it is "constituted" by the totality of hermeneutic procedures by which it is deciphered' (Ricoeur 1989: 107). The shift in Ricoeur's position is marked by his claim that the 'naïve' realism of the unconscious is not something which Freud himself is guilty of. The notion of the unconscious is relative rather than strictly speaking objective, in that 'it is only for someone other that I even *possess* an unconscious' (Ricoeur 1989: 107). This relativity is what rescues the realism of the Freudian unconscious from its naïve variant, but it does so at a price – we must renounce the claim that the unconscious itself thinks:

> Against this naïve realism we must continually emphasise that the unconscious does not think. Freud himself *never* makes the unconscious think, and in this respect the discovery of the term *Es* or id was a stroke of genius. Ucs is the id and nothing but the id. Freudian realism is a realism of the id in its ideational representations and not a naïve realism of unconscious meaning. By a strange reversal, naïve realism would end up by giving consciousness to the unconscious and would thus produce the monster of an idealism of unconscious consciousness. This fanciful idealism would never be anything more than an idealism of meaning as projected into a thinking *thing*. (Ricoeur 1989: 108)

That Lacan should publicly praise this paper is extraordinary, as is his using the occasion to befriend Ricoeur and invite him to attend his seminar, since, even as it advances over the position established in *The Voluntary and the Involuntary* and 'rehabilitates' Freud in terms of phenomenological hermeneutics, it places Ricoeur in diametric opposition to Lacan. That 'it thinks' is central to Lacanian theory; the lecture on 'The Freudian Thing' from 1955, in its claim that 'the thing speaks of itself' (and Lacan spends some two pages telling us what it says) is nothing other than a sustained projection of meaning into a thinking thing. Moreover, what is at stake is also a reading of Freud, a question of how Freud is to be interpreted. Ricoeur claims that Freud never makes the unconscious think, and yet Lacan claims to read Freud aright.

Meanwhile, Ricoeur continues in 'Consciousness and the Unconscious' by pursuing a 'dialectic' of the unconscious: 'consciousness is not a given, but a task', he says, and asks 'What is the meaning of the unconscious for a being whose task is consciousness?' (Ricoeur 1989: 108–9). Dismissing the Freudian claim to 'epigenesis', Ricoeur sees the dialectical task of the 'layman and philosopher' (as opposed to the psychoanalyst) as being one of escaping from childhood concerns into the realm of adulthood. In this respect, the master-slave relationship in Hegel 'is not at all a dialectic of consciousness' (Ricoeur 1989: 110), a claim that again puts Ricoeur at odds with Lacan, who in *The Four Fundamental Concepts of Psychoanalysis* presents the master-slave dialectic as precisely that. For Ricoeur (1989: 110), the master–slave dialectic is a dialectic of the birth of a self, 'the passage out of desire as desire for another into *Annerkennung* or *mutual recognition*', whereas Lacan's reading of Hegel is reversed: the mutual recognition of the master–slave dialectic is what originates desire as desire for another. But for Ricoeur, the dialectic of consciousness is nothing other than the dialectical relationship between phenomenology as one kind of hermeneutics, and psychoanalysis as another kind. Just as phenomenology challenges the naïve realism of the unconscious, so psychoanalysis shows that the consciousness of the phenomenologist can never be the same again. The passage to adulthood mirrors the passage out of pure phenomenology (or pure consciousness) into a new hermeneutical understanding which assimilates the unconscious not as something utterly unknown, but as something disguised, and, hence, knowable through interpretation. This for Ricoeur is the meaning of the Oedipus myth. Contrary to Freud, who saw Oedipus as the embodiment of repressed childhood desires (to kill one's father and marry one's mother), Ricoeur sees the Oedipal myth as a parable of adulthood: it is not Oedipus' desires that are punished (after all, Oedipus did not know that Jocasta was his mother and Laïus was his father, and this unknown is 'external' to Oedipus, not an internalised unconscious unknown), but his presumption and pride in calling down a curse on whoever has blighted the city, without considering that it might be himself. The tragedy is of Oedipus

Rex, not of Oedipus the child. But this alternative reading must nevertheless acknowledge the Freudian reading to which it is in dialectical relation, in order to avoid the charge of the Freudians, that any alternative to their reading is merely an example of the repression that the Oedipus complex itself is intended to describe. Hence, Ricoeur assimilates the Freudian reading of Oedipus into an overarching hermeneutic which accounts for both child and man, just as in life the man also incorporates the child within him. This passage from childhood to adulthood, at once opposing (Freudian) archaeology with (Hegelian) teleology, and incorporating the former within the latter, Ricoeur calls a 'work of culture'. It is culture that is really opposed to the unknown of the unconscious. Thus he concludes his paper with the quotation from Freud which forms the very basis of Lacan's theory: *Wo Es war, soll Ich werden.*

It is clear from this account of 'Consciousness and the Unconscious' that Ricoeur is encroaching very much on Lacan's territory but reaching quite different conclusions. It is clear also that this essay contains in reduced form all of the essential arguments that were to be articulated at greater length in *De l'interprétation*, thus refuting Lacan's claim that Ricoeur had stolen his ideas as a result of attending his seminars – Ricoeur was to attend the seminars on Lacan's invitation, as a result of the latter having heard this paper. What is less clear is why Lacan chose to befriend Ricoeur on the basis of the paper. Nevertheless, on mature reflection, Lacan seems eventually to have perceived the paper's implicit hostility to his own thinking: the discussion following Ricoeur's paper, in which Lacan praises Ricoeur, was removed from the published conference proceedings in 1966 at Lacan's request,[3] while he concludes his own (extensively rewritten) paper, 'Position of the Unconscious', with the snide remark 'The fact that, regarding the Oedipus complex, the last act – or rather the role of warm-up band – went to a hermeneutic feat, confirms my assessment of this colloquium' on its publication in the *Écrits* in the same year (Lacan 2006: 721).[4]

As is well known, Lacan was mortally offended when Ricoeur's *De l'interprétation* was published in May 1965. One of Lacan's disciples, Jean-Paul Valabrega, in a review in *Critique*, complained that Ricoeur had failed to acknowledge that Lacan was the first in France to have introduced the study of language into psychoanalysis, and that, in so doing,

> Ricoeur has made his own many ideas which originally did not belong to him. He allows the impression that the theses he developed from his reading were the fruit of his own solitary meditation, which would be a tremendous and admirable thing, to be sure, but which is not true
>
> (cited in Roudinesco 1990: 395).

Ricoeur's angry reply is to the effect that he had completed the outline of his book before he had read Lacan or attended his seminar, and he concludes by decrying Valabrega's 'propriety mentality', asking rhetorically, 'Are ideas distinct things that one can possess and be robbed of?' (cited in Roudinesco 1990: 396).

Elisabeth Roudinesco's (1990: 395) take on this episode is as follows:

> As far as the use of linguistics was concerned, Lacan did nothing of what Ricoeur claimed. He employed certain concepts from linguistics to effect a rearticulation of Freud's text, but never did he implement the slightest 'linguistic conception of the unconscious'. As for the 'elimination of energetics', it was not part of Lacan's project since that project was concerned with neither energetics nor linguistics as such, nor with any other 'elimination'. Not only did Ricoeur not 'steal Lacan's ideas', but so little did he 'steal' them that he misconstrued them completely. He invented a Lacan whom he was unable to read and whom he tried in vain to confront.

Ricoeur's (1998: 70–1) reply to this charge, that he could not have borrowed from Lacan because he understood nothing of him, is this:

> I have to say that this is true. I do not understand this form of articulation or of thinking; it is entirely foreign to me. I do not understand how this thinking works; at times I am dazzled, as if by flashes, but without being able to follow the thread of the discourse. . . . I have always been sorry about this and quite often have felt it was a kind of infirmity on my part.

If Ricoeur's tone of anger in his reply to Valabrega was uncharacteristic, then his characteristic humility is heightened here to an extraordinary degree. But, on closer inspection, Ricoeur, in generalising Roudinesco's charge, avoids addressing its specifics: that Ricoeur mistakenly characterises Lacan as eliminating Freud's energetics, and that he mistakenly attributes a 'linguistic conception of the unconscious' to Lacan.[5] Actually, the first point is one which appears to have been most responsible for triggering Lacan's ire (cited in Dosse 1997: 332): 'Il y a un philosophe qui a découvert chez Freud un énergétique: Vroum! Vroum! Vroum . . .'. What a curious labyrinth of *méconnaissance*! On the publication of Ricoeur's book, Lacan engages in a characteristic display of anger, but his principal complaint is counter-psychoanalytic: that Ricoeur has stolen his ideas, when, if psychoanalysis teaches us anything, it is that ideas cannot be owned. Meanwhile, Ricoeur displays *un*characteristic anger at the charge that he has stolen Lacan's ideas, but hyper-characteristic humility at the suggestion that he has misunderstood them. But he avoids mentioning the specific idea of energetics, which Lacan oddly ridicules – ridicules because it is Ricoeur's idea, contradicting the notion that Ricoeur has stolen *his* ideas.

This entire labyrinth appears to have been generated from one footnote in *De l'interprétation* – one of only two instances in the entire book where Ricoeur (1970: 367, n. 37) mentions Lacan by name:[6]

> My criticism of the behaviourist 'reformulations' of psychoanalysis is very close to the one that could be drawn from Lacan's article ['Function and Field of Speech and Language in Psychoanalysis']. We diverge, however, when I go on to criticise a conception that eliminates energy concepts in favour of linguistics.

Ricoeur is not claiming here that Lacan has the intention of eliminating energy concepts, merely that this is the effect of his using linguistics as the mechanism for rearticulating Freud's work. And, we might add, this is true: contrary to Ricoeur's self-assessment, he *has* understood Lacan aright on this point, as we hope to demonstrate in Chapter 4 below. But, meanwhile, the sentence to which the words quoted above are a footnote is instructive:

> Analytic experience unfolds in speech[,] and ... within this field, what comes to light is another language, dissociated from common language, and which presents itself to be deciphered through its meaningful effects – symptoms, dreams, various formations, etc. (Ricoeur 1970: 367)

This at once places Ricoeur in proximity to Lacan and, again, separates them. Ricoeur, like Lacan, recognises that Freud's is in effect a theory of language, but we must use the phrase 'theory of language' cautiously. It is a theory of the efficacy of language, which is to say, of both the effects of language in the analytic situation and the role of language in determining the content of psychic phenomena. It is not the same as saying that Freud was a linguist *avant la lettre*. Hence, when Ricoeur writes that 'what comes to light is another language, dissociated from common language', this sounds rather close to Lacan's slogan, 'the unconscious is structured like a language'. But really Ricoeur and Lacan are approaching the problem of the unconscious in relation to language from opposite directions. For Ricoeur, what is operative is a semiotics of symbols that are irreducible to language, a whole rhetoric of the unconscious that is 'concerned not with the phenomena of language but with the procedures of subjectivity that are manifested in discourse' (Ricoeur 1970: 400). Although these phenomena, being infra- or supra-linguistic, are still referred to language – 'we are in the presence of phenomena structured like a language' – 'the problem is to assign an appropriate meaning to the word "like"' (Ricoeur 1970: 400). Lacan, after the publication of Ricoeur's *De l'interprétation,* makes his own attempt at assigning such a meaning – with what success, we shall examine in Chapter 4. But suffice here to say that an inattentiveness on Lacan's part to the meaning of the word 'like' in the formula 'the unconscious is structured like a language' in the years preceding the publication of the *Écrits* might legitimately lead one to believe that he does, indeed and *contra* Roudinesco, 'implement a linguistic conception of the unconscious'. Lacan's is the opposite conception of semiotics from Ricoeur's: for him, all of semiotics is poured into the pint pot of linguistics. Thus, Lacan reduces, following Jakobson, all rhetorical tropes – effects of discourse – to the two tropes of metaphor and metonymy, whereas for Ricoeur 'the procedures of subjectivity that are manifested in discourse' include such distinct entities as synecdoches, euphemisms, allusions, antiphrases, litotes, etc. (Ricoeur 1970: 400). Hence, it is that Ricoeur's insistence on the linguistic dimension of psychoanalysis leads to the opposite conclusion from both Lacan and Roudinesco: it is not a concentration on language that 'leads one to eliminate as an anomaly the interrelationship of hermeneutics and energetics in analytic theory' (Ricoeur 1970: 367), but rather its opposite, a failure to take language into account, that does this.[7]

Méconnaissance is piled on *méconnaissance* in the encounter between Ricoeur and Lacan, however, with the publication of a pro-Lacanian article by Michel Tort (1966). There, he draws a contrast between Ricoeur's view of the Freudian unconscious in *The Voluntary and the Involuntary,* where Ricoeur held that 'the object *par excellence* of psychology as a science is the unconscious', and his view in *De l'interprétation,* that the unconscious is the proper object of psychoanalysis rather than of psychology. Ricoeur had replaced references to his mentor Dalbiez by references to Lacan. This is a more subtle (some would say insidious) criticism of Ricoeur than that to be found in Valabrega, since he is not accusing Ricoeur of the theft of ideas, but rather that, in his own acknowledged similarities with Lacan, Ricoeur could not have written his book had not Lacan been available to Ricoeur's thinking in the intervening years. Roudinesco's (1990: 397) charitable interpretation of this position is that Tort attempts 'to show that the dissemination and existence of Lacanian thought had modified the French intellectual landscape, to an extent allowing thinkers to modify their methods or to imagine theirs were converging with Lacan's'. Ricoeur (1998: 69), however, sees Tort's article as based on a 'misunderstanding', and one which, moreover, 'cast doubt on my good faith':

> This was a devastating article that blasted me and said in essence: Ricoeur spoke once of the unconscious in *The Voluntary and the Involuntary*, he speaks about it a second time in *Freud and Philosophy*. What was there between these two works? Nothing, except Lacan.

Ricoeur's (1998: 69) riposte to this is that there was, actually, something else between *The Voluntary and the Involuntary* and *De l'interprétation*:

> What there was between them was my own exploration of symbolic language in the framework of my book *The Symbolism of Evil*, and, consequently, the emphasis on the linguistic dimension of our relation to the unconscious. This dimension is in fact brought to the fore in Lacan, but I had coordinated it with the energetic, dynamic dimension, instead of opposing the former to the latter as he does.[8]

This suggests that, although arrived at independently, there is a commonality of purpose between *The Symbolism of Evil* and Lacan's linguisticisation of Freud. Hence, the similarities and differences between Ricoeur's 'symbolism' and Lacan's 'symbolic' are something we must confront in the work that follows.

We recall that Lacan's radical translation of Freud's *Wo Es war, soll Ich werden* is 'Where (it) was itself, it is my duty that I come into being.' We have already seen how this translation leads to similarities and differences in the positions of Ricoeur and Lacan regarding the Cartesian *cogito*, the realism of the unconscious, and the language of the unconscious. But we should also note that Lacan's formula, 'It is my duty that I come into being' (which is the part of his translation that is most liberal, allowing the German word *soll* to carry a lot of weight) also pushes Lacanian theory in the direction of ethics. Lacan's ethics are elaborated principally in *The Ethics of Psychoanalysis, 1959–60* (Lacan 1992), and the 1962 article 'Kant with Sade' (Lacan 2006: 645–58). Lacan's position might be described as 'more Kantian than Kant'. Lacan points out that the Kantian categorical imperative, 'act only in accordance with that maxim through which you can at the same time will that it become a universal law' (Kant 1998: 31), is just as capable of taking evil as its mode of practical application as it is good: I can choose to act in an evil way, and will that it become a universal law. (Kant himself implicitly recognises this in his characterisation of 'diabolical evil'; it is just that he refuses to believe that a human being is capable of such evil.) Thus it is that Sade both proves the truth of the Kantian categorical imperative and exposes the dissymmetry between its first formulation and its second, 'So act that you use humanity, whether in your own person or in the person of any other, always at the same time as an end, never merely as a means' (Kant 1998: 38). By 'proving the truth',

Lacan means demonstrating its universal applicability; the categorical imperative, through being universal, allows any form of behaviour to be assimilable to the universal law. Of course, this means that the categorical imperative contradicts itself as a moral imperative; more precisely, a wedge is driven between morality and ethics, since the case of Sade demonstrates that immoral behaviour can just as easily be adopted as a general rule of ethics as can moral behaviour. Hence, Sade negates the second formulation of the categorical imperative by always treating other people as a means rather than as an end rather than vice versa, and yet he is still, through his constancy in this, always in tune with the first formulation of the categorical imperative. And the end towards which Sade uses others as the means is his own enjoyment; his is the pursuit of what Kant calls 'pathological' desire. Hence, *contra* Kant, Lacan sees no distinction between pathological desire and ethical action; ethics is pathological just as desire is ethical.

Ricoeur has an equally ambivalent relation to Kant in his ethics, although not one which follows the Lacanian path. In her *Ricoeur and Kant: Philosophy of the Will*, Pamela Sue Anderson (1993: 5, n.16) 'plac[es] Ricoeur in a precise line with Kant' and, as her subtitle suggests, concentrates on the former's *Philosophy of the Will*. The present work does not seek to reconstruct Ricoeur's Kantianism or to go over the ground already trodden by Anderson; however, it does take seriously Ricoeur's claim to be a 'post-Hegelian Kantian' in ethics, while concentrating on his later works in this area. In his essay 'Practical Reason' (1991: 188–207), Ricoeur explains the dialectic he wishes to establish between Kantianism and Hegelianism. Ricoeur is something of an admirer of Hegelian *Sittlichkeit*, the community founded on constitution but, unlike Hegel, does not see it as leading to 'universal mind', which the totalitarian regimes of the twentieth century have shown to be a dangerous notion. Rather, he sees Hegelian *Sittlichkeit* as being tempered, or limited, by the freedom of individual choice that lies at the heart of the Kantian categorical imperative (whereby I *choose* to act . . .), just as Kantian individuality is reigned in by an adherence to an institutional framework that Hegelian *Sittlichkeit* provides. In other words, Ricoeur returns to the notion of intersubjectivity as formulated by the Husserl of the *Cartesian Meditations* and developed into a concept of *Lebenswelt* in his last writings: for him, a dialectical negotiation between Hegelian *Sittlichkeit* and Kantian individualism is what Husserlian intersubjectivity implies when transposed to the ethical (and concomitantly political) sphere. (Hence, yes, Ricoeur is in a line that extends from Kant, but it is a line which passes through Hegel and Husserl, and so demonstrating Ricoeur's Kantian heritage as such is of limited utility.) It is at this point that once again a similarity emerges between Ricoeur and Lacan: both identify a gulf between the first and second formulations of Kant's categorical imperative. In Ricoeur's terms, the first formulation leans towards Hegelian universalism, while the second insufficiently guards against the 'pathological' desire of the individual that Kant himself warns of (and which Lacan embraces). More simply, the first formulation is a moral imperative and the second an ethical one. Thus far, Ricoeur and Lacan are in agreement. But Ricoeur, unlike Lacan, does not wish to drive a further wedge between the first and the second formulations of the categorical imperative in the name of a pathological desire. Rather, he seeks to bridge the gap between the two formulations. This he does through developing a philosophy of love, of being a neighbour. As Lacan remarks, 'Sade refuses to be my neighbour', but Ricoeur is diametrically opposed to Sade in his promotion of neighbourly love. The New Commandment, to love thy neighbour as thyself (so much misunderstood by Freud, and so disdained by Kant himself), becomes for Ricoeur an enhanced formulation of the second version of the categorical imperative, one which heals the rift between it and the first.

It is against this background that in his later work Ricoeur goes on to develop a 'philosophy of action'. After 1966, however, Ricoeur and Lacan part company in terms of direct contact, and so direct comparison becomes difficult. It is difficult too because a 'philosophy of action' could not be further from Lacan's concerns in the 1970s. While Lacan writes much of 'the ethics of psychoanalysis', his comments are limited to the ways in which psychoanalytic theory critiques philosophical ethics. Lacan does not address the question, What am I to do?, even in the limited sphere of how an analyst should behave ethically towards an analysand, still less with regard to life in general. Therefore, in the absence of writings by the master himself, Chapter 8 takes the work of Slavoj Žižek to be representative of a Lacanian practical ethics. This is not to claim that Žižek simply *is* Lacan, or that a simple substitution of Žižek in the place of Lacan is not problematic. But Žižek, of all avowed Lacanians working today, is the most 'ethico-political', and his work may be taken as a fair representation of what a Lacanian ethics would look like were it applied to a practical political programme. Again, there is both a similarity and a difference between the two thinkers held at a singular point. And the point is this: is a deontological – i.e., non-pathological – desire possible? Reading somewhat against the grain of Lacan's texts, Žižek claims that Lacanian 'desire', as explicated in 'Kant with Sade', is such a deontological, non-pathological desire. But what Žižek does not articulate explicitly, although it is one of Ricoeur's abiding concerns from his earliest writings to his last, is that such a deontological desire entails responsibility. The Hegelian demand for sacrifice, which Lacan conceives as an impossible existential choice, becomes for Ricoeur an opening into solicitude. For Ricoeur, my word is my bond: the promise has solicitudinous efficacy only if one has faith in language. Although Lacan repeatedly insists on speech as the locus of truth, his linguisticisation of Freud may also be seen as a Freudianisation of language: just as, after Freud, one might lose faith in consciousness, so also after Lacan one might lose faith in language. This is something Ricoeur never does.

2

The *Cogito* and its Detractors

Despite their many differences, Ricoeur and Lacan share what might be called a 'post-Cartesian' heritage. In Ricoeur, this is mediated through the existentialism of Marcel and Jaspers, the phenomenology of Husserl, and the ontology of Heidegger; in Lacan, of course, it is mediated through the very notion of the unconscious that is the cornerstone of Freudian thinking. But both lines of scepticism towards the *cogito* can be traced back to a common origin – an origin of the origin, if you will – and that is Nietzsche. In *Beyond Good and Evil*, Nietzsche (1966: 24) writes:

> With regard to the superstitions of logicians, I shall never tire of emphasising a small terse fact, which these superstitious minds hate to concede – namely, that a thought comes when 'it' wishes, and not when 'I' wish, so that it is a falsification of the facts of the case to say that the subject 'I' is the subject of the predicate 'think'. *It* thinks; but that this 'it' is precisely the famous old 'ego' is, to put it mildly, only a supposition, an assertion, and assuredly not an 'immediate certainty'. After all, one has even gone too far with this 'it thinks' – even the 'it' contains an *interpretation* of the process, and does not belong to the process itself. One infers here according to the grammatical habit: 'thinking is an activity; every activity requires an agent; consequently – '.

Contained in this short paragraph are the seeds of two of the major strands of twentieth-century thought: on the one hand, the notion of interpretation prefigures Heidegger's notion that man is primarily an interpreting being: in this view, thought collapses in on itself in its attempt at reflexivity, so that the attempt to think thinking can only be apprehended retroactively, as an interpretation which the thinker is always already engaged in. Interpretation is originary. On the other hand, Nietzsche's opposition between the 'I' and the 'it' opens up the entire field of what will later become known as the 'unconscious'. Indeed, Nietzsche's attack on Cartesian certainty (which is not an attack on certainty as such – but just on *Cartesian* certainty) situates the 'it' as an 'unknown', an *unbewuss*.

It is this *Unbewussheit* of the 'it' that appeals to Freud. At the beginning of his 1923 work *The Ego and the Id*, Freud takes seriously Nietzsche's quip about following the grammatical rule: for Freud (1961a: 13–14), 'being conscious' really *is*

> in the first place a purely descriptive term, resting on perception of the most immediate and certain character. Experience goes on to show that a psychical element (for instance, an idea) is not as a rule conscious for a protracted length of time. On the contrary, a state of consciousness is characteristically very transitory; an idea that is conscious now is no longer so a moment later, although it can become so again under certain conditions that are easily brought about. In the interval the idea was – we do not know what.

The idea which Freud takes, 'for instance' could be, of course, the idea 'I think'. Just as Husserl was to discover in his investigation into time (and also later Heidegger, in his development of time-consciousness as a 'protraction' whereby 'presencing' is maintained through the retention of the past in remembrance),[1] so Freud discovers that the *cogito* requires a constant effort, or renewal of effort, of thinking to sustain itself. Thought is threatened by the void of un-thought – and the 'I' of the *cogito* is threatened by non-existence or, at least, the failure of apodictic certainty of existence – through the lapse of time. Time, in this view, is, precisely, a lapsus: it is the space into which thought falls when it is not being *maintained*.

But this void of thought is merely phenomenological: in other words, thought during this interval of un-thought is 'latent'; it is 'capable of becoming conscious at any time'. Such latent thought Freud calls the 'preconscious', a description consistent with the findings of Husserlian phenomenology. But Freud wants to go further. When we take into account mental dynamics, he says, we see that there is a state in which ideas existed before they become conscious: this state is called 'repression', and the mechanism which prevents certain of its contents from ever becoming fully conscious is called 'resistance'. This, in effect, introduces a 'third term': there is the conscious, which conforms to the Cartesian 'I'; the latently conscious, which is available to philosophical (or phenomenological) description and which Freud calls the 'preconscious'; and, third, the 'unconscious', which is defined precisely as being unavailable to any kind of description which might be called perceptive – it is, rather, the product of a dynamics and can only be uncovered, or described, through the dynamic descriptive process which constitutes psychoanalysis.

This allows Freud to develop what becomes known as a 'topology' of the psyche. In a complex network of 'one downmanship', Freud attributes his discovery of the 'unconscious' in this new sense to Georg Groddeck (1949), who in turn borrowed it from Nietzsche: 'I propose', writes Freud (1961a: 23),

> to take [Groddeck's discovery] into account by calling the entity which starts out from the system *Pcpt.* [perception] and begins by being *Pcs.* [preconscious] the 'ego', and by following Groddeck in calling the other part of the mind, into which this entity extends and behaves as though it were *Ucs.* [unconscious], the 'id'.

What is significant about this development in Freud's thinking is its realism: the unconscious is now, in a manner in which it was not, or at least not explicitly, in his earlier works, a specific 'entity' which has its own 'locus'. The mind is now divided as if it were a material entity, which lends the diagram Freud provides in his *The Ego and the Id*[2] a dubious status: is it a metaphor, existing only in order to demonstrate a *conceptual* relativity between the Freudian concepts heretofore elucidated? Or is it rather a directly representational picture, showing how the mind 'looks'? This question is, of course, unanswerable, a fact that is reproduced in the dichotomous nature of the sentence Freud (1961a: 24) himself employs to address this issue: 'The state of things which we have been describing can be represented diagrammatically . . .; though it must be remarked that the form chosen has no pretensions to any special applicability, but is merely intended to serve for purposes of exposition'.

In his lecture 'The Dissection of the Psychical Personality' (1933), Freud strengthens the 'topographical' description of the unconscious further. Again acknowledging the influence of Nietzsche via Groddeck, Freud (1973: 104) again calls what is unconscious the 'it' (*das Es*, the id):

> The impersonal pronoun seems particularly well suited for expressing the main characteristic of this province of the mind – the fact of its being alien to the ego. The super-ego, the ego, and the id – these, then, are the three realms, regions, provinces, into which we divide an individual's mental apparatus, and with the mutual relations of which we shall be concerned in what follows.

Again, the 'mental apparatus' is accorded the status of a physical region, which is then capable once again of being diagrammatised, as it is in Freud's (1973: 111) new topological illustration, which portrays 'the structural relations of the mental personality'.

Freud (1973: 112) ends his lecture with what has become one of his most famous remarks, *Wo Es war, soll Ich werden* ('Where id was, there Ego shall be'). What in the light of Lacan is often neglected in discussions of this remark is the context established immediately preceding: the intention of the therapeutic efforts of psychoanalysis, says Freud (1973: 112), is 'to strengthen the ego, to make it more independent of the super-ego, to widen its field of perception and enlarge its organisation, so that it can appropriate fresh portions of the id'. From this, two remarks follow. First, the appropriation of fresh portions of the id is seen by Freud as dependent on the ego's being able to become more independent of the super-ego. In psychoanalytic terms, this means lifting repression through overcoming psychic resistance. This, in turn, presupposes, as Freud indeed does, that such characteristics as guilt are the products of the agencies of repression, or, to put it the other way around, that guilt is at once a symptom of repression and one of the means which the super-ego employs in order to subsume repressed material. In both *The Ego and the Id* and the *New Introductory Lectures*, Freud explicitly equates the ego with the conscience, which itself is no longer a Tennysonian 'still small voice', but an interiorisation of societal disapproval of a particular action. This has the effect of implicitly relativising the conscience and its correlate, morality: by implication, there is no absolute right or wrong in Freudian ethics, but merely approval or disapproval. Nowhere does Freud entertain the idea that repression (in the psychic sense) might be a good thing – which is not to say that some things are best left forgotten, but it is to say that the conscience might not, as Freud assumes, be part and parcel of the baggage of the 'super-ego'. Contrary to the implicit view of Freud, conscience and guilt are not the same thing: one can have a 'guilty conscience', and one who is without conscience will always be without guilt, but it does not follow that they are both different names for the same 'agency of repression'. Second, and of direct importance to Lacan's reading of Freud, we should note that Freud's mission is to strengthen the ego, which is entirely consistent with the 'ego psychology' of Lowenstein and others to whom Lacan set up his entire theory in opposition. But here lies the nub of the difference between a Freudian ethics of psychoanalysis and, say, a virtue ethics aiming at the 'good life'. For Freud, psychoanalysis aims at strengthening the ego in its fight against the id by enabling it to appropriate to itself matter from the super-ego. Put another way, the ego is to be strengthened against the unthinking forces of the subject's natural desires by taking unto itself suchlike as moral judgements. Not succumbing to the vicissitudes of the id is, Freud (1973: 112) says, 'a work of culture, not unlike the draining of the Zuider Zee', by which he means that the Ego can become enculturated, responsible only to itself for the task of making moral decisions, and answerable only to its own I-saying self. This is the hidden Nietzschean message of Freud's implicit moral philosophy: such an Ego would be a Nietzschean superman, answerable only to himself. The conscience, or 'super-ego', conceived of as the internalisation of cultural values, would be replaced by self-created values, so that the Ego would be encultured unto himself. All of which is left open to the same objection as that which can be made against Nietzsche: that it leads to unbridled, amoral Egoism, in the common sense of the word. (It springs also, of course, from the same source: an overreaction to the strictures of stifling and hypocritical 'Victorian morality'.)

All of which constitutes a slight detour from Lacan's interpretation of Freud's dictum, *Wo Es war, soll Ich werden,* but one which may serve as a reminder of what is at stake ethically and morally when we come to examine Lacan's own ethics. Indeed, Lacan's analysis of Freud's words is in response to the sort of 'Nietzschean' criticism we have made above: 'The terms in which I am posing the problem of psychoanalytic intervention make it sufficiently clear, I think,' writes Lacan (2006: 346), 'that its ethics are not individualistic'. Furthermore, Lacan's analysis of the Freudian formula is couched in terms of a critique of the American ego psychology with which, on face value and as a result of Freud's own preceding remarks, it appears consistent: the practice of psychoanalysis in the American sphere, writes Lacan (2006: 346), 'has so summarily degenerated into a means of obtaining "success" and into a mode of demanding "happiness" that it must be pointed out that this constitutes a repudiation of psychoanalysis'. In what, then, does Lacan's defence of Freud's *Wo Es war, soll Ich werden* consist, which is nothing other than a defence of psychoanalysis itself?

Lacan calls this defence an 'analysis' of the formula's 'signifying structuration'. What Lacan means precisely by 'signifying structuration' is unclear: the analysis which follows is partly grammatical, and partly semantic; insofar as it is an analysis of language, on the one hand we might say that the term 'signifying structuration' indicates that Lacan's conception of linguistics is indebted to a structuralist model (which is itself problematic to anyone who does not subscribe to this model, as few people do nowadays); on the other hand, as a translative interpretation of the meanings of Freud's words, the term 'structuration' appears to be irrelevant.

Be this as it may, Lacan begins by pointing out that, in distinction to the earlier essay *Das Ich und das Es,* Freud here avoids using the definite articles. In the former essay, claims Lacan (2006: 347), Freud used the articles 'in order to maintain the fundamental distinction between the true subject of the unconscious and the ego as constituted in its nucleus by a series of alienating identifications'. This is an opposing view to the one which is commonly adopted by critics of Freud, and which we ourselves adopted above: that the adoption of the definite articles are consistent with Freud's materialisation of the 'realms' of the psyche as specific topographical loci. Indeed, this problem, of Freud writing as if the unconscious (or the Ego and the Id) were real, identifiable loci within a materially construed psyche, is entirely glossed over by Lacan. Notwithstanding this, we should bear in mind the term 'loci' in Lacan's (2006: 347) particular analysis of *Wo Es war, soll Ich werden* which follows:

> It seems here that it is in the locus *Wo* (Where) *Es* (the subject devoid of any *das* or other objectifying article) *war* (was [*était*]) – it is a locus of being that is at stake, and that in this locus), *soll* (it is a duty in the moral sense that is announced here, as is confirmed by the single sentence that follows it, bringing the chapter to a close) *Ich* (I, there must I – just as in French one announced 'ce suis-je', 'it is I', before saying 'c'est moi', 'it's me') *werden* (become [*devenir*] – not occur [*survenir*], or even happen [*advenir*], but be born [*venir au jour*] of this very locus insofar as it is a locus of being).

Lacan's analysis looks very much like a 'close reading' in the literary critical sense, and it is noticeable that he follows the ordering of Freud's sentence. As a grammatical analysis, it is immediately problematic. His parenthesis describing the *Es* calls it a 'subject': is this a grammatical subject, or the 'subject' of psychoanalysis, what in another parlance might be called the 'person' (bearing in mind that usually in Lacanian theory, these two happily coincide)? If the former, the analysis is simply incorrect. Grammatically, the sentence is analysed as an inversion of *Ich soll werden wo Es war,* in which case the subject and the *Ich* do indeed coincide (and the prepositional phrase *wo Es war* is a complement) – but the *Es* cannot be a subject. This casual grammatical claim is made for the convenience of the latter interpretation, that it is the *Es* which is endowed with subjecthood in the psychoanalytic sense. But analysing the words of Freud's sentence simply in the order in which they appear blinds Lacan to the rhetorical effect of its inversion (putting the complement first), which is to emphasise the temporal ordering: the *Es* exists in some sense *prior* to the *Ich.*

We might also question Lacan's (2006: 347) insistence that 'it is a duty in the moral sense that is at stake here, as is confirmed by the single sentence that follows it'. We recall that that sentence is 'It is a work of culture, not unlike the draining of the Zuider Zee'. This sentence does have a moral implication, as we have already seen: but it is the kind of morality which derives its meaning from cultural values, rather than seeing cultural values as a reflection of pre-existing moral ones. Thus, it is forcing Freud's intention to say that the *soll* carries particular moral force: grammatically, it is ambiguous between epistemic and deontic modality, which is to say, between a prediction and an 'ought to'. But 'duty' is Lacan's word, not Freud's – even if we are to accept the moral force of the *soll,* that this *soll* entails a duty only follows if one holds to a (broadly) Kantian moral theory, which Lacan might (in a highly modified manner, as we shall see below) but which Freud, on the evidence, apparently did not. The point here, of course, is that Kant's categorical imperative claims to be testable objectively, whereas Freud's dictum is implicitly subjectivist in its morality.

Lacan's translation of the *Ich* is also a ruse based on a grammatical misunderstanding: '*Ich* (I, there must I – just as in French one announced "ce suis-je", "it is I", before saying "c'est moi", "it's me")'. The historical change in French grammar from 'It is I' to 'It is me' is a red herring here: the real point is that the 'it' here has no special meaning – it is not assimilable to the Freudian *Es* – indeed, it has no semantic meaning at all, although it does have signification: it functions as what grammarians would call a 'dummy subject'. Thus, when Lacan (2006: 348) remarks that 'the point is not to analyse if and how the I [*le je*] and the ego [*le moi*] are distinct and overlap in each particular subject on the basis of a grammatical conception of their functions', he is being somewhat disingenuous, since that is precisely what his preceding analysis has done – except that grammar is not Lacan's strong point.

But we risk being disingenuous ourselves if we do not get to the crux of Lacan's point in his translative interpretation of *Wo Es war, soll Ich werden.* And that is that Lacan's (2006: 347–8) own version of this formula is '"Where it was" [*Là où c'était*], one might say, "Where (it) was itself" [*là où c'était*], as I would like it to be heard, "it is my duty to come into being"'. Translations, or problems of translation, seem to be multiplying themselves, remembering that Freud's *Wo Es war, soll Ich werden* is a reworking of Descartes' *cogito ergo sum.* (Here we might pause to note that its being such a reworking of Descartes has become a philosophical commonplace, partly because of the influence of Lacan, and partly because an educated readership of Freud picks up on the allusion. But it *is*, precisely, an allusion: nowhere does Freud explicitly say that he is attempting to supplant the Cartesian view, and the whole concept of 'allusion' here opens up the question of 'what Freud intended'.) The original English translation appears at fault for interpolating too much: 'Where the Id was, there the Ego shall be.' This reinstates the definite articles which Freud himself had used in 1923, but which are not to be found in his text of 1932; it Latinises the *Es* and the *Ich*; and it resolves the ambiguity of the *soll* into an exclusively epistemic modal meaning. Lacan's translation, meanwhile, interpolates too much in the opposite direction: *'là où c'était, c'est mon devoir que je vienne à être'* ['Where it was itself, it is my duty to come into being']. Bruce Fink's English translation of Lacan, like that of Alan Sheridan before him, omits the *là*, 'there', of the French translation of Freud which Lacan takes as his starting point, so that a more literal translation would read: 'There where it was ...'. Lacan retains this *là*, and in so doing strengthens the notion of 'locus of being' that he has introduced, while giving the formula a Heideggerian flavour: *là c'était* chimes with *Dasein*. Moreover, the elided *c* in the French rendering of 'it is' (*c'est*) 'suggests to' Lacan (2006: 347) 'the production of a verb, *s'être*, which would express the mode of absolute subjectivity'. Lacan's neologism is not entirely original: an equivalent can be found in Gerard Manley Hopkins' use of the word 'self' as a verb (as in 'Selves, goes itself, myself it speaks and spells'), and its origin is in Heraclitus. But we might want a stronger reason for coining the neologism than the suggestion of a homonymy. And if this is something which 'suggests' itself to Lacan, then it is an even bigger leap to attribute the thinking behind it to Freud, 'who truly discovered it in its radical eccentricity', according to Lacan (2006: 347). The homonymic neologism is a Heideggerian one, both in terms of content (it plays between the ontic and the ontological) and in terms of philosophical strategy (it is not unlike Heidegger's use of questionable etymologies in appropriating the thought of the pre-Socratics). But there is a difference between, on the one hand, assimilating Freudianism and Heideggerianism, and, on the other, claiming that Freud unwittingly anticipates, or at least is consistent with, Heidegger, which Lacan implicitly does but which would have bemused both thinkers.

This leaves us with the second half of Lacan's formula, 'it is my duty that I come into being'. This takes the opposite route to James Strachey's English translation of Freud: rather than divest the German *soll* of its deontic meaning in favour of its epistemic one, it divests it of its epistemic meaning in favour of the deontic one. Moreover, 'come into being' has a particular resonance lacking in Freud's *werden*, which translates simply as 'become'. Does 'become' mean the same as 'come into being'? Only a believer in the mystical power of etymology would answer 'yes, always'. Those who believe that meaning derives from use would look to the context. And in the context of Freud's sentence, the *Wo* is the giveaway: as Lacan points out, it identifies a locus. So, in this context 'become' means 'occupy the place of'; 'I should be in the place of where it was.' If we are to look to a later philosophy to accord with Freud's theory at this point, Sartrean being-through-action comes much closer than Heideggerian *Dasein*, except that the 'action' in Freud is a mental action.

All of this could be an argument in favour of literal translation: 'Where it was, should I become'. If it is an oversimplification to claim that 'Freud was really a very simple man',[3] nevertheless it is true that Freud (unlike Lacan!) liked to write in a very simple style: *Wo Es war, soll Ich werden* is persuasive (which is not the same as true) in its elegant simplicity, which is lacking in Lacan's convoluted version.[4]

Some nine years earlier, in 1946, writing against his erstwhile mentor

Henri Ey,[5] the proponent of 'Cartesian psychogenesis', Lacan had posited his own interpretation of Descartes. Contrary to Ey, who attributes to Descartes 'an absolute dualism between the organic realm and the psychical realm', Lacan (2006: 128) sees Descartes' dualism as, rather, one of 'extension and thought'. For Lacan (2006: 129), it is important that 'the first judgement of certainty that Descartes bases on the consciousness that thinking has of itself is a pure judgement of existence: *cogito ergo sum*'. Some years later, in 'The Instance of the Letter in the Unconscious' (1957), Lacan (2006: 429) writes that, '"I am thinking, therefore I am" (*cogito ergo sum*) is not simply the formulation in which the link between the transparency of the transcendental subject and his existential affirmation is constituted'; to avoid the Cartesian *cogito* 'is also to deny oneself access to what might be called the Freudian universe'. Lacan thus co-opts Descartes to Freudianism, which, on the face of it, might seem odd, insofar as Cartesianism is commonly considered to be a philosophy of consciousness, and certainly it is this interpretation of Descartes that has made him important to Husserlian phenomenology, which, in its denial of the Freudian unconscious, is the philosophy of consciousness *par excellence*.[6] But Lacan reads Descartes as if he were an existentialist – which entirely erases the existentialist critique of the *cogito*, to the effect that it already presupposes the being that it predicates. 'Is the place that I occupy as subject of the signifier concentric or eccentric in relation to the place I occupy as subject of the signified? That is the question', says Lacan (2006: 430), equating, through his own linguistic detour, Hamlet's existential question with the question of 'What can I know?' raised and answered by the *cogito*. Lacan (2006: 430) continues: 'The point is not to know whether I speak of myself in a way that conforms to what I am, but rather to know whether, when I speak of myself, I am the same as the self of whom I speak'. This formula opens up what Lacan calls a 'schism' in the *cogito*, between the 'I' of the 'I think' and the 'I' of the 'I am': Descartes' utterance of the *cogito* stood at the apex of the historical reflection on the conditions of science, but its schism reminds us that even science depends on the subjective element, that of the subject who is necessary to perceive its empirical data. Hence, 'the philosophical *cogito* is at the centre of the mirage that renders modern man so sure of being himself in his uncertainties about himself' (Lacan 2006: 430). The *cogito*, then, is at once the starting point for philosophical reflection on the Freudian universe, the initial spur to the development of the distinction between the *Ich* and the *Es* that is encapsulated in Freud's *Wo Es war, soll Ich werden* and something which must be radicalised, in a way that a radical reading of Freud's *Wo Es war, soll Ich werden* achieves, in order to open the Freudian worlds of the psyche to analytic scrutiny. Hence, there is a line from Descartes through Freud to Lacan, a line of 'interpretive translation', which proceeds from Descartes' *Cogito ergo sum*, through Freud's *Wo Es war, soll Ich werden*, to Lacan's (2006: 430) own: 'I am not, where I am the plaything of my thought; I think about what I am where I do not think I am thinking'. Again there is an unspoken Nietzschean echo here: it is the indirection of attention to thought that allows in the possibility of the Freudian unconscious.[7]

The three intellectual figures, meanwhile, which are to determine Ricoeur's thinking throughout the 1950s are Husserl, Marcel and Jaspers. But how does Ricoeur reconcile the existentialism of Jaspers and Marcel with Husserl's phenomenology, bearing in mind that the two former take what Ricoeur himself was later to call the 'direct route' to ontological understanding, while the latter takes the more circuitous route that Ricoeur was later able to develop into his hermeneutics? The answer lies in their respective treatments of the Cartesian *cogito* and Ricoeur's appropriation and development of them. The *cogito*, and what is in effect a mediation between its existential dismissal and a certain Husserlian Cartesian movement, is the site of a negotiation in Ricoeur's early thinking, which establishes an attitude (in the phenomenological as well as the everyday sense) towards being and existence which will enable Ricoeur not only to establish the parameters of his investigation into Freud in the 1960s, but also by extension to develop a philosophical theory of consciousness and self-knowledge which can accommodate both the Husserlian–Cartesian apodictic Ego, and a modified version of the Freudian unconscious.

To understand how this can be, it is necessary first to establish what Ricoeur finds in common between Jaspers and Marcel. The subtitle of Ricoeur's first single-authored book, *Gabriel Marcel et Karl Jaspers*, is *Philosophie du mystère et philosophie du paradoxe*, and this effectively summarises what is original about the philosophies of these two thinkers respectively. The notion of 'mystery', we recall, is summarised most succinctly in Marcel's 1933 essay 'On the Ontological Mystery', where 'mystery' is defined as something which, although we do not know the answer to it, does not require an answer. This is in contradistinction to a problem, which requires a solution. Indeed, for Marcel the mystery is *meta-problematical*. He illustrates this through an example. Suppose, he says, 'I have made an encounter which has made a deep and lasting trace on all my life' (Marcel 1948: 10). Suppose also that this encounter takes place at an Italian health spa. A rational explanation might be that the same person shares a similar taste for scenery, or suffers from a similar ailment. But this only explains the encounter; it does not explain why we should have been brought together in the deep sense of finding a life-changing affinity. To take this explanation to be causal would amount to a transgression of the very causal reasoning that has explained the fact of the meeting in the first place. Hence a mystery is 'rooted in what is beyond the domain of the problematical properly so called' (Marcel 1948: 11). In the example given, we cannot 'avoid the difficulty by saying that it was after all nothing but a coincidence, a lucky chance', since this would be a 'vain negation of what I apprehend with the deepest of my being' (Marcel 1948: 11). Note here that Marcel (and through his own admission) is not being, strictly speaking, philosophical: the 'coincidence theory' is a perfectly valid piece of philosophical reasoning; what negates it is not philosophical rationality, but faith. What Marcel does not acknowledge at this particular point of his argument, but which is intrinsic to his thinking as a whole, and which he does articulate elsewhere, is that mystery is that which confronts philosophy with faith, the fact of faith being that which philosophy as such runs up against in vain, if by 'philosophy' we mean a rational chain of reasoning leading to causal explanation.[8] So, then, a mystery is distinct from a problem; insofar as the language of 'problem' is appropriate to it, a mystery is 'a problem which encroaches on its own data': going back to Marcel's (1948: 11) example of the encounter with a significant other,

> I who enquire into the meaning and the possibility of this meeting, I cannot place myself outside it or before it; I am engaged in this encounter, I depend upon it, I am inside it in a certain sense, it envelops me and comprehends me – even if it is not comprehended by me.

At this point we see a first point of contact between Marcel and Jaspers. Marcel's mystery might be described as a 'limit concept' (or 'boundary situation'), a notion Jaspers (1970: 177–222) develops in his *Philosophy* to describe a reality that philosophy can only stare in the face but not overcome – the reality *that I exist*, for example. And for Marcel (1948: 11–12), too,

> To think, or, rather, to assert, the meta-problematical is to assert it as indubitably real, as a thing of which I cannot doubt without falling into contradiction. We are in a sphere where it is no longer possible to dissociate the idea itself from the certainty or the degree of certainty which pertains to it. Because this idea *is* certainty, it *is*, the assurance of itself; it is, in this sense, something other and something more than the idea.

We might immediately note that the certainty involved here is not Cartesian certainty. This is not to say that it is not a 'certain certainty'; rather, that the certainty is not arrived at through a Cartesian route. The thinking subject does not comprehend his own thinking to arrive at the one thing he cannot doubt; rather, the thinking involved here is not strictly speaking essential to the certainty as such. The certainty lies in the idea as a *récu*; it is the content of the idea that is certain, not the fact of thinking it (as if the thinking it were separable from the idea as such anyway). It follows that this 'deep' idea, that I have met this other person for a purpose, cannot be a unique idea, in the same way that the Cartesian *cogito* is unique. Indeed, the kind of universal scepticism that pertains *en route* to the *cogito* (and the counterpart to its uniqueness) is for Marcel (and here he may be indebted to Kierkegaard) a version of despair.

This brings us to a first point of contact between Marcel and Jaspers to be noted by Ricoeur, which is on the question of liberty, or freedom. Ricoeur (1947: 19)[9] says that 'the meaning and quality of my liberty' is quite different from one of these philosophers to the other. Ricoeur points out that there are two senses of the word 'I': the first is the classical one associated with Descartes, which has a role of personal attention in the knowledge of truth: it is this which Kantianism, for example, dispenses with in the establishment of a possibility of universal knowledge. As Ricoeur (1947: 20) puts it, 'I' is no longer 'me', but 'the thought in me'. On the other hand, the 'I' can be seen as that which positions itself against its life, events, society, etc.; the 'I' is less a thing I am through nature, than something that I bring into existence through the exercise of choice. This is the 'I' of Jaspers, and it is one he derives from Kierkegaard: for example, Jaspers is impressed by Kierkegaard's reading of Abraham, since Abraham defines his being *qua* Abraham through the exercise of a counter-intuitive choice (to sacrifice Isaac). It is this exercise of choice that, for Kierkegaard, makes Abraham a supra-ethical being; for Jaspers, as Ricoeur (1947: 21–2) points out, this *freedom* of choice enables Abraham to transcend mere empirical existence (if 'empirical' is construed as a passive perception); his being is indissociable from his action.

Ricoeur points out the importance of being incarnated for Marcel, especially insofar as it constitutes a critique of Cartesianism:

> Being or having a body, this body, my body, and, through its mediation without analogue in the reign of objects, being squarely with the world, that is what it is to be. Ideas come from that which does not exist. That which does not exist, is the *subject* which has these ideas, whereby ideas are its *objects*. Briefly, the opposite of existence, is not the being-there (Dasein) of the thing, but the abstract couple that comprises the *objectivity* of thoughts of geometry, physics, biology, sociology, and the *subject* of these thoughts, when the subject is no longer an incarnated being, but a function of the *a priori* conditions of united knowledge of its life and times, of love and of death. The discovery of the *Cogito* by Descartes essentially signifies for Marcel the access to the *subject* of knowledge. But it is a gain in the order of objectivity, it is a *part* of the

> dimension of existence. The *Cogito* is the 'non-inserted', more: 'the non-insertion in the course of an act'. In the course of this act of exile, the plenitude of a presence such as nature, work of art, friendship, God, risks being the torture of Tantalus of a thought which triumphs in the vanity of transparency to itself. (Ricoeur 1947: 27–8)

That the Cartesian *cogito* should isolate the 'subject', but in so doing, actually deprive it of existence, will become a clue to understanding Lacan's claim that the proper subject of psychoanalysis is the Cartesian subject. What Ricoeur appreciates is that for Marcel, the Cartesian subject is not a whole self: in effect, for Marcel the Cartesian 'subject' is the self minus the body. Being incarnated has existential significance: it is incarnatedness that enables the self to participate in the world, to be a being in the world. The achievement of Descartes is to have discovered the modern 'subject' (again, this anticipates Lacan's claim that the modern subject is the scientific subject; that science is not possible without the 'subject'), but at a terrible price, that of surrendering the being-in-the-world of the self incarnate. Hence, the Cartesian subject is 'transparent to itself', but the transparency of the *cogito* is mere vanity. Existence, for Marcel, is being-in-the-world; since the Cartesian subject is an idealisation, it does not 'exist' in the sense of being in the world. Comprehending the subject is a philosophical problem – *the* philosophical problem since Descartes – but still it fails to address the mystery of being.

Ricoeur's perceptive move is to find something in common with this Marcelian mystery and Jaspers' 'paradox', even though on the face of it 'mystery' and 'paradox' in the senses of Marcel and Jaspers appear incompatible. There is, says Ricoeur (1947: 28), a 'surprising meeting' between the two philosophers: 'the theory of incarnation is found again in Jaspers under the name of "historicity" or of "limit situations", which comprise the moment of arrest of the world of free existence through a moment of engagement with the world'. For Ricoeur, Marcel's 'incarnation' is nothing other than Jaspers' 'historicity' or 'limit situation', in that in both Marcel and Jaspers 'engagement with the world' is the overriding principle of their philosophies. Incarnation, historicity and limit situation all ground the subject in existence and ensure that the subject is not merely a subject, but a self. 'It is nonetheless remarkable', says Ricoeur (1947: 29), that Marcel and Jaspers each find, without mutual influence, the word 'situatedness' 'to designate this adherence of the concrete subject to its flesh and its world. It is above all remarkable that they have both recognised in incarnation or in historicity the anchoring point of metaphysics.'

Although the future direction of Marcel's philosophy is to develop an 'ontology of faith and hope', whereas Jaspers' will culminate in

Transcendence, it is the route to these respective problematics through the common source of being-in-the-world that interests Ricoeur, and which for him, despite the difference between 'paradox' and 'mystery', makes the philosophies of Jaspers and Marcel assimilable to one another:

> In effect, our situation is an *ordeal* that is not susceptible to pure description, but which is caught within a dialectic of surpassing whereby its sense changes completely, only when I run up against these real lesions through the affirmation of a Being that all the time envelops and surpasses the misery of my condition, or only when I cede to the invitation to despair that follows from all of my faults. The surpassing of the ego through Transcendence is thus sustained on the part of the other through the checks of the incarnated condition; it anticipates anew, as if to say in an instant, the tensions of Jaspers .... (Ricoeur 1947: 29)

Although the expressions 'paradox' and 'mystery', then, become clarified by a working-through of a critique of knowledge and of the existential respectively, in them we 'are presented only with a difference in complexion in a simple elucidation of the human condition' (Ricoeur 1947: 31).

Ricoeur's writings on Husserl from the 1940s and 1950s, meanwhile, are conveniently collected in English translation in *Husserl: An Analysis of His Phenomenology* (Ricoeur 1967a). These include the Introduction to his French translation of *Ideas I*, but Ricoeur's real interest at this time is in Husserl's treatment of the problem of 'constitution' and, more specifically, with providing a critique of the idealistic and egological strands of Husserl's phenomenology – a critique which Husserl himself develops in *Ideas II* and, especially, in *Cartesian Meditations.* Ricoeur's writings on Husserl are mainly introductory – apart from the 'Introduction' to *Ideas* itself, there are encyclopedia entries and other articles aimed at explaining Husserl to an unfamiliar French public – but it is the specific direction of the course which Ricoeur steers through Husserl that is of interest here, and his choice of aspects of Husserl's thinking that he brings to the fore.

In '*Ideas II*: Analyses and Problems' Ricoeur (1967a: 35–81) points out that *Ideas II* at once tests the method of 'intentional analysis' advanced in *Ideas I* and anticipates the systematic expression of Husserl's doctrine of 'transcendental solipsism' that is to be found in *Cartesian Meditations.* It is this latter doctrine that is of primary interest to Ricoeur, since its 'transcendental' element is precisely that which protects Husserlian phenomenology from the philosophical error of pure solipsism – an error that the 'subjectivity' of the starting point of the eidetic reduction has left open to accusation by unsympathetic critics.

An important aspect of Husserl's doctrine that Ricoeur (1967a: 36–7) notices is that 'the return to the ego leads to a monadism according to which the world is primordially the sense that my ego lays out'. This monadism is, of course, in distinction from Cartesian dualism, despite the Cartesian origin of the problematics which lead to the development of 'transcendental solipsism' in the first place. It is a point of contact between Husserl and those whom Ricoeur calls the 'existential phenomenologists', Marcel and Jaspers. As is to become a theme of his later philosophy, Ricoeur is keen to find points of contact between these apparently disparate thinkers, his own philosophy being indebted to those very points. In this case, Ricoeur (1967a: 37) notices that

> Husserl, lucidly assuming the responsibility of 'transcendental solipsism', tries to find something in the understanding of the Other that would resolve the extraordinary paradox of constituting 'in' me the primary 'outsider', the primordial 'Other', which, pulling me out of the domination of subjectivity, reorganises the sense of the world around it and inaugurates the intersubjective adventure of objectivity.

Objectivity allows phenomenology to assume the scientific footing which had to be presupposed in order for phenomenology to be initiated. But in the course of passing from subjectivity to objectivity, we should pause at intersubjectivity. The relationship with the 'Other' which this entails has implications for ethics (which is why *Ideas II* was significant to Merleau-Ponty and Lévinas), as well as offering a point of comparison with Lacan.

Ricoeur goes on to examine the three objects of Husserl's investigation in *Ideas II*, namely the 'thing', the 'soul', and *Geist*. Regarding the thing, Ricoeur points out that, once the phenomenological attitude has been adopted, the Kantian 'thing itself' can be interrogated. Such an interrogation is a 'noematic' reflection, 'because it is the cogitatum, not the cogito – the noema and not the noesis – that is elucidated' (Ricoeur 1967a: 41). What distinguishes the thing itself from *Geistigheit* is both extension and the essential attribute of thinghood. The latter half of this definition might sound circular, but Husserl's point is that extension and thinghood are mutually dependent: extension cannot be an attribute unless it is an attribute of a thing, just as a thing cannot exist without extension. As Ricoeur indicates, this facilitates comparison with Kant's Transcendental Aesthetic. Whereas for Kant space as a transcendental *a priori* was distinct from the things that occupied it, for Husserl 'the division of space is a division of the thing itself. Every quality appears or disappears in space, in some way "fills" it' (Ricoeur 1967a: 42). But what is more important for our purposes is that, as Ricoeur (1967a: 42) writes, 'an interesting notion for future analyses of the psyche is introduced here', which is that, in contradistinction to the thing, 'the psyche is not extended, it does not fill a space, and it is not spatially divisible'. However, 'it is localised in space, which is not the same thing, or, so to speak, it is ordered to space' (Ricoeur 1967a: 42).

This subtle analysis of the relation of the foundation of the psyche to things provides a useful clarification of the confusion generated by Freud's vacillation in *The Ego and the Id* and 'The Dissection of the Psychical Personality' between taking his topology of the psyche as a metaphor, and understanding it as a mapping of a real locus. Being *ordered to,* rather than *ordered in* space, is the crucial distinction here. The psyche, as an indissociable part of the monadistic subject, addresses objects in space through apprehending them, and this constitution of the psyche in relation to the mutual dependency of things-in-space orders the 'point of view' of that psyche – it is a Kantian law essential to its foundation and governing its apprehension – without granting to the psyche as such the status of 'thing as such', i.e., as something extended in space and itself thereby affecting space.

Such a line of thought is anticipated by Husserl himself in his description of the process of 'transfer' from an understanding of the Other to an understanding of the self. One of the consequences of Husserlian 'empathy' (that I realise by analogy that the Other is just like me in terms of his phenomenological constitution and, equally importantly, I realise that I am just like the Other in being presentable as well as being appresentable – that my personhood can be apprehended as a brain located within a body, for example) is 'the quasi-localisation of the soul'. By virtue of the correlation of the psychic with the corporeal that empathy of and with the Other entails, we realise that

> the soul is nowhere, but yet its connection with the body places it somewhere. It is localised only because it is ordered in relation to a place by an empirical rule. In this sense, man moves about, moves away, and moves back. By this quasi-localisation a man is incorporated with his subjectivity into my spatial surrounding world. The analogue of myself is over there. (Ricoeur 1967a: 66)

This raises the question of whether, for Husserl, intersubjective experience is prior to the solipsistic activity of the phenomenological reduction – in a footnote, Ricoeur (1967a: 66, n.20) suggests that Husserl 'does not reach a primitive experience of the psyche in the second person' because he is 'inhibited' by the 'descriptive method' of phenomenology. This notwithstanding, we might remark two features of Husserl's introduction of a phenomenology of intersubjectivity in *Ideas II.* First, Husserl arrives by a roundabout route at what Marcel took as a pre-given, namely incorporation as an essential attribute of the monalogical thinking subject – Husserl's phenomenology at this point is united with, or at least consistent with, what Ricoeur calls the insistence on the *corps propre*, or ownmost body, of the 'existential phenomenologists'. Second, Ricoeur brings out a privileging of the Other within a field of intersubjectivity which has obvious points of comparison – some of them sympathetic, some of them less so – with Lacan, which we shall examine below.

In his elucidation of *Ideas II*, Ricoeur repeatedly draws attention to its anticipation of, and points of contact with, *Cartesian Meditations*. In his discussion of that work, and particularly in his discussion of the Fifth Cartesian Meditation, Ricoeur returns to the 'problem of the Other'. According to Ricoeur, the whole of the Fifth Meditation is devoted to addressing the paradox that is at the heart of Husserlian phenomenology, and which leaves it open to the charge of solipsism:

> On the one hand, it must follow the reduction through to the end and maintain its wager on the constitution of the sense of the alter ego 'in' and 'arising from' the ego; on the other hand, it must account for the originality, the specificity, of the experience of the Other, precisely as the experience of someone other than I. (Ricoeur 1967a: 116)

As Ricoeur (1967a: 131) goes on to say, 'we must learn to coordinate empirical realism, for which communities are real beings, with transcendental idealism, for which all being-sense is drawn from the ego'. Again, as in *Ideas II*, it is the constitution of the psyche in relation to the owned body that resolves this paradox. As Ricoeur (1967a: 137) puts it:

> The psyche, like the owned body, is a naturalisation and a reification of the ego. On the basis of this naturalisation something like a 'reciprocity of Others' can be instituted. I see myself within the world as psyche among psyches, as psyche equalised with, separated from, and tied to the other psyches. Each man appears to each other man in an intra-psychic manner. . . .

The Other, then, comes to occupy a central place in Husserl's later philosophy, but also in Ricoeur's understanding of Husserl. It is the operations of 'transference' (not in the psychoanalytic sense, although we should note the resonance) from the ego to the other and vice versa that enables Husserl to realise the constitution of man in the world, which has universal applicability, and which opens the way to the concept of 'life-world' which Husserl developed in the 1930s. According to Ricoeur (1967a: 141), this transferential process between ego and Other 'disassembles the mechanism of Husserlian explication', by which he means, the mechanism of phenomenological description. It is this which enables Husserlian phenomenology as a whole to realise 'a harmonious equilibrium between tendencies which, were they separated, would lead back to the constructivism of German idealism and to the empiricism of the British tradition' (Ricoeur 1967a: 141).

This leads Ricoeur to a comparison between Descartes's *cogito* and what he calls the 'Husserlian *cogito*'. Whereas for Descartes the *cogito* 'furnishes the first link in a chain of truths', phenomenology cannot be so systematic: 'The Husserlian *cogito* is not a truth to be followed by other truths in an "order of reasons". The *cogito* plays, rather, the role of "origin" (*Ursprung*), of "antecedent foundation", instead of that of initial theorem' (Ricoeur 1967a: 141). Note here that the *cogito* is still the *cogito*: Husserl does not challenge the content or validity of the Cartesian *cogito* as such, nor does Ricoeur claim he does. But the *cogito* takes its place in Husserlian phenomenology as part of what Ricoeur was later to call the 'long route' to understanding. Whereas Marcel and Jaspers, and, in a different way, Heidegger, short-circuited the hermeneutic journey through an insistence on the primacy of (embodied) ontology, what is appealing about the *cogito* for Husserl is that it locates the origin of thinking in thinking. Even if it is true, as Nietzsche claimed, that the *cogito* proves nothing because it is a circular argument, the circle is worth traversing. In Ricoeur's later works it is to become, in effect, a variation of the hermeneutic circle.

3

From the *Cogito* to the Unconscious

If *Karl Jaspers and the Philosophy of Existence, Gabriel Marcel and Karl Jaspers* and the essays collected in *Husserl: An Analysis of his Phenomenology* were primarily 'explicatory' works, then *The Voluntary and the Involuntary* is Ricoeur's first attempt at an original philosophy. Although this work is primarily Husserlian, it nevertheless marks an important shift in emphasis from Husserl's thought. In '*Ideas II*: Analyses and Problems' Ricoeur (1967a: 41) had remarked that

> If it is true that consciousness is an 'I can' (as Husserl repeats in every extended philosophical exposition of his method), then this is why the power of consciousness does not interest him insofar as it is liberating but rather interests him insofar as it is legislative. Phenomenology is a philosophy of 'sense' more than a philosophy of 'freedom'.

The Voluntary and the Involuntary, by contrast, takes freedom as its primary concern,[1] while still more or less following Husserl's phenomenological method.

There, Ricoeur takes up the theme of ambivalence towards the *cogito* once again. He writes that in order 'to understand the relations between the involuntary and the voluntary we must constantly reconquer the *cogito* grasped in the first person from the natural standpoint' (Ricoeur 1966: 9). This effectively encapsulates the entire project of Husserl's Fifth Meditation. The Natural Standpoint is, we recall, the pre-phenomenological standpoint, the standpoint from which the objects of perception in nature are viewed and considered as 'real' – these include the Cartesian 'mind'. It is only by performing the *epochē* or phenomenological reduction that the natural standpoint can be held in suspension in favour of an apperception of thinking from the standpoint of thinking, a self-awareness of thinking which short-circuits the Nietzschean objection that there is no guarantee that it is 'I' who thinks. However, again reprising his own conclusions regarding the route to understanding which *Ideas II* and *Cartesian Meditations* have taken, Ricoeur reminds us that the 'reconquest' of the *cogito* 'can make use of the Cartesian *cogito*'. Ricoeur also reminds us that for Descartes himself, we 'learn to conceive of the union of the soul and the body' when we turn to the discourse of ordinary life, and refrain from meditation and the 'study of all that makes use of the imagination' (1966: 9). So, the possibility of Cartesian dualism being overcome is acknowledged by Descartes himself, although for Descartes this leads to a contradiction to be avoided. This is the same contradiction as the paradox that confronted Husserl, when he sought to reconcile the objective world implied by intersubjectivity with the solipsism implied by egology.

Be this as it may, 'the reconquest of the *cogito* must be complete', says Ricoeur (1966: 9), if we are to address the task of describing the voluntary and the involuntary. We must be receptive to the *cogito*'s complete experience, which means not only 'I think' as such (the privileged site of phenomenological apperception), but also each of the various modes of thinking. Moreover, these modes of thinking are to be examined intentionally, in the Husserlian sense: need is to be treated as 'I have need of . . .', desire as 'I have desire of . . .', etc. Here we might pause to note that such intentional desire is overlooked, or occluded, in Lacan's formula, 'Desire is the desire of a desire'. This formula effectively reduces all intentionality (in the sphere of desire) to what we might call 'apperceptive desire'. If the initial phenomenological descriptive moment is one of bracketed-off thinking that one is thinking, and if the 'intersubjective' trajectory of Husserl's *Ideas II* and Fifth Meditation show that this is only a preliminary stage in the reconquest of the *cogito*, then by analogy Lacanian desire as an apperceptive process fails to overcome the solipsistic temptation. The 'Other' in Lacanian theory would thus be merely a projection of the self, lacking the 'reciprocity' which Husserl identifies in analogical empathy. Indeed, 'empathy' is a quality distinctly lacking in Lacanian thinking, which may be a reason to be sceptical regarding the efficacy of Lacanian psychoanalysis as a curative process.

But back to Ricoeur. If Lacan reduces each of the modes of intentionality of the *cogito* to 'desire', Ricoeur on the contrary lists desire as but one of the *cogito*'s modes, along with 'I can', 'I intend', 'I have a habit of', and all of the other intentionalities which together constitute a person's character. If we are to divide this list into 'voluntary intentions' and 'involuntary intentions', we see that the involuntary ones are sustained by the body. Again, we might remark in passing that there are two divergences from Lacan here. First, the fact that Lacan does not make a primary distinction between voluntary and involuntary (which is both cause of and consequent upon his blindness to intentionality), suggests a certain deterministic strand to his thought, which would be consistent with his adherence to structuralism in linguistics, itself implicitly (and sometimes explicitly) deterministic and behaviouristic in the philosophical conclusions that follow from it. Second, the body here (in Ricoeur, as it is in Husserl) is a real body, not the subject's phantasmatic projection of his imagined body, and not a body that the subject 'owns' in the same way as one might own a cream cake or a car. This is the point of the notion of *corps propre*, perhaps misleadingly translated as 'ownmost body'. For me to own my body I would have to stand outside it 'objectively', so that it would be a 'thing' for me. But the Husserlian analysis of space suggests that, on the contrary, 'I' and my body are not dissociable in such a way. As Ricoeur (1966: 9) puts it, 'the *cogito*'s experience, taken as a whole, includes . . . my existence as a body', and further, 'the subjectivity of the *cogito* is the intersubjectivity of the "I" function extended to the body itself as a personal body' (Ricoeur 1966: 11). Ricoeur's treatment of this is directly Husserlian; indeed, it is more or less a reprise of the conclusion he reached in summarising Husserl's Fifth Meditation:

> On the one hand, my consciousness is profoundly transformed by the reoccurrence of the other's consciousness in it. I treat myself as a you which in its external appearance is a presentation of the other. From this viewpoint, to know myself is to anticipate my presentation to a you. On the other hand, knowledge of myself is always to some extent the guide for deciphering the other, even if the other is in the first place and principally an original revelation of empathy. The you is an other myself. (Ricoeur 1966: 11)[2]

This, however, leads to a problem. There ought to be a 'relation between the body as mine or yours and the body as an object among the objects of science' (Ricoeur 1966: 12), since they are the same body. The relation is not one of correlation, however, but of the diagnosis of a symptom. A doctor, for example, might detect a secretion, say, in the object body, and this might be diagnosed as a symptom that indicates an intention on the part of the body belonging to the subject, which finds its expression in the language of the *cogito*. But this is difficult: it is quite normal for the 'subjective equivalent' of the diagnosed symptom to be 'quite ambiguous'. And, says Ricoeur (1966: 13), 'in some cases it will appear almost impossible to discover the subjective indication, in the language of the *cogito*, of a function or an occurrence which is well known in biology or in empirical psychology'. And one of Ricoeur's examples of these 'almost impossibilities' is the unconscious.

Before turning to Ricoeur's critique of the Freudian unconscious, however, we should note that Ricoeur (1966: 13–14) encounters a stumbling block in his pursuit of phenomenological method in practice:

> Far from being overcome by the discovery of a common subjective standard between willing and the body, the epistemic dualism seems in a way to be raised by the descriptive method to the essence of the *cogito*

> itself. The triumph of description is distinction rather than a reuniting leap. Even in the first person, desire is something other than decision, movement is other than an idea, necessity is other than the will which consents to it. The *cogito* is broken up within itself.

At this point the Lacanian might cry 'yes!'. And Ricoeur (1966: 14) appears to be heading in a psychoanalytic direction himself when he goes on to explain why the *cogito* should be so broken:

> Extension of the *cogito* to include personal body in reality requires more than a change of method: the Ego must more radically renounce the covert claim of all consciousness, must abandon its wish to posit itself, so it can receive the nourishing and inspiring spontaneity which breaks the sterile circle of the self's constant return to itself.

But such a renunciation does not involve, for Ricoeur, an admission of the Freudian unconscious. Rather, it is at this point that he imports the Marcelian 'incarnation as a mystery' to come to the aid of a Husserlian method pushed to the limits of its adequacy. According to Ricoeur, Marcel's rediscovery of incarnation bursts thought by object: the reorientation from 'problem' to 'mystery' consists of a conversion from 'objectivity' to 'existence'. Ricoeur claims that the analyses in *The Voluntary and the Involuntary* are based on Marcel's notion of the mystery of incarnation: the overall methodological strategy adopted is one of reconciling Husserlian description of the subjective structures of the voluntary with an 'encompassing sense' of the mystery of incarnation, the latter of which, of course, corresponds to the involuntary.

Ricoeur does, however, address Freud directly when he analyses 'experienced necessity'. He embarks on an analysis of the Freudian unconscious by exposing what he calls a 'false dichotomy' between what is 'hidden' when my freedom deceives itself, and the hidden of the unconscious, which must be forcibly extracted through some such 'scientific' technique as psychoanalysis. The former are 'lies', which may be exposed to the self through self-searching; the latter Ricoeur (1966: 375) defines by way of a question: 'Is it possible ... that my decisions are false decisions, my reasons sham motives which *stand for* unconscious motives which I cannot compare because of some mysterious hindrance?'. The interrogative mood indicates a certain scepticism on Ricoeur's part towards the very notion of the Freudian unconscious at this point in the development of his thought, a scepticism which is lent weight by Ricoeur's belief that the dichotomy between the two types of the hidden is a false one anyway, the result of 'a double obstacle':

the obstacle of a dogmatism of the unconscious which commits the error and the fault of attributing *thought* to the unconscious, and the obstacle of dogmatism of consciousness which commits the error and perhaps also the fault of pride, of assigning to consciousness a transparence which it does not have. (Ricoeur 1966: 375)

Perhaps 'false dichotomy' is not quite an accurate term here (even though it is Ricoeur's own), since what Ricoeur is objecting to is the tendency of psychoanalysis to take the second type of hiddenness as if it were the first type. In other words, if something is hidden to myself (the first type), then by self-examination I can recover what is hidden; I can do this because, up until that point, I am in a sense lying to myself. Psychoanalysis, meanwhile, presents 'any relation between appearance and being of human thought which is not immediately transparent ... as a kind of lie' (Ricoeur 1966: 375). The upshot of this is that 'it is rather tempting to shift all responsibility to the ruses of that unconscious demon which I claim to bear within me' (Ricoeur 1966: 375); hence, psychoanalysis leads not only to moral relativism, but also to the abnegation of moral responsibility: 'It wasn't me, guv, it was me unconscious!' Moreover, just as psychoanalytic 'hiddenness' appropriates to itself territory occupied by the self-deception type of hiddenness, so too does the psychoanalyst appropriate responsibility to himself:[3] the one remaining difference between the two types of hiddenness is that in the psychoanalytic type, it is the psychoanalyst who reveals to the patient the truth behind the lies of his unconscious – the patient is unable to do this himself.

The first fault, of attributing thought to the unconscious, is, says Ricoeur, one of a realism of the unconscious, while the second is one of idealism of consciousness. In *The Voluntary and the Involuntary*, Ricoeur attacks both of these faults. Taking the second first, Ricoeur adopts the position already taken by Wittgenstein (1966) in the 1930s (but unpublished at the time Ricoeur was writing, and so he could not have been aware of this), that in the case of dreams, for example, psychoanalysis presupposes that every dream has a 'meaning, that is, can be explained by causes' (Ricoeur 1966: 382). This confuses, as Wittgenstein put it, a necessary explanation with a plausible one: the internal logical coherence of Freud's theory makes it seductively plausible, but it does not follow from this that it is necessarily true.[4] Ricoeur's (1966: 381) original insight concerning this is that this attribution of cause is an indissociable part of psychoanalytic *method*: 'the psychoanalytic method ... consists of gathering indications whose convergence leads us to the hidden *cause*'. Without the adoption of this 'naturalistic standpoint', psychoanalysis as such is impracticable. 'This is a point', says Ricoeur (1966: 381), 'we cannot overstress': in the same way that biology is only possible if we treat the body as an object, so psychoanalysis is only possible if we treat the psychology of the subject as if the subject himself is incapable of discovering the facts that serve as indications of his unconscious processes.

But, of course, the existential phenomenological tradition which takes its lead from the Husserl of *Ideas II* and the Fifth *Cartesian Meditation,* and which is prefigured by Marcel, discovers a domain of the body other than that understood by biology, namely, the *corps propre* or ownmost body, that which is not only perceived *by* the subject, but is also that *through* which the subject perceives as a monadological unity. Indeed, only the most diehard of naturalistic, mechanistic and behaviouristic biologists would claim that biology explained the totality of 'what it means to have a body'. And yet Freudian psychoanalysis presumes to explain the totality of the psyche. As Ricoeur wishes to stress, this is not merely a matter of doctrine, but is intrinsically necessary to psychoanalytic method.[5]

We have already seen how Freud's clearest articulation of the 'realism of the unconscious' is to be found in Lecture 32 of the *New Introductory Lectures.* But it is to this place in the Freudian corpus that Ricoeur turns to attack its counterpart, the idealism of consciousness. Echoing Freud's lecture, Ricoeur (1966: 384) writes that the 'heart of psychoanalysis' is 'a means of extending the field of consciousness'. Thus, Ricoeur finds the heart of psychoanalysis in the same place as Lacan – the end of Lecture 32 of the *New Introductory Lectures* – but his view of it is entirely different. Another point that Ricoeur 'cannot overstress' is that 'the grasp of consciousness is not reducible to a simple theoretical understanding' for psychoanalysis. This was a point Freud himself discovered as early as the late 1890s, and which forms the subject of (his discussion of) the dream of Irma's injection.[6] The patient cannot just 'accept the cure', if the cure is simply an explanation of the symptoms. Rather, repression must be lifted in order to bring about the cure. While 'interpretation is not repression', as Ricoeur (1966: 384) puts it, nevertheless, 'interpretation by the other is a necessary detour between a sick and healthy consciousness', it is that which causes the repression to be lifted, not the subject simply 'knowing' what their symptoms 'mean'. *By the other*: this is the essential point that Ricoeur (1966: 384) takes from Freud's lecture:

> Someone *other* (this other can be myself, in some special circumstances, difficult to bring about) has to interpret and know in order for me to be able to become reconciled with myself. Someone other has to treat me as an *object,* as a field of causal explanation, and to consider my consciousness itself as a symptom, as the sign-effect of unconscious forces, in order for myself to become the master of *myself* once more.

But in order to have got this far, we must believe that there is such a thing as repression. And as we have seen and as Ricoeur (1966: 383, n. 34) notices in a footnote, 'The Dissection of the Psychical Personality' introduces the theory of the 'super-ego' to shift 'interest from the repressed to the repressing unconscious'. The repressing unconscious is a psychic mechanism; hence, once again, 'ethical and social *values* which inhibit incompatible tendencies function as a psychic *force*, construed by the analyst on the model of physical forces' (Ricoeur 1966: 383). For Ricoeur, this very terminology of forces rather than values exposes the error of psychoanalytic doctrine on this point: 'censorship', 'guardian consciousness', 'disguise', etc., are 'dangerous metaphors', and it is important that we remember that they *are* metaphors.

Having addressed the 'idealism of consciousness' in Freudian theory, Ricoeur turns his attention to the 'realism of the unconscious'. This is perhaps the point of greatest divergence between Ricoeur and Lacan. Both agree that, as Ricoeur (1966: 385) puts it: 'The concept of the "meaning" of unconscious thought itself is at stake here'. Moreover, Ricoeur (1966: 385) uses the same term as Lacan, 'Copernican revolution', to describe the effect of Freud's discovery of the unconscious: 'the centre of human being is displaced from *consciousness and freedom* as they give themselves to the unconscious and the absolute involuntary of which we are ignorant and which are known by a new natural science'. What, then, is the essential disagreement on this point between Ricoeur and Lacan?

The answer lies in the 'it thinks' of the realism of the unconscious. This is for Lacan (2006: 458) the most important lesson to be derived from Freud:

> Freud discovered that, without us thinking about it, and thus without anyone being able to think he thinks about it better than anyone else, it thinks. It thinks rather badly, but it thinks steadily. It is in these very terms that Freud announces the unconscious to us: thoughts that . . . are certainly articulated.

Whatever the secret affinities we might have detected between Lacan and Ricoeur, on this particular point the two could not be further apart, Ricoeur being adamant that 'it' cannot 'think'. Reprising both *The Ego and the Id* and 'The Dissection of the Psychical Personality', Ricoeur (1966: 386) writes that for Freud,

> consciousness is understood as a part of the unconscious, as a small circle included within a larger circle. Freud represents the unconscious as thought homogenous with conscious thought and lacking only the quality of consciousness. In this sense the unconscious is really the essence of the psyche, the psyche itself, and its essential reality.

Ricoeur (1966: 386) calls the alleged 'it thinks' of the unconscious a 'chimerical interpretation', and in attacking it, he eulogises the Descartes of the *Treatise on Passions.* If the point of Husserlian phenomenology was not so much the freedom of consciousness as the rational law of its description, this is by no means true of Ricoeur himself, who is fulsome in his praise of Cartesian 'generosity'. This generosity lies in 'knowledge, action, and feeling'. As in Descartes, so in Ricoeur: the certainty prompted by the *cogito* becomes elevated to an ethical principle. Knowledge is 'A knowledge beyond suspicion: namely that in every man "there is nothing which belongs to him truly other than this free disposition of his will, nor for which he could be praised or blamed except for the good or bad use he makes of it"' (Ricoeur 1966: 386). The action is a promise, which many years later Ricoeur would elevate to almost ontological status in his *Oneself as Another*: it is, in the words of Descartes, 'a firm and constant resolution to use them well, that is, never to lack willingness to undertake and execute all the things which he judges to be best; this is what following virtue perfectly means' (cited in Ricoeur 1966: 386). The feeling, meanwhile, is 'respect for myself as free "so that we do not lose, through cowardice, the rights it gives us"' (Ricoeur 1966: 386). Thus, even relatively early in his career, Ricoeur is anticipating many of the themes that are to occupy him in *Oneself as Another* and beyond, as well as anchoring the 'will' side of the central antinomy of *The Voluntary and the Involuntary* in an ethics: 'When I conceive of my unconscious as thinking', he writes, 'I yield to this "cowardice", to this "misconception of myself", which in Descartes' eyes is the opposite of generosity' (Ricoeur 1966: 386).

But, thus far, Ricoeur's praise of the Cartesian will in the face of the Freudian unconscious is merely a counter-assertion of an ethics: it does not address the Freudian (or Lacanian) assertion that 'it thinks' through argument. For that, a return to phenomenology is needed. The phenomenological moment – the moment of apperception, of the phenomenological perceiving that one is perceiving – is not, Ricoeur (1966: 387) reminds us, 'an added operation, grafted onto perception from without, but the explanation of an intrinsic moment of perception'. For the phenomenologist, consciousness is 'unreflected', and 'it is this conception of unreflected consciousness which justifies the use of the word consciousness to designate perception itself' (Ricoeur 1966: 387). This leads us back once again to intentionality: 'As Husserl says, consciousness is consciousness of. ... Intentionality and consciousness belong together' (Ricoeur 1966: 387).

Once Ricoeur has reminded us of this link between consciousness and intentionality, he is able to ask what we conclude from this. And the answer is not 'that there is no unconscious', but, precisely, that 'the unconscious does not think, does not perceive, does not remember, does not judge' (Ricoeur 1966: 387). 'And yet', writes Ricoeur (1966: 387), '"something" is unconscious, something which is akin to perception, akin to memory, akin to judgement', and which psychoanalysis reveals. What is this 'something'? At this point, Ricoeur's (1966: 387) argument departs from the Cartesian–Husserlian phenomenological path it has thus far taken: 'There is in that "something" *that which* sustains an act of perception, but is not yet an act of perception but an impressional matter not yet brought to life by an intentional aim. ... Briefly, it is not yet a consciousness of ...'. This is a significant step beyond Husserl, and a point at which phenomenology is forced to make a concession, a chink in the armour of pure consciousness: 'Psychoanalysis forces us to admit that the infra-perceptive "impressions" can be dissociated from their corresponding intentionality and undergo alterations such that they are cloaked by an apparent meaning which seems absurd' (Ricoeur 1966: 387–8).

This is not, for Ricoeur, a matter of 'splitting hairs' with the psychoanalyst. For him, 'the "working realism" of a psychoanalyst is not philosophically tenable' (Ricoeur 1966: 388). Just like ions and electrons, which, Husserl reminds the physicist, are 'original perceptions' rather than *Dinge an sich*, so the unconscious, Ricoeur (1966: 388) reminds the psychoanalyst, 'is a "psychological" object which refers to certain impressional aspects implied in some way by the unreflecting consciousness'.

Despite the concession made to psychoanalysis by phenomenology in the acknowledgement of this 'something', Ricoeur's analysis from this point on becomes resolutely phenomenological. Psychoanalysis, he says, *gives* a meaning to dreams and neuroses. 'What is this meaning?', he asks (Ricoeur 1966: 389). The answer is that 'desires expressed in waking language – hate of father, love of mother, return to the womb, etc. – are only desires as conceived by the psychoanalyst or by the subject himself as he adopts them' (Ricoeur 1966: 389). When the psychoanalyst talks of 'latent meaning', he is not altogether wrong: 'The "latent meaning" is that "something" which, if it were thought completely by a waking consciousness, would be what the psychoanalysts call "meaning"' (Ricoeur 1966: 389–90). But just because, in the experience of analysis, everything takes place as if the latent meaning 'were already hidden behind the manifest contents' (Ricoeur 1966: 390), it does not follow that it really is so. Rather, in the case of dreams, it is not the nocturnal consciousness that has the wherewithal to perform the four stages of what Freud calls the 'dream-work': it is, rather, 'the analyst who thinks, who is intelligent, and his patient after him' (Ricoeur 1966: 390).

Thus it is that in the 1950s, culminating in the 'Experienced Necessity' chapter of his *The Voluntary and the Involuntary*, Ricoeur is essentially unsympathetic to Freudian psychoanalysis. He attacks both the 'idealism' and the 'realism' of the unconscious. Its idealism lies in its false attribution of causality to the 'psychic processes': plausibility of explanation is not the same as truth. Its realism lies in taking the unconscious as a thing and, moreover, as a thing that thinks, that in some sense has a 'consciousness' of its own. From Ricoeur's phenomenological standpoint, this is inherently contradictory, since such a thing would be a consciousness without intentionality – which is not consciousness at all. This is not to say that Ricoeur dismisses the unconscious altogether. He acknowledges that psychoanalysis teaches phenomenology a lesson, and that is that thought is not transparent: the Cartesian *cogito* must henceforth be conceived of in a new way to account for this. But the opacity of certain regions of thought to the subject does not entail that those thoughts inhabit a separate domain within my psyche, inaccessible to me but accessible to another, the psychoanalyst. Freudian psychoanalysis, thinks Ricoeur, cedes too much power to the analyst – the analyst becomes what Lacan would later call a *sujet supposer savoir*, a subject who is supposed to know. This not only flies in the face of the Socratic dictum 'know thyself', of which Husserl was a great admirer, but also carries with it an abnegation of moral responsibility on the part of the subject. All of this can be summarised as a suspicion on the part of Ricoeur (1966: 400–1) that psychoanalysis leads to determinism and, hence, to the opposite of freedom:

> If the unconscious were purely and simply a 'thing', a 'reality' homogenous with the nature of objects subject to the law of determinism, it would no longer have room for a voluntary and free superstructure. Man in his entirety would be given over to determinism. This is in fact how the Freudians interpret human psychic life. Freud's entire work breathes his mistrust of the place of the will and of freedom.

The realism of the unconscious, the 'it thinks' of the unconscious, drives a wedge between Ricoeur and Lacan. But, as we shall see in the next chapter, in the 1960s, in *De l'interprétation* (*Freud and Philosophy*) and the associated essays collected in *The Conflict of Interpretations*, Ricoeur becomes more accommodating to Freud, proportionately as he leaves behind a pure phenomenology in favour of one mediated by hermeneutics. This 'hermeneutic turn' leads Ricoeur to acknowledge as many points of contact between phenomenology and psychoanalysis as differences; it also propels him into the realm of language and discourse, which will enable direct comparison between Ricoeur and Lacan.

4

The Unconscious and Language

Through the working-through of the symbolics of *The Symbolism of Evil*, Ricoeur has by the 1960s become more receptive to the mediation of language in the process of understanding being-human and of human understanding. He has also approached Freud anew, without the predisposition to 'attack' him, but rather from a position of sympathy towards psychoanalysis as a hermeneutic project. At the end of the last chapter, we remarked that this propulsion of Ricoeur into the realm of language and discourse places him in proximity to Lacan. It is to their respective treatments of the question of language – or, more precisely, of 'the symbolic' – that we now turn.

In 'A Philosophical Interpretation of Freud' (Ricoeur 1989: 160–76), which serves as a justification for both the writing of *Freud and Philosophy* as such and the methodology adopted therein, Ricoeur explains his project to be one of 'reflective renewal' of Freudian concepts, rather than one of critique as such. His guiding question is, 'What happens to a philosophy of reflection when it allows itself to be instructed by Freud?' (Ricoeur 1989: 171). This represents quite a significant reversal in Ricoeur's thinking: in *The Voluntary and the Involuntary*, it was Freud who was to be instructed by reflective philosophy, and found to be wanting, to boot. But now, Ricoeur (1989: 171) wants to know 'what happens to the subject of reflection when the guile of consciousness is taken seriously and consciousness is discovered as false consciousness, which says something other than it says or believes it says?' This 'taking seriously' is something that does not, ultimately, interest the Ricoeur of *The Voluntary and the Involuntary*, where, as we have seen, it is not consciousness which is deemed to be 'false', but rather psychoanalysis's implicit dichotomy between a deceived consciousness and a lying unconscious. Indeed, it is a mark of the shift in Ricoeur's position that he is able to say that he has 'followed Freud' in saying 'that one can no longer establish the philosophy of the subject as a philosophy of consciousness' (Ricoeur 1989: 172) (which was Husserl's life project and one which determined the entirety of Ricoeur's *Philosophy of the Will* – could this be the reason he abandoned the projected third volume?): 'Reflection and consciousness no longer coincide' (Ricoeur 1989: 172).

This is not to say that Ricoeur has the zeal of a convert to Freudianism. Far from it: the critique of *The Voluntary and the Involuntary* remains essentially intact, but now, Ricoeur seeks to supplement it with a more positive interpretation. So, Freud's 'naturalism' is still held to be 'unjustifiable', and the 'realism' of 'psychic "places"' (the allusion is once again to *The Ego and the Id* and 'The Dissection of the Psychical Personality') is still 'philosophically insupportable' (Ricoeur 1989: 172).

Ricoeur (1970: 420) begins his meditation on 'Freud and the Question of the Subject' by remarking that 'Freud very clearly ignores and rejects any problematic of the primal or fundamental subject', which, if true, would mean that Freud does not have the Cartesian *cogito* in mind when he advances his formula *Wo Es war, soll Ich werden,* which in turn would mean that Lacan's interpretation of Freud on this point would be an interpolation to serve Lacan's own (philosophical) ends. But, nevertheless, it *is* a question of the *cogito* for Ricoeur (1970: 420–1), too, insofar as for him Freudianism is a 'flight from the question of the *I think, I am*': the *cogito* is 'the very factor that escapes analytic conceptualisation'; the result of finding the id when we look for the ego in psychoanalysis is that the '*ego* of the *cogito sum* has escaped'. Ricoeur's philosophical move is, rather than to take the Freudian flight from the ego and the *cogito* to be a failure, to take it to be a moment of reflection, which oddly unites it with the problematics raised by Husserlian reflective phenomenology.

To this end, Ricoeur (1970: 421) cites Husserl's famous remark in the *Cartesian Meditations,* that 'adequacy and apodicticity of evidence need not go hand in hand', which for Ricoeur 'provides the framework in which the Freudian problematic can be thought and reflected upon'. The phenomenological reduction – in its 'bracketing off' of the question of the veracity of perception – leaves open the possibility entertained in passing by Descartes on his route to the *cogito,* that I am deceived; moreover, this is 'co-extensive with the certitude of the *I think*' (Ricoeur 1970: 421). The very phenomenological reduction itself reveals that

> At the very heart of the certitude of the *I am* there remains the question: 'How far can the transcendental ego be deceived about itself? And how far do these components extend that are absolutely indubitable in spite of such possible deception?' (Ricoeur 1970: 421)

This represents an advance in Ricoeur over his position in *The Voluntary and the Involuntary,* in that he his now moving towards what is to become a recurring theme of his life's work, that of the 'secret communion' between two apparently irreconcilable philosophical points of view. Whereas in *The Voluntary and the Involuntary* Freudianism was problematic on the side of the involuntary, here it is in communion with the possibility of doubt that lies at the heart of Husserlian egology. Despite all the seeming obstacles, psychoanalysis has now been admitted into the tradition of phenomenological philosophy.

But what is its effect? Earlier in Book III of *De l'interprétation*, Ricoeur had approached the same problem from the opposite direction, which is to say, he approaches the psychoanalytic field phenomenologically, rather than approaching the phenomenological field psychoanalytically. There, as well as reminding us that, in the phenomenological reduction, 'immediate consciousness is deposed along with the natural attitude' (so that 'phenomenology begins by a humiliation or wounding of the knowledge belonging to immediate consciousness', a wounding akin to that which it receives from the theory of the unconscious), the notion of intentionality can also be construed as a 'step toward the Freudian unconscious' (Ricoeur 1970: 377).[1] Intentionality is 'both commonplace and unfathomable': it is part of the structure of intentional acts that they are 'unreflected', i.e., the *cogito* is operative 'prior to being uttered' in them (Ricoeur 1970: 378). More simply, if I utter an intentional statement such as 'I believe it is raining', the *cogito* is implicit in this 'I believe', even though I do not reflect on this fact – one could say, it is unconscious. Or, as Ricoeur (1970: 379) puts it in more abstract terms,

> This unawareness proper to the unreflected marks a new step toward the Freudian unconscious; it means that the co-implicit or co-intended cannot completely attain to the transparency of consciousness precisely because of the texture of the act of consciousness, i.e. because of the invincible unawareness of self that characterises intentionality in act.[2]

Now, intentionality, like the *cogito* itself, is dependent on language, as our example of 'I believe it is raining' demonstrates (such an example is not provided by Ricoeur, who could be more explicit on this point). Lacan and Ricoeur agree on a further point: that psychoanalysis as an 'archaeology of the subject' (tracing the origins of the subject's neuroses, etc., through the recollection of memory) 'lies at the intersection of desire and language' (Ricoeur 1970: 395). A question of epistemology is raised by the coordination of the 'economic language' of psychoanalysis (that the discourse of the subject is determined by the libidinal drives of the psychic system) and the 'intentional language' of phenomenology. Despite their point of contact, 'phenomenology is not psychoanalysis', and the language of each (or, more properly, the ways in which each construe 'language' respectively) cannot be reduced to the other.

However, when Ricoeur (1970: 395) takes 'the linguistic aspects of the unconscious as our guide', he immediately takes issue with Lacan's claim that 'the unconscious is structured like a language'. For Ricoeur, Freud himself does not see his as being a linguistic theory. We recall that Lacan, in 'The Instance of the Letter in the Unconscious', insists that the theory of dream interpretation, and of the associated rebus,[3] is a linguistic theory:

> In Freud's complete works, one out of three pages presents us with philological references, one out of two pages with logical inferences, and everywhere we see a dialectical apprehension of experience, linguistic analysis becoming still more prevalent the more directly the unconscious is involved.
>
> Thus what is at stake on every page of *The Interpretation of Dreams* is what I call the letter of discourse, in its texture, uses, and immanence in the matter in question. (Lacan 2006: 424)

Now, using philological references, however frequently, does not make one a philologist, in the same way that driving a motor car does not make one a mechanic. Nor does using logical inferences make one a logician – it just means that one is rational. But notwithstanding this, how does Lacan's claim, that Freud was really a linguist, stand up? First, we might wonder why Freud never says 'I am a linguist'. Is this because he was one without admitting it to himself, or because he was one without realising it? This is not an entirely facetious question: the two alternatives it presents correspond to the two types of non-consciousness identified by Ricoeur: that of the self-deceptive lie, and that of the unconscious – and neither can be explained away by the merely circumstantial fact that Freud was unaware of Saussure. (*The Interpretation of Dreams* pre-dates the *Course in General Linguistics,* but if the later Freud of the 1920s and 1930s really saw himself as a linguist, he would surely have sought out the principal figures in the discipline of linguistics as it had then become established.)

But there is no need to dwell on the facts of the case of whether Freud read linguistics or saw himself as a linguist. The pertinent question is whether Freud's theory lends itself to an interpretation that sees the theory as a 'linguistic' one. We recall that in Chapter VI of *The Interpretation of Dreams* ('The Dream-Work'), the dream-work is analysed as consisting of four stages: condensation, displacement, figurability and secondary revision. The first three, being processes in converting psychic material into 'the language of the dream', are what concern us here.

It is tempting to read these processes linguistically, especially in the light of the structural linguistics of Roman Jakobson. Hence, figurability and displacement are both examples of code-switching, of moving from pictorial code to linguistic code, and vice versa. In this very notion of 'code' Jakobson – quite aside from Lacan – is assuming pictures to be a 'code' in just the same way as language is, or at least, that they are 'encoded' is the common defining feature that essentially unites them, regardless of the specificities of their instantiations independent of such encoding.[4] If one has such a 'semiotic' view of the world, that language, pictures, sounds, etc. – in short, the entire domain of the perceptible – is governed by the dynamic of encodability or *signification,* then it becomes very easy to see Freud's 'rebus' as a mode of encoding and decoding in this structuralist sense. Freud sees the interpretation of dreams to be a following of the process of the dream-work in reverse. In the structuralist linguistic view, this process, of creating or deciphering (encoding and decoding) a rebus becomes a process of translation:[5] in the dream-work, first, an element in pictorial code is translated into verbal code, and, second, the element in the verbal code is translated into an alternative, homonymous element within the same verbal code.

It is against this intellectual background that Lacan explains the first three terms of the Freudian dream-work. Transposition, he writes, 'is what I designated earlier, with Saussure, as the sliding of the signified under the signifier, which is always happening (unconsciously, let us note) in discourse'. Condensation, meanwhile 'is the superimposed structure of signifiers in which metaphor finds its field', while displacement is the 'transfer of signification that metonymy displays' (Lacan 2006: 425).

Here we have got to the heart of Lacan's linguisticisation of Freud. And it is true that, presented in this way, structuralist linguistics maps very neatly on to Freudian theory. But we need only be convinced by Lacan's theory to the extent that we are convinced by structuralism as an adequate theory of language (and, of course, to the extent that we are convinced by Freudianism in the first place – but that is another matter): Lacan appropriates the structuralist model of language unquestioningly, and so his theory is open to question to the same extent that that structuralist model is open to question.

But this itself presupposes that Lacan has appropriated the structuralist model accurately. The 'sliding of the signified under the signifier' is attributed by Lacan to Saussure, but earlier in 'The Instance of the Letter in the Unconscious', Lacan (2006: 415) concedes that the algorithm S/s, although it 'should be attributed to Ferdinand de Saussure', 'is not reduced to this exact form in any of the numerous schemas in which it appears in the printed version of the various lectures from the three courses he gave'. This is somewhat disingenuous: in fact, Lacan has introduced a significant variation in the Saussurian 'algorithm' (Saussure himself does not see it as an algorithm) by inverting it. The doctrine of the 'primacy of the signifier over the signified' is all Lacan's, not Saussure's. Indeed, Saussure's metaphors to describe the relationship of signifier to signified make it clear that they are equal to, and simultaneous with, one another in his psychic model: they are two sides of the same coin, or

> A language might ... be compared to a sheet of paper. Thought is one side of the sheet and sound the reverse side. Just as it is impossible to take a pair of scissors and cut one side of paper without at the same time cutting the other, so it is impossible in a language to isolate sound from thought, or thought from sound. To separate the two for theoretical purposes takes us into either pure psychology or pure phonetics, not linguistics. (Saussure 1983: 111)

If for Lacan Freud was a secret Saussurian, then so too was Saussure a secret Freudian. Yet there is nothing in Saussure's *Course* to suggest this: when he says that a signifier must necessarily call to mind its corresponding signified and vice versa, it is the purely conscious mind that Saussure is envisaging.

This leaves open the questions of whether 'condensation' is assimilable to 'metaphor', and whether 'displacement' is assimilable to 'metonymy'. We shall return to these questions below. For now it is sufficient to note that for Lacan (2006: 424) 'the linguistic structure that enables us to read dreams is at the crux of the "signifierness of dreams"'; the 'rebus' is a *linguistic* puzzle (and, moreover, he attributes this view to Freud). In opposition to this, Ricoeur (1970: 399) writes:

> If we take the concept of linguistics in the strict sense of the science of language phenomena embodied in a given and therefore organised language, the symbolism of the unconscious is not *stricto sensu* a linguistic phenomenon. It is a symbolism common to various cultures regardless of their language; it presents phenomena such as displacement and condensation which operate on the level of images, and not that of phonemic or semantic articulation.

Ricoeur goes on to claim that dream mechanisms blend the infralinguistic and the supralinguistic (to borrow Benveniste's terminology): they both fall short of the level of language as a rule-governed system, and, insofar as they are akin, as Freud himself points out, to 'proverbs, sayings, folklore, myths', 'it is on the level of rhetoric rather than linguistics that the comparison should be made' (Ricoeur 1970: 399–400). Rhetoric, of course, includes metaphor and metonymy among its tropes, but these are 'concerned not with phenomena of language but with procedures of subjectivity that are manifested in discourse' (Ricoeur 1970: 400).

However, 'to call these mechanisms infra- or supralinguistic is, of course, still to refer them to language' (Ricoeur 1970: 400). Hence, says Ricoeur (1970: 400), 'we are in the presence of phenomena structured like a language'. This places Ricoeur in direct engagement with Lacan. For Ricoeur (1970: 400), 'the problem is to assign an appropriate meaning to the word "like"'. This is a problem addressed by Lacan himself, at almost exactly the same time that *De l'interprétation* was published, on the occasion of his introducing his work to the American academic public. In his lecture 'Of Structure as an Inmixing of an Otherness Prerequisite to Any Subject Whatever' Lacan (1972: 188) claims that, 'properly speaking', to say that 'the unconscious is structured as a language ... is a redundancy because "structured" and "as a language" for me mean exactly the same thing. Structured means my speech, my lexicon, etc., which is exactly the same as a language'. Clearly, for Lacan here 'like' (or 'as', *comme*) means 'in the same way as', so that 'the unconscious is structured in the same way as language is structured'. This is not exactly how Ricoeur (1970: 400) views the matter: for him, 'it is in the interplay and blending of the infra- and supralinguistic that we shall find something *like* the instituting of meaning with which phenomenology is familiar'. Like Lacan, however, in investigating this question, Ricoeur begins from the standpoint of desire. What distinguishes desire from need, for Ricoeur (1970: 400), is that it is 'capable of being stated'; a desire is therefore 'an appeal and a demand'. Such a definition of desire equates it with demand, in contrast with Lacan, who places desire (as having a metonymic structure) in opposition to demand (as having a metaphorical structure). We must return to this. Meanwhile, however, for Ricoeur (1970: 400) it follows from this that 'it is on the level of the instinctual representatives that we must look for something like a language'. Again, Lacan (1972: 189) responds allusively to this claim in 'Of Structure as an Inmixing' by asserting that 'the unconscious has nothing to do with instinct': if 'the unconscious is structured as a language', then language has nothing to do with instinct, either. But, to some extent, Ricoeur agrees, or, at least, sees the relation between language and instinct as problematic: that dreams are expressed in narratives and that their elements cluster around 'switch-words' for him exactly demonstrates that '"the capture of instincts in the nets of the signifier" pertains to the order of language in a different way from what is disclosed through an observation of organised language' (Ricoeur 1970: 400–1).

Yet still, Ricoeur (1970: 401) asks, 'But what about language?' Rather than reprising Lacan's 'Instance of the Letter in the Unconscious' in developing 'in detail the interpretation of condensation as metaphor and displacement as metonymy', Ricoeur (1970: 401) follows Lacan's disciples Laplanche and Leclaire, presumably because the schemata presented in the work of the latter are simpler, while remaining faithful to the Lacanian idea. In 'The Instance of the Letter in the Unconscious', Lacan had rendered the processes of metaphor and metonymy as algorithms. The process of metaphor is rendered by Laplanche and Leclaire as their 'Formula 1', $(S'/S) \times (S/s)$, signifying that in metaphor 'a new signifier *S'* replaces the signifier ...; but the former *S*, instead of being suppressed, drops to the rank of the signified' (Ricoeur 1970: 401). Laplanche and Leclaire then transform Formula 1 algebraically into 'Formula 2', thus: *S'/s / S/S.*

Ricoeur has reservations about 'these purely algebraic operations', asking rhetorically 'what possible meaning can be assigned to the multiplication *(S'/S)* × *(S/s)* which allowed Formula 1 to be transformed into Formula 2?'. Nevertheless, writes Ricoeur (1970: 402), 'the final formula deserves to be taken, if not as a true formula, at least as a useful schema for study'. Following Laplanche and Leclaire, who in turn follow Lacan, Ricoeur (1970: 402) remarks that the bar separating the two relations expresses the double nature of repression, being at once a barrier separating the systems, 'and a relating that ties together the relations of signifier to signified'. We might pause here to note that this much is implicit in Saussure, when he writes that the bar signifies at once the indissociability of signifier and signified, and their radical difference, and that this unity-in-difference is both a linguistic (in the sense of its being a fact of the nature of language as such) and a psychic phenomenon (Saussure 1983: 67).[6] And for Ricoeur (1970: 402) too, 'the bar may be said to be not only the symbol of a linguistic phenomenon, a relating of relations consisting solely of signifiers and signified, but also a dynamic phenomenon – the bar expresses repression which impedes transition to a higher system'. However, for him the point is that the second of these two phenomena – repression – is distinct from the first. That the bar is able to express both is an 'artifice' arising from the construction of the diagram, according to which 'repression and metaphor exactly parallel one another'. But bringing this parallelism to the fore in a diagram does not mean that 'metaphor is nothing other than repression, and vice versa' (Ricoeur 1970: 402); Lacan's diagrams and the formulae of Laplanche and Leclaire might make metaphor and repression look as if they coincide, but this is an effect of the diagrams and formulae, not (of) reality. We could say, perhaps, that metaphor is a metaphor of repression – but it is not repression itself. Therefore, according to Ricoeur (1970: 403), we have 'everything and nothing' to gain from the Lacanian algebraism. On the one hand, every economic process (in the Freudian sense) can be seen to have 'a corresponding linguistic aspect' (Ricoeur 1970: 403); on the other hand, Freud's economic explanation itself prevents the linguistic explanation from being assimilable to it: primal repression, in Freud's theory, is constituted precisely by a denial of entrance into the conscious of the instinct as represented in discourse. In other words, repression 'is not a phenomenon of language' (Ricoeur 1970: 403), since it is the repression of the ability to render instinctual material into discourse. Hence, 'the interpretation of repression as metaphor shows that the unconscious is related to the conscious as a particular kind of discourse to ordinary language' (Ricoeur 1970: 403), but nevertheless the two discourses are separate. The algorithm *S/s*, despite Lacan's attributing it to Saussure, has no 'linguistic parallel', since it entails the element *S* occupying the position of both signifier and signified. Such an entity cannot be a sign at all: it is a mere image (or imago, in psychoanalytic parlance), lacking any linguistic characteristics. The upshot of all of this is that, in Ricoeur's (1970: 404) words, 'the mechanisms of the unconscious are not so much particular linguistic phenomena as they are paralinguistic distortions of ordinary language'.

But is Lacan really saying anything other than this? At the end of 'Of Structure as an Inmixing', there is the following exchange between Lucien Goldmann and Lacan (Lacan 1972: 198):

> GOLDMANN: I think you said that the unconscious is the ordinary language, English, French, that we all speak.
>
> LACAN: I said *like* language, French or English, etc.
>
> GOLDMANN: But it's independent from this language? Then I'll stop; I no longer have a question.

Here Lacan echoes Ricoeur's (1970: 400) insistence that 'the word "like" must receive no less emphasis than the word "language"'. However, earlier, when asked by Harry Woolf whether 'this fundamental arithmetic and this topology are not in themselves a myth or merely at best an analogy for an explanation of the life of the mind' (a question akin to the possibility mooted above that metaphor is a metaphor for repression), Lacan (1972: 195–6) replies:

> Analogy to what? 'S' designates something which can be written exactly as this S. And I have said that the 'S' which designates the subject is instrument, matter, to symbolise a loss. A loss that you experience as a subject (and myself also). In other words, this gap between one thing which has marked meanings and this other thing which is my actual discourse that I try to put in the place where you are, you as not another subject but as people that are able to understand me. Where is the analogon? Either this loss exists or it doesn't exist. If it exists it is only possible to designate the loss by a system of symbols. In any case, the loss does not exist before this symbolisation indicates its place. It is not an analogy. It is really in some part of the realities, this sort of torus. This torus really exists and it is exactly the structure of the neurotic. It is not an analogon; it is not even an abstraction, because an abstraction is some sort of diminution of reality, and I think it is reality itself.

Here we come to the crux of the matter of Lacan's so-called 'materiality of the signifier', which was articulated in 'The Instance of the Letter' in the diagram of the toilet doors, in which he 'silence[s] the nominalist debate' by insisting on the importance of the reality of the 'little enamel plaques' which serve to ensure that the 'natural needs' of Western Man are subjected 'to the laws of urinary segregation' (Lacan 2006: 417). Are we from this to conclude that the result of Lacan's 'linguisticisation of Freud' is that, just as Freud grants ontological status to the unconscious (it is an 'it'), so likewise does Lacan grant an unwarranted material reality to the unconscious through his insistence on the 'materiality of the signifier'? This is a problem identified by Fredric Jameson as 'the fundamental enabling device of structuralism in general': the ambiguous nature of language itself (manifested in the discontinuity between the *énoncé* and the subject of enunciation) leads to a 'shifting back and forth between a conception of speech as a linguistic structure, whose components can then be tabulated, and that which, now on the contrary understanding speech in terms of communication, permits a virtual dramatisation of the linguistic process (sender/receiver, destinaire/destinateur, etc.)' (1982: 364). Again, this ambiguity is held in play by the word 'like' in the formula 'the unconscious is structured like a language'.

Thus, on the one hand, Lacan (1993: 166) explains that his formula 'does not mean that the unconscious is expressed in discourse'. In what looks like an anticipation of Ricoeur's objection to his algorithms, Lacan (1993: 166–7) says that

> the analytic phenomenon as such, whatever it may be, isn't a language in the sense in which this would mean that it's a discourse – I've never said it was a discourse – but is structured like a language. This is the sense in which it may be called a phenomenal variety, and the most revealing one, of man's relations to the domain of language. Every analytic phenomenon, every phenomenon that comes from the analytic field, from the analytic discovery, from what we are dealing with in symptoms and neurosis, is structured like a language.

Lacan's explanation here of what he means by 'structured like a language' is more precise than the oblique one given in 'Of Structure as an Inmixing': 'This means it's a phenomenon that always presents the essential duality of signifier and signified. This means that here the signifier has its own coherence and nature which distinguish it from every other species of sign' (Lacan 1993: 167). Some of the confusion arises from Lacan's insistence on *a* language, rather than simply on 'language': in 'Of Structure as an Inmixing' he insists that 'when I say "as a language" it is not as some special sort of language, for example, mathematical language, semiotical language, or cinematographical language. Language is language and there is only one sort of language: concrete language – English or French for instance – that people talk' (Lacan 1972: 188). But in that case, why insist on *a* language, rather than just on 'language'? The answer is that not only must the signifier be conceived of as material, but also that language has specificity: Lacan often insists that 'the unconscious is the discourse of the Other'. This is the other hand of the ambiguity: if 'the unconscious is the discourse of the Other', does this not mean that the unconscious simply *is* the speech of whoever is speaking to the subject? This would solve quite neatly the difficulty arising from Freud's vacillation between seeing the unconscious as a working analytic hypothesis, and as a topographical feature of the mind. In this new formulisation, Lacan's linguisticisation of Freud would simply mean: the unconscious *does* exist as a reality, and it can be specifically identified – it is the language that the subject hears the Other speak to him.

But things cannot be that simple in the Lacanian schema. To define 'the Other' as 'whoever is speaking to the subject' would, in effect, be to define the Other phenomenologically: it would be the Other who forms the basis of Husserl's 'analogical' apprehension of other *cogitationes* just like mine, and the existence of whom provides an opening into ethics, as developed in Merleau-Ponty's famous remark, 'I borrow myself from others'. (This is the same Other that appears in other of Husserl's successors: in Lévinas, for example.)

But Lacan does not conceive of the Other in this way. As Jameson (1982: 364) puts it, Lacan's Other is the locus of the very superposition of speech conceived as linguistic structure, and the dramatisation of the linguistic process, 'constituting at one and the same time the dramatis personae of the Oedipal situation ... and the very structure of articulate language itself'. Lacan not only defines the unconscious as the discourse of the Other; he equally defines the Other as the place from which the discourse of the unconscious emanates. Again, there is a vacillation: this time, between seeing the Other as language as such (thus, if the unconscious is structured like a language, and the unconscious is the discourse of the Other, then the Other is the place from which the linguistically structured discourse of the unconscious emanates), and seeing the Other as figures who utter such a discourse. The two sides of this antithesis are co-dependent, but even if we were to choose the second to the exclusion of the first, we would still not be with something that looked like the phenomenological Other. Instead, we are with the three terms of the Oedipal relation (as 'On a Question Prior to Any Possible Treatment of Psychosis'[7] explains), which are part of what Lacan calls the Symbolic Order. Hence, they are symbolic figures that are at work here: the *I* as the ego-ideal (articulated through the disjunction between *énoncé* and *énonciation*); the

M 'as the signifier of the primordial object'; and *P* 'as the position in *A* [for '*Autre*'] of the Name-of-the-Father' (Lacan 2006: 462). In the Lacanian version of the Oedipal relation, it is an alienated-through-language subject, a signifier of a primordial object, and the Name-of-the-Father who symbolically act out the drama. This at once gets round the problem in Freud of taking the Oedipal complex literally – these are not real people playing out a drama in front of the subject, but the privileged signifiers of the subject's symbolic order – and creates a new problem, insofar as, precisely, we are no longer dealing with real people. This problem is particularly acute in the case of the Other, which is granted a particular privilege in being identified with the Name-of-the-Father. Once again, the Other is conceived linguistically – it is the invocation of the Law, an articulation of a threat of deprivation (of maternal love) or of displacement (the Other is in the place where 'I' wish to be) – but, once again, this is at the expense of conceiving the Other as a real person, moreover, as *any* real person, with all of the ethical possibilities and responsibilities that that entails.

There is, thus, in Lacanian theory something dispiriting, in the same way that there is something dispiriting in Freudian theory. Ironically, for all their differences, Freud and Lacan never really escape the position Husserl occupied in *Ideas I*, and which Husserl was able to think his way out of in *Ideas II* – namely, a position of auto-reflexivity. 'Why should my reflections perpetually centre upon myself?' cries the hero in what is often regarded as the world's first psychological novel,[8] and the tone of despair is telling. Husserlian phenomenology in its early phase ('early' in terms of the chronology of Husserl's development, but also 'early' conceptually, in terms of the procedural order of phenomenological method) is caught within a Cartesian reflexive moment, whereby the solitary ego questions the apodicity of evidence as presented to his solitary self. Without the perception of the Other, and, hence, the notion of empathy, in *Ideas II*, which ultimately leads to the development of the notion of the *Lebenswelt* in Husserl's late works, phenomenology would be, if not strictly speaking solipsistic in the philosophical sense, at least a lonely affair. For all its dependency on the Other, and on the analyst (through the process of transference, these come to mean the same thing), psychoanalysis is equally lonely, with the added poignancy of an attached irony. Whether one chooses to read Freud's *Wo Es war, soll Ich werden* with the ego psychologists as a call to strengthen the ego, or with Lacan as a call to confront the primal alienating effect of language as such, there is still no room in the theory for the Other in the phenomeno-ethical sense of any other person who can take me by the hand or look me in the face, an Other my relationships towards whom are not motivated by desire, and particularly by the desire either to have sex with them, do them harm, or both.

Above, we promised to return to the question of whether figurability and displacement are assimilable to metaphor and metonymy respectively. A way into this question is through an essay by Jean-François Lyotard (1989) entitled 'The Dream-Work Does Not Think'. It is worth remarking the reason for Lyotard's title, since it touches on the notion of desire. If the whole purpose of *The Interpretation of Dreams* is to demonstrate that 'a dream is a (disguised) fulfilment of a (suppressed or repressed) wish', then Freud's theory of dreams and dream interpretation has to be consistent with his theory of repression. Hence, if we look at the dream-work of condensation, we see that it constructs 'word-things'; indeed, in the process of interpreting a dream, the (surface) 'wordiness' of words must be disregarded in order to arrive at the meaning that attaches to their deep 'thingness'. To take a well-known example from 1980s beer advertising, in order to interpret a picture of a ladder propped against an enormous shin, followed by a picture of an old tin can, as 'Heineken', we must disregard the 'wordiness' of the words attaching to the pictures, 'high knee can'. In other words, there is a disjunction in rebuses (and the dream-work consists in the construction of rebuses) between *meaning* and *signification*, and it is the signification that must be disregarded in order to arrive at the meaning. Here, following a hint from both Lyotard and, in a different way, Ricoeur, we might remark that rebus or dream interpretation is not *linguistic* interpretation as such, but is, rather, an interpretation of the distance between language and its concrete other, the kind of meaning that can attach to symbols quite apart from the language used to name or describe them. Hence, Lacan's 'materiality of the signifier' is something of a red herring: it would be more accurate to say that material objects can signify to an 'interpretant' directly, without the need of the mediation of language, and, moreover, if and when language does mediate, it is not necessary for the object-meaning and the linguistic signification to coincide.

But back to Lyotard's title. The point of the assertion 'the dream-work does not think' (which is to be found in Freud himself) is that, as Lyotard (1989: 25) puts it, 'there is no need to imagine that the id has an idea at the back of its head'. In other words, there is no third party which embellishes the 'text' of the dream for the benefit of its interpreters; if the dream is a disguised desire, then 'the disguise does not result from the alleged deceiving intent of desire; the work itself *is* disguise' (Lyotard 1989: 25). This at once follows from and entails the dream-work (and its reverse-process, dream interpretation) not being a linguistic process as such, but rather 'violence perpetrated on linguistic space'.

As we have said, the implication of Lyotard's (1989: 30) argument is 'that the dream is not a discourse, because the dream-work is intrinsically different from the operations of speech'. This, of course, is in direct opposition to Lacan's position, and it hinges as much on a reading of Jakobson as it does on a reading of Lacan. Jakobson, in a cluster of articles on aphasia, draws an essential distinction between what he calls 'selection' and 'combination'. Developing a hint from Saussure, he explains:

> Selection (and, correspondingly, substitution) deals with entities conjoined in the code but not in the given message, whereas, in the case of combination, the entities are conjoined in both, or only in the actual message. The addressee perceives that the given utterance (message) is a *combination* of constituent parts (sentences, words, phonemes etc.) *selected* from the repository of all possible constituent parts (the code). The constituents of a context are in a state of *contiguity*, while in a substitution set signs are linked by various degrees of *similarity* which fluctuate between the equivalence of synonyms and the common core of antonyms. (Jakobson 1971: 243)

It follows from this that there are two 'poles' of language, the metonymic, corresponding to combination and contiguity, and the metaphoric, corresponding to selection and similarity (or difference). The study of aphasia reveals something about discourse generally, namely that

> one topic may lead to another either through their similarity or through their contiguity. The *metaphoric* way would be the most appropriate term for the first case and the *metonymic* way for the second, since they find their most condensed expression in metaphor and metonymy respectively. (Jakobson 1971: 254)

Hence, 'metaphor' and 'metonymy' are overarching terms which cover aspects of discourse not only at the level of trope (simile, synonymy, antonymy, paraphrasis, etc., are all sub-divisions of metaphor, while synecdoche is a sub-division of metonymy), but also at the level of genre (the novel is predominantly metonymic, while poetry is predominantly metaphorical), and at the level of school (Romanticism and Symbolism are predominantly metaphorical, whereas Realism is predominantly metonymic).

This is the model that Lacan appropriates, or attempts to appropriate, in his linguisticisation of Freud. Lyotard's first move is to indicate a point at which Jakobson and Lacan disagree: Jakobson places Freud's 'condensation' under the category of combination, or metonymy, whereas Lacan places it under the category of selection, or metaphor. Jakobson (cited in Lyotard 1989: 33) himself attributes this disagreement to Freud's own imprecision in his concept of condensation, which 'seems to encompass cases of both metaphor and synecdoche'. But, for Lyotard

(1989: 33), the confusion arises from 'applying to one field of expression categories borrowed from another': the two operations of selection and combination are being 'bent' by Jakobson and Lacan in order to make them fit – Jakobson bends them one way, and Lacan the other. Again, for Lyotard, the 'language' of the dream is not modelled on 'articulated discourse', which is to say, it is not modelled on *a* language, 'English or French for instance[,] that people talk', as Lacan (1972: 188) would have it. Rather, 'metaphor and metonymy must, therefore, be understood ... in a sense which is itself metaphoric' (Lyotard 1989: 33). The imprecision lies not with Freud, but with Jakobson.

Lyotard takes further issue with Jakobson. For Jakobson (1971: 255), a metaphor is 'the capacity for two words to replace one another ... and [be] linked ... by semantic similarity (or contrast)'. But for Lyotard (1989: 34), this definition neglects that which is most essential to metaphor, or at least, to poetic metaphor: that the substitution '*is precisely not authorised by usage*, is not inscribed in the paradigmatic network surrounding the supplanted term'. This oversight is a result of Jakobson's structuralism, or at least, of his having developed his concept of metaphor from Saussure's concept of selection. Thus, for Saussure, a speaker must both select a word from a range of possibilities (the cat *or* feline, pussy, kitten, animal, dog) and combine it with an appropriate contiguous collection of other words (sat on the mat). Whichever possibility is chosen, usage authorises that it be understood as something which sits on a mat. Saussure, of course, is merely describing what he considers to be the psycholinguistic process – he is not claiming that this process is metaphorical. A better example of a *metaphor* is the one actually provided by Lacan (2006: 422): 'His sheaf was neither miserly nor spiteful'.[9] Sheaves cannot, literally, be miserly nor spiteful, whereas cats can, literally, sit on mats. Hence, although he believes he is indebted to Jakobson, Lacan is actually arriving at a truer definition of metaphor than Jakobson's, one of an uncommon or unexpected substitution: it is this uncommonness or unexpectedness that leads to the 'overdetermination' of the statement which Freud finds to be a feature of condensation. When the substitution *is* authorised by usage, however, 'we no longer have anything like metaphor in Lacan's sense of a *figure* of style. We have simply an instance of a choice between terms which stand in paradigmatic relation to each other, any one of which would serve equally well at that particular point in the chain' (Lyotard 1989: 34).

This brings us to the main thrust of Lyotard's argument against Lacan's reading of Jakobson. In 'Two Aspects of Language', Jakobson (1971: 254–5) points out that metaphor and metonymy have two 'aspects': positional and semantic. Hence, in a word-association test, for example, 'hut' can either be substituted by 'cabin', 'palace', etc., or it can gain a positional aspect such as 'has burned down' or 'is a wretched little house'. The second of these is metaphorical, both substitutionally and positionally, since 'a wretched little house' is a substitute for 'hut'. Hence, a metaphor must always be semantically substitutive, but it may or may not also be a positional predicate, whereas 'metonymical responses to the same stimulus, such as *thatch*, *litter*, or *poverty*, combine and contrast the positional similarity with semantic contiguity' (Jakobson 1971: 255). It follows from this that, in the words of Lyotard (1989: 35), 'a statement such as "his sheaf was neither miserly nor spiteful" would be entirely unacceptable as a metaphor for Jakobson', because 'on the semantic level they are not amenable to substitution'. Here Lyotard appears to be in error, since he also claims that 'the terms constitute a clearly predicative statement', which would not be a reason for Jakobson to exclude its being a metaphor – it would be a metaphor in its positional aspect as well as its semantic one, as Lyotard self-contradictorily acknowledges in the previous paragraph. The confusion arises from Lyotard's assertion that it is 'clearly' 'a predicative statement': what he fails to notice is that the predicate here is adverbial, whereas in Jakobson's example it is a noun phrase. What Jakobson calls 'positional similarity' cannot be possible if the grammar of the statement will not allow substitution as such, nor does Jakobson claim that it is.

The 'predicative statement' part of Lyotard's argument may thus be dispensed with, and it seems that his whole detour into Jakobson's 'positional aspects' is unnecessary to the essential part of his argument, which is this: that Lacan confuses metaphor with metonymy, according to Jakobson's definitions: 'it seems to me that "his sheaf" is a good instance of metonymy, the sheaf being understood as an emblem of Booz, while the use of the imperfect confers, in addition, a typically narrative connotation on the statement' (Lyotard 1989: 35–6). This is surely right insofar as 'his sheaf' refers to Booz: 'sheaf' is associated with Booz by being a synecdoche, which is a sub-division of metonymy, and over the whole sentence there is a narrative progression which is an example of contiguity in the positional aspect, although this is aided by the simple past rather than the imperfect (this is true in the original French as it is in English translation).

Lyotard (1989: 36) immediately proceeds to ask, 'given Lacan's interpretation of metaphor, how can one say that condensation is one?' To answer, Lyotard reproduces the algorithm in 'The Instance of the Letter in the Unconscious' which Ricoeur avoided in favour of the simpler one by Leclaire and Laplanche:

$$f\left(\frac{S'}{S}\right)S \cong S(+)s$$

However, Lyotard's interpretation is the same as that provided by Ricoeur: 'The metaphoric function of the signifier is congruent with the emergence of signification. The metaphoric function is transcribed f(S'/S), the emergence of signification S(+)*s*'. What is interesting here is Lyotard's (1989: 36) remark concerning 'the notation of the metaphor itself (S')': 'it conforms to Lacan's own definition: S' is the stated term which eclipses the signifier S, just as his sheaf is supposed to eclipse Booz'. This is true, except that Lyotard has already demonstrated that what Lacan means by 'metaphor' is, in fact, metonymy, at least according to Jakobson's definition. Lyotard (1989: 36) does not address the implications of his own insight here when he goes on to ask whether what Lacan says about metaphor can also 'be said for condensation in the dream-work'.

Lyotard (1989: 37) has what he calls 'the strongest reservations' about such a mapping. For Lyotard, Lacan distorts Saussure's meaning as much as he distorts Jakobson's. Lyotard reminds us of what we noticed above: that Saussure places the signified *above* the signifier, and that, moreover, the bar in Saussure, insofar as it is used consistently at all, shows the transparency of signified to signifier, not its hiddenness: 'Lacan ... omits to say that Saussure's reflection on the linguistic sign takes its departure from the transparency necessary to interlocutory experience' (Lyotard 1989: 37). But neither of these accusations are seriously damaging to Lacan. Just as he might have misread, or misappropriated, Jakobson, so too he may have done the same with Saussure, in order to further his own intellectual ends. Lacan is not about an accurate reading of his predecessors and influences – he is about a theory of the psyche. His theory might still stand up, regardless of the (deliberate) misreadings on which they are based.

The plank of Lyotard's (1989: 37) argument that gets to the heart of Lacanian theory as such, rather than merely attacking his understanding of others, is this: 'in Lacan's thought there is a confusion between *signification* in the strict sense Saussure accorded the term by shifting it back to linguistic value, ... and *meaning*'. Lyotard illustrates this confusion by means of the French idiom *la nuit tombe* (night is falling). There are two ways in which this can be seen as a metaphor. First, we can analyse it at the level of what Saussure would call 'signification', according to the value attaching to the signifiers comprising it. So, night does not literally *fall*; 'fall' is what Lakoff and Johnson (1980: 14–21) would call an orientational metaphor, the signifier 'fall' being a substitute for any number of other words (it is a mark of how deeply ingrained metaphorical thinking is that it is difficult to think of substitute words that are not themselves metaphorical, such as 'comes' or 'approaches') which have a predicative relationship with 'night'. Second, the *whole sentence* can function as a metaphor for something else, something, that is, unconnected with discourse about the setting of the sun and the time of day. Hence, to borrow Lyotard's example, 'night falls' could be a metaphor for the accession of Hitler to power. This, in Lyotard's terminology, would involve an investigation into the metaphor's meaning, as opposed to its signification – and the 'meaning' is dependent on the place of the sentence within the context of a field of discourse.

According to Lyotard (1989: 37), 'the manner in which Lacan understands metaphor has to do with meaning, not signification', which is why it cannot be Jakobson's metaphor (or, we might add, Saussure's). Now, if this is the case, then for Lyotard it becomes impossible to describe Freud's dream-work in terms of metaphor and metonymy. According to Freud, condensation is necessary owing to limitations of space, 'the locus of dreams being narrower than the locus of our thoughts' (Lyotard 1989: 38). Condensation is not a linguistic operation. Although the work of condensation may be best grasped when it seizes on words and names, the dream-work treats words as if they were things. As Lyotard (1989: 39) puts it: 'Substitution, for Jakobson, was *constitutive* of discourse; condensation, for Freud, is a transformation *dismissive* of discourse'.

Lyotard (1989: 39) is equally dismissive of the attempt to assimilate metonymy to the Freudian dream-work:

> It doesn't matter that Jakobson and Lacan agree, this time, to ascribe displacement to metonymy; it takes a real play on words to do it. Metonymy is already hard-pressed to play in rhetoric the role that Jakobson attributes to combination in the speech act and to the syntagmatic relation in the table of language. The difficulty is aggravated if, leaving discourse behind, metonymy is required to function as mainspring for oneiric displacement.

This leads Lyotard (1989: 40) to a conclusion concerning the dream being 'articulated like a language' (which, by extension, we may apply to the formula 'the unconscious is structured like a language'):

> It must then be accepted that the word 'language' loses its precision conferred on it by post-Saussurian linguistics. It refers to a study not of language, but of enunciation. It is particularly the theory of signification as a value, and of value as a syntagmatic and paradigmatic framework that must be, if not abandoned, at least completed by a theory of meaning.

This appears to dish Lacan's theory of metaphor and metonymy quite comprehensively. However, we remarked above that Lyotard does not follow through his own insight, that Lacan confuses Jakobson's metaphor and metonymy in the use of his example, 'His sheaf was neither miserly nor spiteful'. This is because Lyotard's argument is really about the applicability of metaphor and metonymy to the Freudian model: if neither metaphor nor metonymy map on to the Freudian topography, then it does not matter whether we call 'metaphor' 'metonymy' or vice versa. But we should pursue this question further, partly because Lacan's confusion reflects a problem with Jakobson's theory of metaphor and metonymy that is worthy of investigation in its own right, and partly because metonymy, which is given only scanty discussion by Lyotard, is perhaps more important than metaphor in Lacan, since it is (allegedly) the structure of desire, and Lacan's theory, like Freud's and like any psychoanalytic theory, is a theory of desire.

Let us then turn again to 'His sheaf was neither miserly nor spiteful'. This is what Lacan (2006: 422) has to say about it:

> In Hugo's verse, it is obvious that not the slightest light emanates from the assertion that a sheaf is neither miserly nor [spiteful], because it is clear that the sheaf has no more the merit than the demerit of these attributes, since miserliness and hatred, along with the sheaf, are properties of Booz, who exercises them when he uses the sheaf as he sees fit, without making his feelings known to it.

Lyotard points out that, if the sheaf belongs to Booz, then 'sheaf' is a metonymy, since there pertains a contiguous relationship of owned and owner. Lacan himself says as much in alluding to the 'properties of Booz', without realising that in so doing he is giving a definition of metonymy, not of metaphor: 'If "his sheaf" refers back to Booz . . ., it is because it replaces him in the signifying chain – at the very place that awaited him, because it had been raised up a step by the clearing away of miserliness and hatred' (Lacan 2006: 422). The relationship of possessor to possessed is clearly – in Jakobson's terms, but also according to the entire history of commentary on the trope – a case of metonymy. As Ricoeur (2003: 210) will go on to show some years later in *The Rule of Metaphor*, mere substitution as such cannot be taken to be the defining characteristic of metaphor, since metonymy is a kind of substitution too. Yet this is precisely what Lacan is doing here: taking the fact that the line *substitutes* Booz for his sheaf to be decisive in attributing a metaphoric quality to the process. Moreover, since Lacan's thinking here is overly influenced by the Freudian assault on the Cartesian *cogito*, Lacan (2006: 422) goes on to make an existential claim about metaphor in this line: 'the sheaf has thus cleared this space of Booz, ejected as he now is into the outer darkness where miserliness and hatred harbour him in the hollow of their negation'. This is to cast metaphor in the light of Hegelian dialectic – which Lacan will go on to do more explicitly in *The Four Fundamental Concepts of Psychoanalysis* – which, if Lacan wishes to declare himself a Hegelian, is fine, except that Jakobson cannot be assimilated to a Hegelian model, since (Saussurian) binarism is not 'dialectical' in the sense of entailing an *Aufhebung* – and in any case, we are presented with a metonymy here, not a metaphor.

But this *méconnaissance* on the part of Lacan is pushed to its limits a few pages further on in 'The Instance of the Letter', when he explicitly relates metonymy and metaphor to the wound inflicted on the *cogito* by Freudianism. At this point, Lacan (2006: 430) addresses the means by which the subject confronts the 'suspicion' of which Ricoeur speaks, a suspicion concerning the centrality of the ego to Being:

> It is nonetheless true that the philosophical *cogito* is at the centre of the mirage that renders modern man so sure of being himself in his uncertainties about himself, and even in the distrust he has long since learned to exercise regarding the pitfalls of pride.
>
> Now if, turning the weapon of metonymy against the nostalgia that it serves, I stop myself from seeking any meaning beyond tautology, and if, in the name of 'war is war' and 'a penny's a penny', I resolve to be only what I am, how can I escape here from the obvious fact that I am in this very act?

Jakobson, however, explicitly describes tautology as the ultimate example of a metaphor, not of a metonymy, since for him both contrast and similarity are alike examples of the kind of substitutability that metaphor entails: they are alike syntagmatic in their relation, rather than contiguous. Hence, in discussing patients who have defects in substitution (and perhaps Lacan's error can be forgiven, since metonymy is also a form of substitution, as Jakobson fails to realise), Jakobson (1971: 247) writes: 'Told to repeat the word "no", Head's patient replied "No, I don't know how to do it". While spontaneously using the word in the context of his answer ("No, I don't ..."), he could not produce the purest form of equational predication, a = a: <no> is <no>'.

Tautology, then, is the purest form of metaphor, its zero-point. But could we not say the same of metonymy? Jakobson defines metonymy sometimes as contiguity and sometimes as association, as if contiguity and association were the same thing (while it is true that 'knife and fork' shows both an associative and contiguous relation between the two terms it contains, association and contiguity do not *necessarily* go together). To take one of Lacan's examples, 'war is war', this reaches the zero-point of metonymy just as it reaches the zero-point of metaphor, since contiguity is present by virtue of the predicative process initiated by the 'is', while what could be more associative than a thing with itself? Seen in this way, metaphor and metonymy are reducible to the same thing. But that is because both metaphor and metonymy are versions of substitution, and tautology is pure substitution. Thus, when we turn to Lacan's (2006: 430) next sentence in 'The Instance of the Letter' after the one quoted above, we hear the question 'How – in going to the other, metaphoric pole of the signifying quest, and dedicating myself to becoming what I am, to coming into being – can I doubt that, even if I were to lose myself there, I am there?' This question presupposes that metaphor is at the opposite pole of the 'signifying quest', whereas actually, in the Saussure–Jakobson–Lacan scheme of things, it shrivels to the same place as metonymy.

But it is clear that there is metaphor present in the sentence 'His sheaf was neither miserly nor spiteful' somewhere: it is not literally the case that the sheaf is neither miserly nor spiteful; it is only metaphorically so. So, once a metonymy has been introduced, a metaphor is sure to follow; in this example at least, the metaphor which unfolds over the sentence as a whole appears dependent on the metonymic substitution with which it begins. This is not, moreover, a peculiarity of this particular sentence but appears to be a general rule regarding metaphor or metonymy. Thus, to move to the level of genre, as does Jakobson, we might agree that the novel is 'predominantly metonymic' in its structure – at the level of enunciation, we might say. But at the level of meaning, the novel often stands for – is a substitute for – a set of circumstances in real life: its mimetic quality is, precisely, metaphorical. This becomes clearer if we take an example from American poetry of the 1930s, which is often described as 'predominantly metonymic', as opposed to the metaphoric nature of most poetry. In William Carlos Williams' poem 'Nantucket', each of the descriptive elements constituting each stanza is metonymic of the Nantucket of the poem's title: each is a representative sample, as it were, of the whole, as is confirmed by the absence of punctuation at the end of the poem, which implies that the list could go on indefinitely. The effect of this cumulative metonymy, when combined with the title, however, is a metaphor: the poem is constructed through metonymy, but in order to become a metaphor, a reproduction, of the experience of visiting Nantucket, which the poem is a substitute for. Metonymy cannot exist in isolation from metaphor, or at least, it cannot according to the definitions of 'metaphor' and 'metonymy' posited by Jakobson.

We should look at those definitions again. Actually, in his writings on aphasia other than 'Two Aspects of Language', Jakobson hardly mentions metaphor and metonymy. In 'Aphasia as a Linguistic Topic', for example, he writes merely that 'the two opposite tropes, metaphor and metonymy, present the most condensed expression of two basic modes of relation: the internal relation of similarity (and contrast) underlies the metaphor; the external relation of contiguity (and remoteness) determines the metonymy' (Jakobson 1971: 232). Here metaphor and metonymy are relegated to being merely sub-divisions of what really interests Jakobson in his writings on aphasia: similarity (selection) and contiguity (combination). In his other writings on aphasia, such as 'Toward a Linguistic Classification of Linguistic Impairments' (Jakobson 1971: 289–306) and 'Linguistic Types of Aphasia' (Jakobson 1971: 307–33), metaphor and metonymy are not mentioned at all. In passing, Jakobson wants to draw some parallels between aphasic conditions and culture at large, and metaphor and metonymy are the vehicles by which he does it, but they are not the central concerns that the psychoanalytic and philosophical readings of Jakobson would imply.

Furthermore, we might suspect that Jakobson leads himself astray in introducing metaphor and metonymy in relation to similarity and contiguity respectively. The problem lies in the structuralist drive to classify everything in a bipolar fashion. Hence, the definition of metaphor is forced to fit the model of similarity and selection, while the definition of metonymy is forced to fit the model of contiguity and combination. Thus, according to Jakobson, the use of metaphor is achieved by appealing to the 'code'; 'metaphor' is the general name of the phenomenon of selecting from the code. 'Metonymy', meanwhile, appeals to both code and context; it consists in the combination of words (or morphemes) in a sequence, but, of course, that combination is a combination of words which have also been *selected.* This aligns – in the practical study of aphasic discourse – metonymy with 'minor words' that provide contexture, such as articles, prepositions and pronouns, and metaphor with the major word classes of noun (especially), verb and adjective. Moreover, it explains the asymmetry in aphasic ailments: a patient who suffers predominantly from encoding disorder is also likely to suffer from decoding disorder to some extent, whereas a patient suffering predominantly from decoding disorder is unlikely to suffer from encoding disorder also. The aphasic choice appears to be decoding disorder plus encoding disorder, or decoding disorder only. This is because the encoder has to appeal to both code and context, whereas the decoder already has the context provided for him by the encoded message which he receives.

This may constitute a plausible linguistic classification of aphasias, but is it consistent with an understanding of metaphor and metonymy as such? In short, whatever the merits of Jakobson's development of the Saussurian distinction between selection and combination, does the ascription of *metaphor* and *metonymy* to these respectively hold good? There are two reasons to think that it does not. First, Jakobson is not consistent in his definition of metonymy. In 'Aphasia as a Linguistic Topic', Jakobson describes a hypothetical patient 'focused upon contiguity'; in other words, suffering from decoding disorder. 'He will', says Jakobson (1971: 236),

> not react to the stimulus word *champagne* with metaphors such as *ginger pop* or *geyser* or *mistress*, which suggest some analogy between two images, but he will readily resort to metonymical shifts from the cause to the immediate or further effect (*tipsiness* or *hangover*), from the thing contained to the container (*bottle*), from the goal to an auxiliary tool (*corkscrew*), and from the whole to a part (*foam*).

One wonders whether this hypothesis accords with clinical experience. Jakobson's hypothetical patient appears to have no difficulty selecting major word classes; the principle of selection is merely one of association rather than similitude or difference. But similitude and difference on the one hand *versus* association on the other appears an arbitrary means of drawing a distinction: why not (more intuitively) similitude and association *versus* difference? If metonymy is a species of substitution, substitution as such cannot be the defining criterion of metaphor (or its absence of metonymy). The essential distinction in aphasia, according to Jakobson's own investigations, is not between various modes of selection, but between the ability to select as such *versus* the ability to combine. A response of *fizz* to the stimulus-word *champagne* is not an example of combination at the expense of selection.

This leads us to the second problem with Jakobson's theory, which is one of the epistemology of the subject. Jakobson calls *ginger pop* a metaphor of *champagne*. In some contexts it could be. But this presupposes much about a patient who would give such a response. A patient might not know that *ginger pop* is (or was, in the 1950s) used as a metaphor for champagne, but might have a personal association with ginger pop and champagne, in which case, the words would for him be a metonymy, not a metaphor.

This leads us to Ricoeur's critique of Jakobson in *The Rule of Metaphor*, which was written a decade after Ricoeur's engagement with Lacan but which helps our case here in elucidating why Jakobson's is not an adequate theory of metaphor and metonymy. Ricoeur (2003: 210) writes that 'the strength of Jakobson's schema is also its weakness'. Its strength lies in its generality and simplicity, through which the concepts of metaphor and metonymy are no longer restricted to tropology but are applicable throughout the domains of semantics and semiology (and it is an effect of Jakobson's schema that these become conflated). But 'a heavy price' must be paid for this, and that is that the field of tropology, in all its diversity, is reduced to just two tropes. For example, Ricoeur again mentions Freud: if, for Freud, displacement and condensation are two distinct features of the dream-work, the effect of Jakobson's subsuming synecdoche under metonymy is to conflate (or, to put it unkindly, confuse) condensation (synecdoche) with displacement (metonymy). Moreover, Ricoeur (2003:

212) chides Jakobson for leaving out 'the predicative nature of metaphor'. Here, once again, we can say (although he is not mentioned anywhere in *The Rule of Metaphor*) that Lacan has a better idea of metaphor than Jakobson, even though he pays deference to Jakobson in his formulation. To take another example favoured by Lacan, 'Love is a pebble laughing in the sunlight', we can see that (a) love is not, literally, a pebble (first metaphor), and (b) neither love nor pebbles laugh (second metaphor). Both of these metaphors are created over the whole sentence, through the predicative work of the word 'is'. Jakobson's, like Aristotle's and Fontanier's before him, is ultimately a theory of metaphor at the level of individual words, rather than at the level of the whole sentence or beyond.

But Ricoeur's (2003: 212) most serious charge is that

> the fundamental problem of the difference between newly invented metaphor and metaphor in common use vanishes with the omission of the predicative character of metaphor, to the same extent that the degrees of freedom in combination affect the syntagmatic and not the paradigmatic side of language.

This difference is the most important point on which Ricoeur wants to insist in *The Rule of Metaphor*, remembering that the French title of that work is *La Métaphore vive*, 'Metaphor Lives' or 'Living Metaphor'. It is the newly invented metaphor, living metaphor, which provides the interpreter of the metaphor with a new insight into the world, and which, thus, elevates discourse to a new level of phenomenological truth. Failing to distinguish between living metaphor and dead metaphor thus threatens that moment of freedom Ricoeur discerns in the phenomenological reduction, the adoption of the bracketed standpoint, as such: for him, the predicative function of the 'is' in, say, 'Achilles is a lion' is metaphor's expression of intentionality, intentionality being that which characterises my freedom as a thinking being.

Thus, there is an inexorable logic behind Ricoeur's critique of Jakobson: failure to appreciate the predicative ability of metaphor goes hand in hand with failure to distinguish 'living' from 'dead' metaphor, both being variations on denying metaphor's intentionality, which, as a mode of intentionality as such, is indicative of human freedom. Indeed, Jakobson (1971: 236) talks of the limits to the freedoms enjoyed by aphasics: 'Of the two relative freedoms of the speaker – free selection of words and their free combination into larger contexts – the former is limited in cases of similarity disorder, and the latter in cases of contiguity disorder . . .'. Freedom for Jakobson is relative, bounded by the very structural dichotomy between metaphor and metonymy which he describes – the constraints on that freedom endured by the aphasic are the same constraints which we must all endure to a degree. This is a far cry from the absolute freedom entailed by the intentionality latent within the Cartesian *cogito* and which phenomenology draws out. Ricoeur (2003: 213) blames Jakobson's failure to grasp this on his 'semiological monism', whereby 'the difference between sign and discourse is itself minimised'. Since newly invented metaphor is an attribution to discourse, any theory which obliterates the distinction between sign and discourse must be blind to it. Insofar as we can accept at all Jakobson's schema of combination taking place in the code, while selection operates between entities associated in the code,

> in order that selection itself be free, it must result from an original combination created by the context and therefore distinct from performed operations within the code. In other words, it is in the region of unusual syntagmatic liaisons, of new and purely contextual combinations, that the secret of metaphor is to be sought. (Ricoeur 2003: 213)[10]

We have taken something of a detour into a critique of Jakobson, in which we have been anachronistically aided by Ricoeur, in order to bring out the weaknesses in Jakobson's theory. This, in turn, is in order to question Lacan's theory of desire and demand, insofar as it is based on a Jakobsonian model. This will be our task in the next chapter, when we will contrast Lacan's and Ricoeur's respective treatments of symbolism.

5

From the Symbolic to the Ethical

If, as we have seen, Lacan's theory of metaphor and metonymy is based on a misreading of Jakobson's untenable theory, where does that leave all that follows from the notions of metaphor and metonymy in Lacan, namely, the theory of demand and desire which correspond to them respectively? This is a serious question, since demand and, in particular, desire are central to what we might call 'Lacanianism'; Lacanian psychoanalysis, like the Freudian, is predicated on a philosophy of desire, the belief that all of man's ways of being in the world are explainable in terms of desire. This, of course, forms the basis of one of Ricoeur's criticisms of Freudianism: that, even if Freud's (and, we might say, by extension, Lacan's) philosophy of desire is a good philosophy of *desire*, it does not necessarily follow that desire accounts for the whole of human existence, or that psychoanalytic theory is thus generalisable into a 'philosophy' properly speaking.

The Freudian 'discovery' of the unconscious is, for Lacan, a discovery on a par with the great discoveries of science, such as that the earth revolves around the sun. For Lacan (2006: 430–1), truth is evoked

> only in that dimension of ruse whereby all "realism" in creation derives its virtue from metonymy, as well as this other fact that access to meaning is granted only to the double elbow of metaphor, when we hold in our hand their one and only key: namely, the fact that the S and *s* of the Saussurian algorithm are not in the same plane, and man was deluding himself in believing he was situated in their common axis, which is nowhere.

This presupposes much. That the S and *s* of the Saussurian algorithm are not in the same plane is not a 'fact' in the same way that it is a fact that Jacques Lacan was born in 1901: it is an interpretation of a theoretical position and, as we have seen, both the theoretical position and its interpretation are open to question. But, of course, what Lacan is really getting at here is that for at least 250 years (between Descartes and Freud) man was deluded in a self-assurance of '*I* think; *I* am', whereas the alleged existence of the Freudian unconscious means that, in Lacan's (2006: 430) formulation, 'I am thinking where I am not, therefore I am where I am not thinking'. The difficulty here lies in the linguisticisation of Freud invoked by Lacan's importation of Saussure. For Lacan, it is the language of the unconscious that constitutes the fundamental alienation that is at the *Kern unseres Wesen*, in Freud's phrase. We have already seen how this language is a discourse, and how its discursive meaning does not require a linguistic analysis to be uncovered, just as we have seen how the 'algorithm' of the sliding of the signified under the signifier is not, in fact, Saussure's. But the essential point is that for Lacan, the sliding of the signified under the signifier *is*, precisely, metaphor as such, in its most reduced and purest form. If the sliding of the signified under the signifier constitutes metaphor (just as its concomitant, the displacement of one signifier by another, constitutes for Lacan 'metonymy'), then it follows that, for Lacan, metaphor and metonymy are elevated to ontological status in the constitution of the human subject. Metaphor is nothing other than the process of 'coming into being' that Freud invokes in his 'work of culture' that follows from the formula *Wo Es war, soll Ich werden*, whereas metonymy is nothing other than the process of desire that acts as a counterweight to this becoming.

This elevation is formulated by taking metaphor to be the defining characteristic of demand, just as metonymy is the defining characteristic of desire. It is to the Lacanian thesis of desire and demand that we must now turn, in the light of what we have already said concerning metaphor and metonymy as such.

Lacan's theory of desire owes much to that found in Plato's *Symposium*: Socrates is 'the precursor to psychoanalysis', says Lacan (2006: 699). We recall that in the *Symposium*, the truth of desire is spoken by an old woman, Diotima, who speaks from the heart of a text which has a 'Russian doll' structure: Apollodorus meets Glaucon in the street, who tells of Aristodemus' visit to the dinner party many years ago, where Socrates recounts what Diotima told him many years prior to that. What is significant about this textual structure from a Lacanian perspective is that truth is arrived at indirectly; it may reside at the heart of the text, but it is hidden. And when that truth is the truth of desire, desire itself is revealed by Diotima to have the same structure of elusiveness: desire is the desire for that which one does not have, for a lack, but desire can never, by definition, be fulfilled, otherwise it would no longer be desire. The structure of the text also enables this elusive truth to be demonstrated through its replication in the relationship between Alcibiades and Socrates. Alcibiades desires Socrates – who, like Diotima, is old and ugly – for the knowledge that Socrates possesses, but he is chided by Socrates, who asks him whether by sitting next to him he hopes to have this knowledge poured into him as wine is poured from a bottle.

From this brief sketch, we can see how Diotima's words on desire anticipate Lacan's formula that desire is a desire of a desire, since in this 'metonymic' formulation lies the potential for interminability of desire that Diotima identifies. The 'of' in 'desire is a desire of a desire' can be read both 'subjectively' and 'objectively': desire is both a desire to be desired, and the desire that comes from the Other. This leads immediately to Lacan's slogan, 'Desire is desire of the Other', which can likewise be read in the double sense of 'desire for the Other' and 'the Other's desire'. Here we should remember the definition of the 'Other' ('Autre' with a capital 'A') in Lacan: that it is the locus from which is heard the discourse that constitutes the unconscious.

All of this must be set against the background of the 'three terms of the Oedipal relation'. Lacan's linguistic reworking of the Freudian interpretation of Oedipus emphasises not the direct desire (to kill the father and marry the mother – after all, Oedipus cannot have a direct desire to do these things, since he is unaware that Laïus is his father and Jocasta his mother), but rather the indirection of desire that is determined by displacement: the subject wishes to be in the place where the father is. This, consistent with the *Symposium*, sees the desire of the subject as determined by a lack: the absence of the mother as determined by paternal displacement.

If the terms of the Oedipal relation are what determine man in his primal being, then, in everyday life, desire manifests itself in desires for others, ruses which repression sets up in order to deflect the subject from the true path of desire, the path towards the truth of 'where I come from'. Lacan explains this, for example, in his reading of *Hamlet*, in which Ophelia is described as 'the bait in the trap that Hamlet doesn't fall into' (Lacan 1982: 11–12): she is a desired and desirable object (at least, at one point in Hamlet's past), but only as a result of Hamlet's *méconnaissance* of the true object of his desire, which is to restore his succession to his father's place that has been usurped by Claudius. This refers back to 'The Mirror Stage' (Lacan 2006: 75–81), where identification with the *I* in imaginary space is held to be possible only through acknowledgement of the other objects in the field of vision which the ideal ego of reflection is defined dialectically against, and through which understanding of the place of the *I* is mediated. Hence, the road to *connaissance*, to a Socratic 'knowing thyself', can only be taken via the detour of *méconnaissance*, the deflection of desire onto an object occupying a place less than that of truth in the institution of the human condition.

This object is the *objet petit a* of Lacanian theory, and its place is articulated in another algorithm: $\$\diamond a$. This algorithm is to be read as deriving from Lacan's Schema L:

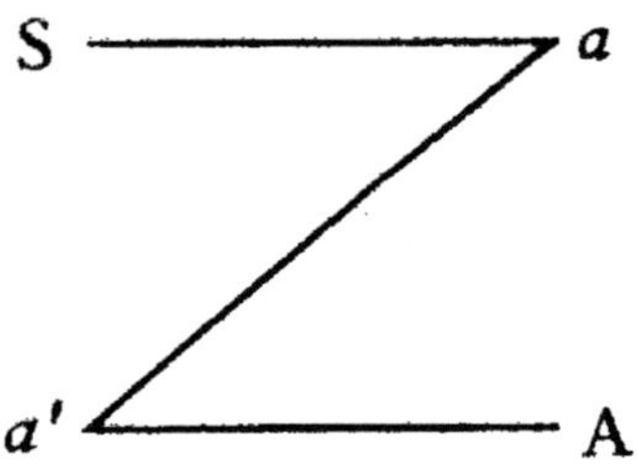

L Schema

which 'signifies that the condition of the subject, S . . . depends on what unfolds in the Other, A. What unfolds there is articulated like a discourse (the unconscious is the Other's discourse). . .' (Lacan 2006: 458–9). This unites the formulae 'the unconscious is the discourse of the Other' and 'the unconscious is structured like a language', but, again, we should note, *contra* Lacan, that discourse analysis and linguistic analysis are not the same thing, or, more particularly, that analysis at the discursive level requires an enquiry into meaning that the linguistic analysis of signification cannot attain. That aside, the interest of the subject in this discourse lies in his being 'drawn to the four corners of the schema: namely, S, his ineffable and stupid existence; *a*, his objects; *a'*, his ego, that is, his form as reflected in his objects; and A, the locus from which the question of his existence may arise for him' (Lacan 2006: 459).

Our interest here is in the *a*, the *objet petit a*, which is the locus of the objects of fantasy, the privileged objects of the subject's desire, but which are lures away from the true object of desire, the truth that is articulated by the Other in posing the question of his existence – by the fact of speech, which for Lacan is metaphorical as such. In other words, the question here is of the relationship between the metonymy of desire and the metaphor of a demand of being which the discourse of the Other poses as a question, as Lacan (2006: 459) puts it, a question of 'What am I there?'

It is thus that the algorithm $\$\Diamond a$ is the algorithm of 'fantasy itself'. It may be read as 'the subject is in dialectical relation with his objects'. Since his objects are the objects of his desire, we might also read this as the algorithm of metonymy, as the algorithm of the dialectic of desire. And further, since desire is the desire of the Other, the algorithm $\$\Diamond a$ entails the further algorithm, $\$\Diamond D$, which may be read as 'the subject is in dialectical relation to demand'. This is because the Other, as locus of the question of being for the subject (and, hence, of metaphor, which, as the process of displacement of one signifier for another, is the locus of the discourse that is the unconscious, if we believe with Lacan that 'language' and 'discourse' are the same), places the subject in the position of having to answer the question, 'What am I' – the answering of which constituting the 'work of civilisation, akin to the draining of the Zuider Zee', that is the work done by the subject in addressing Freud's *Wo Es war, soll Ich werden.* These algorithms together encapsulate the essence of Lacanian theory. The barred $ of the subject is constituted through the alienation that is indissociable from being a speaking being, since language as such is a metaphorical, or displacing, process of substituting one signifier for another which leads the signified to become permanently eclipsed. This barred subject is in dialectical relation to both desire – the metonymic desire that can never be fulfilled because its true object always escapes, fetishised though it might be by metonymic substitutes in the subject's fantasy – and to demand, the very demand to 'come into being' posited by the initiation of the subject into language as such, which is a metaphorical process.

This much will doubtless sound a familiar précis of Lacan. The purpose of reprising thus far the basic theory is to arrive at the point at which desire and demand meet. We have already seen how metaphor and metonymy, in Jakobson's schema, reduce to a zero-point of the tautology of pure repetition. We have also noted that the '◇' of Lacan's algorithms can be read as 'is in dialectical relation to'. But what does this mean? In addressing this question, we will also see what happens to metaphor and metonymy when they are recast as demand and desire respectively.

If the ◇ signifies a 'dialectical' operation, a good place to start would be by looking at Lacan's explanation of this 'lozenge'. He claims that the lower half signifies a 'v' for *vel*, which should be understood, as it is in logic, as an 'inclusive *or*', meaning 'either one or the other or both'. Incidentally, we might remark in passing that logic is not Lacan's strong point, as is shown by his explanation of the *vel*:

> There is a *vel* that is worth illustrating, in order to differentiate it from the other uses of the *vel*, of the *or*. There are two of them. You know, from your earliest lessons in logic, that there is the exclusive *vel* – I go *either* there *or* there – I have to choose. There is another way of using *vel* – I go to one side or the other, I don't care, one's as good as the other. These two *vels* are not alike. Well, there is a third, and in order not to mislead you, I will straight away tell you what it is intended for. (Lacan 1979: 210)

This is, frankly, pure nonsense. The earliest lessons in logic actually teach the distinction between *vel* and *aut*. There is no such thing as an 'exclusive *vel*', since the exclusive meaning of 'or' is covered by *aut*. And the second meaning of *vel* that Lacan identifies, 'I go to one side or the other, I don't care, one's as good as the other', is actually a confused variation of the first: it is (logically) still an *aut*, since an exclusive choice is still made, and the subjective vacillation of the chooser *en route* to that choice is entirely irrelevant to the objective logic of the operation. What makes Lacan's confusion on this point all the more breathtaking is the glib arrogance with which he dismisses Russell's paradox and its attempted solutions by professional logicians:

> The solution is very simple, it is that the signifier with which one designates the same signifier is evidently not the same signifier as the one with which one designates the other – this is obvious enough. The word *obsolete*, in so far as it may signify that the word *obsolete* is itself an *obsolete* word, is not the same word *obsolete* in each case. (Lacan 1979: 210)

Clearly, Lacan's familiarity with Russell does not extend as far as his theory of definite descriptions.

All of this notwithstanding, when Lacan says *vel*, he does indeed mean *vel* as it is understood in symbolic logic, which is to say, as an 'inclusive or', 'either one or the other or both'. But Lacan's route to truth is not the same as that to be found in a truth table. Rather, his purpose in introducing the *vel* is Hegelian, 'since it is a question of nothing less than that operation that we call *alienation*' (Lacan 1979: 210), and Lacan conceives of alienation in Hegelian terms. 'The *vel* of alienation', he says, 'is defined by a choice whose properties depend on this, that there is, in the joining, one element that, whatever the choice operating may be, has as its consequence a *neither one, nor the other*' (Lacan 1979: 211). Lacan (1979: 212) illustrates this by means of an example: '*Your money or your life!* If I choose the money, I lose both. If I choose life, I have life without the money, namely, a life deprived of something'. Thus, it is that 'the choice ... is a matter of knowing whether one wishes to preserve one of the parts, the other disappearing in any case' (Lacan 1979: 211).

This choice is dialectical in the Hegelian sense, in that the situation can also be viewed from the perspective of the highwayman (the 'Other', to pursue the analogy). The highwayman in this situation has nothing to lose, just as the subject must lose something. There is, therefore, an asymmetrical relationship between the victim and the highwayman, or between subject and other. Just as the victim must either surrender his money, or his money and his life, so the highwayman gains either the money, or both the money and the life of the victim. This is interesting in its own right, but we should note once again that logic is not Lacan's strong point – what is being described here is not a *vel* as commonly understood, or as previously described by Lacan as according with symbolic logic. The formula here is not 'either one or the other or both', nor is it even, as Lacan claims, 'neither one nor the other'.[1] The formula is, rather, '$(\sim P) \vee (\sim Q)$', where 'V' is understood as *vel*, thus: 'either not-P or not-Q or both not-P and not-Q'.

Perhaps it does not matter that Lacan has arrived at the formula 'either not-P or not-Q or both not-P and not-Q' by a confused and erroneous route. The point is that this is a Hegelian formula:

> It is in Hegel that I have found a legitimate justification for the term alienating *vel*. What does Hegel mean by it? To cut a long story short, it concerns the production of the primary alienation, that by which man enters into the way of slavery. *Your freedom or your life!* If he chooses freedom, he loses both immediately – if he chooses life, he has life deprived of freedom. (Lacan 1979: 212)

Thus the Terror is a Hegelian moment: in the revolutionary cry *Freedom or death!*, 'the only proof of freedom that you can have in the conditions laid out before you is precisely to choose death, for there, you show that you have freedom of choice' (Lacan 1979: 213). The invocation of Hegel here once again puts demand on an existential footing. The *soll Ich werden* of *Wo Es war, soll Ich werden* becomes the choice of a subject confronted with the void of non-Being; that Lacan should rephrase the dialectic of the master and slave in Hegel in terms of the highwayman is apt, in that it foregrounds the nature of *demand* that is placed on the subject, a demand made by being itself insofar as the subject exists as a speaking being.

If such is the way of demand, then we have still to confront desire in relation to it. Reminding us that the 'of' in the formula 'desire is the desire of the Other' can be read in two ways, both as 'from' and as 'for', Lacan (2006: 690) explains:

> This is why the Other's question – that comes back to the subject from the place from which he expects an oracular reply – which takes some such form as '*Chè vuoi*', 'What do you want?', is the question that best leads the subject to the path of his own desire, assuming that, thanks to the know-how of a partner known as a psychoanalyst, he takes up that question, even without knowing it, in the following form: 'What does he want from me?'

Thus, we see that desire is as dialectically structured as is demand. Indeed, the desire of the Other is made manifest by his demand. But, thus far, we have not addressed what lies at the heart of Lacanian theory, that which makes it a properly Freudian theory – and that is that the dialectic of desire and dialectic of demand are sexualised. Lacan's is not merely a theory of subjectivity, but of intersubjectivity, and, moreover, it is a theory of intersexual relations.

That the dialectics of desire and demand govern intersexual relations is already implicit in the diagram of the toilet doors in 'The Instance of the

Letter', whereby his 'doubling' of the diagram Lacan attributes to Saussure symbolises 'the imperative [Western man] seems to share with the vast majority of primitive communities that subjects his public life to the laws of urinary segregation' (Lacan 2006: 417). But when Lacan moves into an explicitly Hegelian exegesis of desire and demand, what is desired and what is demanded in their dialectical relation determines the sexual locus of the subject. This is dependent on the 'phallus' as a master signifier: 'The phallic signifier clearly constitutes [the woman] as giving in love what she does not have' (Lacan 2006: 583). She does not have it, because she *is* it. The man, meanwhile, cannot *be* it, because he has it. Thus, the Freudian displacement of the Oedipal relation can be rewritten (taking a hint from Ernest Jones) as: a woman desires to have what the man has, and the man desires to be what the woman is. A 'desire to have' is a demand: the woman demands something of the man. The man, conversely, desires to be in the place where he can make that demand. Thus, the master–slave dialectic is played out between the sexes, with the woman occupying the place of the master (or of the highwayman): she is in the position of being able to make a demand, which the man can only satisfy by surrendering something of himself. But as readers of Hegel know, the master is not unassailable, and what keeps the slave alive – keeps him from not choosing death – is the hope that in the future he too will become master. Such is the nature of desire for the man, that the woman will sacrifice herself. For that is what she must do if she is to fulfil the desire of the man: she must not give something *of* herself, but give herself as such, and, thus, suffer symbolic death as master. In such a self-sacrifice, the Hegelian dialectic is *aufgehebt* in the transformation of the man's desire into an existential demand to which the woman accedes. As Lacan (2006: 581) writes in 'The Signification of the Phallus': 'The phallus is the signifier of this very *Aufhebung*, which it inaugurates (initiates) by its disappearance. That is why the demon of *eidos* (*Scham*) springs forth at the very moment the phallus is unveiled in the ancient mysteries', and, further, in 'The Subversion of the Subject', 'Such is woman concealed behind her veil: it is the absence of the penis that makes her the phallus, the object of desire' (Lacan 2006: 699). Hence, a woman's love being the gift of that which she does not have.

But all of this hinges on the meaning of 'phallus' (and not, as Lacan thinks, on 'the signification of the phallus', since, as we have seen, he is mistaken to conflate meaning with signification). Once again, we are cast into the problematic of the realism of Freudianism. Freud, as is well known, gave the castration complex a biological basis: 'penis envy' is so called, and not called 'phallus envy', because the little girl sees the little boy's penis and becomes conscious of a lack of one herself, whereas the little boy sees the little girl's lack, and becomes (according to the boy's infantile theory of castration) anxious that he could become so deprived himself someday. Does Lacan's recasting of the Freudian castration complex in terms of Hegelian dialectic (which is ultimately the same thing as recasting it linguistically, despite the questionable assimilation of structural linguistics to Hegelianism that this entails) divest his theory of the biologism to be found in Freud?

Lacan, of course, claims that it does. But in answering this question, we must investigate the nature of the 'phallus' in Lacan's thought. On the one hand, it is a signifier; on the other hand, there must be some referential link – or at least some link of signification, some signified that this signifier has slid under – between this signifier and a material object. We are driven to ask – why *this* signifier, rather than any other? Why should the *phallus* have the privilege of master signifier? Indeed, it gains determining mastery over the subject's discourse by fulfilling the same role in Lacanian theory as does the copula in Heidegger. The word 'is' for Heidegger simultaneously names being and indicates that being itself is not a thing, we cannot say of Being, that it has being. Being is not an attribute of Being itself; Being is not a thing. Likewise, for Lacan (2006: 579)

> the phallus is a signifier, a signifier whose function, in the intrasubjective economy of analysis, may lift the veil from the function it served in the mysteries. For it is the signifier that is destined to designate meaning effects as a whole, insofar as the signifier conditions them by its presence as signifier.

But we have still not got to the very kernel of this matter: why is the *phallus* accorded the privilege in Lacan (2006: 579) of being the signifier 'that is destined to designate meaning effects as a whole', as opposed to the signifier 'is' (and we should note the shift in Lacan to a noun from the Heideggerian verb)? In Heidegger, the choice of the word 'is' as primordial signifier (not that Heidegger would talk using such terminology) is determined by his entire project of fundamental ontology. We might say that Lacan's choice of the phallus as master signifier is equally determined by his project of fundamental sexuality, whereby the Being of Man is conceived of as fundamentally sexual: Lacan's is a sexual ontology. If the child's question and the philosopher's question are the same – 'Where do I come from?' – then Lacan is able to give the same answer to both questioners.

At this point, we could reprise the critique of Derrida and his followers, and charge Lacan with *phallogocentrism*. But our purpose here is, rather, to move the discussion into the ethical sphere, a movement which is more implicit than explicit in Derrida's argument. Specifically, we must question what happens in Lacanian theory when Lacan moves from the analysis of

Freudian 'intrasubjective economy' to a theory of intersubjectivity. When we do, we see at once that Lacan's is a theory of sexual relations. This means both relations between the sexes and sex as a determining factor in intersubjectivity. It is not so much that psychoanalysis is a discourse of desire but that it is specifically a discourse of sexual desire, and this is as true of Lacan as it is of Freud. But for all our detour through Lacanian theory, are we in any better position than we were at the outset to respond to a complaint often made by laypeople against psychoanalysis, that 'It's all about sex'? What underlies this complaint is the feeling that, actually, life is not all about sex, or, more accurately, that the joys and vicissitudes of life are not all reducible to a sexual explanation. Freud certainly thinks they are; Lacan, although he shifts the terms of the debate from the biological to the significatory level, still implicitly thinks they are. It is to Ricoeur that we turn to find a philosophy of the non-sexual dimensions of life. Whenever Lacan writes of 'desire', for example, he always means 'sexual desire', since, following Freud, all desire is at bottom sexual for him: desire for happiness in the future, world peace, or a cream cake, are all variations on the theme of displacement, and what is displaced is the desire of the Other, which is desire for the phallus. The phallus may be a signifier in Lacan, and not a physical organ, but it is still specifically a sexual signifier, since it determines the locus of the subject within the Oedipal framework. After all, Lacan insists on the materiality of the signifier, and the phallus only has the signifying function of the phallus if it looks, well, *phallic.*

What Ricoeur, meanwhile, admires about Freud from a philosophical point of view is that, like Heidegger in a different way, he reminds us – and this strikes to the heart of psychoanalysis conceived as a hermeneutics – that 'consciousness is not a given but a *task*'. And it follows from this that for 'the layman and the philosopher' (i.e., for anyone who is not a professional practising psychoanalyst), this opens the way to an understanding of the unconscious that is 'no longer *realist* so much as it is *dialectical*'. This looks promising from a Hegelian point of view: by placing Freud's realism in antithesis to dialectics, it looks as if Hegelianism could be made compatible with Freud: after all, Hegel's is a philosophy of consciousness, and if the final sentences of 'The Dissection of the Psychical Personality' are interpreted as a rallying call to consciousness, then the Hegelian dialectic might be the route to be taken to attain consciousness in the Freudian sense.

However, Ricoeur, unlike Lacan, sees Freud and Hegel as being in confrontation. While it may be true, as Ricoeur (1989: 109) remarks in 'Consciousness and the Unconscious', that 'The only forms which would be irreducible to Freud's key signifiers – the Father, the Phallus, Death, the Mother – in which, psychoanalysis teaches us, all other chains of signifiers are anchored, must be similar to those marked out in the

Phenomenology of Spirit', this does not account for the fact of the difference between Freudian and Hegelian genesis. Ricoeur repeatedly criticises Freudianism for being an archaeology: psychoanalysis is a technique for recovering the origins of the individual; insofar as it is teleological, the telos is merely the cure facilitated by the return to the archaeological state prior to the trauma that caused the neurosis, or whatever. Unlike Hegelianism, which is teleological in a grander sense of aiming for the 'ends of man' in an ever-ascending state of consciousness, psychoanalysis is not 'forward-looking'. In terms of the individual, this means that psychoanalysis seeks its explanations in childhood: Hegelianism, meanwhile, is explicitly a philosophy of adult consciousness.

Such is the nub of Ricoeur's criticism of Freud's reading – which he sees as a misreading – of *Oedipus Rex*. Ricoeur (1970: 516) reminds us that 'at the beginning of the play Oedipus calls down curses upon the unknown person responsible for the plague, but he excludes the possibility that that person might in fact be himself'. For Ricoeur, 'the entire drama consists in the resistance and ultimate collapse of this presumption'. Now, 'this presumption is no longer the culpable desire of the child, but the pride of the king; the tragedy is not the tragedy of Oedipus the child, but of Oedipus Rex' (Ricoeur 1970: 516). It follows from this that it is possible to apply to the play what Ricoeur calls an 'antithetic of reflection'. On the one hand, there is the initial drama, which actually takes place before the start of the play and is recalled by the characters retrospectively: this is the drama of the death of the father and the marrying of the mother. On the other hand, there is the second drama, that of Oedipus' hubris, which is presented in the play directly. The first drama is a drama of childhood and comes 'within the province of psychoanalysis'. The second drama, however, 'Freud seems to reduce to the status of secondary revision ...[,] although it actually constitutes the true tragedy' (Ricoeur 1970: 517). What is significant about this opposition which Ricoeur establishes between the two dramas – and, hence, between the two readings of the play which follow from each – is that while he associates the first with Freud, he also sees the second as being Hegelian:

> As in the Hegelian dialectic, Oedipus is not the centre from which the truth proceeds; a first mastery, which is only pretension and pride, must be broken; the figure from which truth proceeds is that of the seer, which Sophocles describes as "the force of truth". This figure is no longer a tragic one; it represents and manifests the vision of the totality. (Ricoeur 1970: 517)

Hence, the supplanting of the first drama by the second represents an *Aufhebung*, and, moreover, one which is teleological, since Tiresias represents not merely the truth of the drama of the adult in isolation, but rather the truth of the drama of the adult that comprehends the drama of the child, just as in real life the adult contains within him the child which he once was. Thus, the Ricoeurean 'antithetical' reading as such is itself Hegelian: the two readings are not in simple antithesis, but, rather, the first is subsumed under the second. We might note in passing, too, that with specific regard to the Oedipal drama, Tireseas embodies both masculine and feminine attributes. In Lacanian terms, he would occupy the position of phallus, the locus from which truth speaks, which would explain his feminine guise. But this would be to confuse Tiresias as commentator *on* the first drama with Tiresias as embodiment of the truth of *both* dramas.

To return to Ricoeur's essay 'Consciousness and the Unconscious', then, Ricoeur (1989: 109–10) argues that 'man becomes an adult only by becoming capable of new key signifiers which are similar to the moment of spirit in Hegelian phenomenology and regulate spheres of meaning which are absolutely irreducible to Freudian hermeneutics'. It is this 'absolute irreducibility' which places Ricoeur in antithesis to Lacan, carrying with it as it does the notion of replacing the key signifiers of Freudianism, the signifiers of the Oedipus complex. These are the signifiers that are as central to Lacanian theory as they are to Freud's: indeed, by calling them 'signifiers', Ricoeur is already shifting the debate onto Lacanian terms, although he does not in this essay mention Lacan by name. But the implication is clear: Lacan, like Freud, is condemned to an archaeological theory of childhood rather than a prospective theory of adulthood. It follows from this that, while both Ricoeur and Lacan make use of Hegel, Ricoeur's Hegel is a means of moving beyond psychoanalysis, not something which psychoanalysis can appropriate.

To hammer this point home, it is to the dialectic of the master and the slave, on which Lacan bases his understanding of Ernest Jones's 'aphanisis' as the logic of the *vel* (and, by extension, the dialectic of desire, or the dialectic between desire and demand), to which Ricoeur (1989: 110) turns:

> This is not at all a dialectic of consciousness. What is at stake here is the birth of the Self or, in Hegelian terms, the passage out of desire as desire for another into *Anerkennung* or *mutual recognition*. What happens in this process? Nothing less than the birth of the Self through a disremption of consciousness. There had been no Self before this dialectic. . . .

Is Ricoeur saying something vastly different from Lacan here? No, but the difference, however subtle, is profound. Lacan and Ricoeur agree that the master–slave dialectic is not a 'dialectic of consciousness'. They might also agree that 'there had been no Self before this dialectic', were the language of the Self assimilable to Lacanian discourse. But here is the first point of departure: Lacan speaks not of a Self, but of a subject. Selfhood can only be attained, precisely, through 'the passage out of desire as desire for another'. The master–slave dialectic, for Ricoeur, is not an example of the kind of dialectic that takes place *within* desire; it does not explain desire. When Ricoeur writes that the master-slave dialectic is not a 'dialectic of consciousness', he is presumably (from his remarks on Marx further in his essay) alluding to the Leninist doctrine of 'raising of consciousness', through which reading, the slave (proletariat) will become master in turn once the reality of his situation and the possibility of changing it has become apparent to him. But this is Lenin, not Hegel: Hegelian hope lies in recognition (of the other), not in (self-)consciousness of a situation. Ricoeur's reading of the dialectic as 'the birth of the self' through recognition of the other aligns Hegelian phenomenology with the phenomenology of, say, Merleau-Ponty.

But is not the Lacanian variant on Hegelianism doing the same thing? After all, Lacan claims that his theory of the 'gaze' is based on the philosophy of Merleau-Ponty (presumably the reference is to *The Visible and the Invisible*[2]): narcissism, says Lacan (1979: 74), is a satisfaction in the specular image which 'gives the subject a pretext for ... a profound *méconnaissance*'; this is a satisfaction deriving from what Merleau-Ponty calls the *speculum mundi*, 'that gaze that circumscribes us, and which in the first instance makes us beings who are looked at, but without showing this' (Lacan 1979: 75). But in Merleau-Ponty, just as in Hegel, cognition is cognition and recognition is recognition – it is not misrecognition (*méconnaissance*).

The crux of the difference in Hegelianisms between Ricoeur and Lacan is that for Lacan, the dialectic of desire is explainable in Hegelian terms, whereas for Ricoeur, the master–slave dialectic shows how desire can be left behind. For Lacan, desire is a form of entrapment that is governed by the Hegelian dialectic: the *Aufhebung* confirms the subject as a desiring being. Desire (of the slave) is the desire to be in the place of the Other (the master). This desire can only come to an end when life does: death is the absolute master. But, for Ricoeur, both slave and master are able to live their lives once they recognise each other: this is mutual recognition, not the *méconnaissance* of 'primary narcissism'; the absolute master is not death, but life; life is lived in mutuality once desire has been left behind. Desire, for Ricoeur, is essentially childish, which is why psychoanalysis is good at explaining it. But once I recognise the Other, the time has come to put away such childish things.

It does not matter whose is the more accurate reading of Hegel – Ricoeur's or Lacan's. The point is that an ethics is implied by both readings, since both entail an opening into the sphere of the Other. But a Lacanian ethics can only be an ethics based on desire, just as psychoanalysis as a whole sees desire as everything. This is problematic in its implication that the Other, as a locus of discourse, is *merely* a locus of discourse: at best, a fantasmatic projection of the subject, and not a Self, just as the subject is not a Self. Ricoeur's ethics, meanwhile, is capable of discussing 'intersubjective relations' in the sense of 'inter-*self* relations', since leaving desire and the signifiers of the Freudian topography behind opens the way to spheres of human existence other than those governed or determined by desire. As Ricoeur (1989: 110) puts it, 'The stages of this mutual recognition bring us across "regions" of human meaning which are essentially nonsexual'. In a slightly later essay,[3] Ricoeur (1989: 324–5) makes what is at stake even more clear and, while he is writing of Freud, the comparison he draws between psychoanalysis and a phenomenology of the Other is, by extension, equally applicable to Lacan:

> After Freud, the only possible philosophy of consciousness would be one that is related to the Hegelian phenomenology of Spirit. In this phenomenology consciousness does not know itself. To employ once again our previous mode of expression, I will say that man becomes adult, becomes 'conscious', if and when he becomes capable of these new figures, the succession of which constitutes 'Spirit' in the Hegelian sense of the word. An exegesis of consciousness would involve an inventory and a step-by-step constitution of the spheres of meaning which consciousness must encounter and appropriate for itself so as to reflect upon itself as a self, as an adult, human, ethical self. Such a process is by no means a type of introspection or immediate consciousness; it is by no means a figure of narcissism... .[4]

This is a work, says Ricoeur (1989: 324), of discovering 'new figures, new symbols, which are irreducible to those rooted in the libidinal ground'. It is at this point that we must examine the different conceptions of symbolism in Lacan and Ricoeur.

'The symbolic' as a major concept in Lacan, part of the triad *symbolic, imaginary,* and *real,* is first introduced in the Rome Report ('The Function and Field of Speech and Language in Psychoanalysis'[5]) in 1954. There, Lacan (2006: 245) sets out to show how the 'conception of language as signs' is inadequate; in other words, how 'language' is more than mere 'communication'. This he does by drawing a contrast between language and the 'wagging dance' of bees, as observed by von Frisch.[6] This dance 'is distinguished from language precisely by the fixed correlation between its signs and the reality they signify' (Lacan 2006: 245). This distinction is rather typical of definitions of language dating from the early 1950s. In

Peirce's terms,[7] language is distinguished from mere 'communication' by being 'symbolic' as well as 'indexical'; in other words, it has the capacity for what Saussure calls 'arbitrariness', or, more accurately, a non-essential link between signifier and signified (there is nothing tree-like about the word 'tree'), as opposed to the index, which is a type of sign that is in existential relation to what it signifies.

Lacan (2006: 246) makes the symbolic quality of language its defining feature:

> In a language, signs take on their value from their relations to each other in the lexical distribution of semantemes as much as in the positional, or even flectional, use of morphemes – in sharp contrast to the fixity of coding used by bees. The diversity of human languages takes on its full value viewed in this light.

But human language is not unique among communication systems in being 'arbitrary' or symbolic in this sense: bird song, for example, is similarly symbolic. Symbolisation can, therefore, not be the *defining* characteristic of a 'language' as opposed to a mere communication system. It was some three years later, in his review of B. F. Skinner's *Verbal Behaviour*, that Chomsky (1959) identified this defining feature as creativity. We need not here go into whether Chomsky is correct in identifying creativity in language as a uniquely *human* capability: suffice to say, of all the observed communication systems, only human language has this feature naturally, whether or not other animals might be artificially taught a language that incorporates it. That Lacan should identify symbolisation as the most important characteristic of human language makes him very much a man of his time in this respect, rather than the innovator he thinks he is: it aligns him not only, once again, with the structuralists, but also (unwittingly, perhaps) with a certain deterministic behaviourism.

This is not to say that when Lacan writes of the 'Symbolic' he simply means 'language'. Far from it. The symbols of the symbolic are not, to adopt Peirce's terminology again, icons: they are not physical objects reflexively signifying themselves, but signifiers, in the same way that the signifiers of language are signifiers. They signify something else, something other than their objective appearance, just as do the signifiers of language. So, although both language and the symbolic order are comprised of symbols, this does not mean that they are the same thing but merely that there are other kinds of symbols – other kinds of signifiers, Lacan would say – than those found in language. The field of the symbolic might encompass language, but it also exceeds it. But the problem we have identified in seeing symbolism as the defining characteristic of language may be carried over, *mutatis mutandis*, to Lacan's entire symbolic order: namely, that it is a closed system. If Chomsky's language is open, unbounded and infinite, it is because Chomsky focuses on grammaticality as its defining characteristic. It is because grammar is a *system* rather than a *set* that it is open to the infinitude of human creativity. If Ricoeur opposes Hegel to Freud, so also might we oppose Chomsky to Lacan (which is not to imply that Chomsky may be compared to Hegel): Lacanian psychoanalysis works with the fixed stock of the symbolic order, whereas Chomskian grammar works with the infinite possibilities opened up by human creativity in language. (This is why Chomskian 'deep structure' cannot be equated with the unconscious, as some have claimed.)

If the symbolic order is closed for Lacan, then it is also an order in which the subject is trapped, just as in Freud the subject is trapped by his childhood. This leads to a concept of symbolisation quite contrary to that of Ricoeur. The symbolic stumbles in its attempt to arrive at the Real. While everyday reality might be perfectly knowable, the Real of the subject is ineffable. The symbolic order may be closed, but it is not necessarily complete: the Real is that which it lacks. Such is the effect of that which constitutes symbolisation: the constant sliding of the signified under the signifier. There is always something else, something other, which escapes, an unknown which is unfathomable to the analytic experience (Freud's 'analysis interminable'). In effect, the symbolic order mediates between reality and the Real of the subject, but in so doing acts as a kind of barrier between them. If psychoanalysis aims at the Real through an interpretation of symbols, it is also suspicious of those symbols, and carries with it a certain defeatism. 'The deep truth is imageless'.[8]

Ricoeur's (1969: 347–57) slogan, meanwhile, is 'The symbol gives rise to thought'. At a certain level, Lacan would agree: there can be no thought without symbolisation. But there the similarity between Ricoeur and Lacan on the nature of symbols ends. For Ricoeur, the symbol giving rise to thought is like an invitation, an invitation, precisely, to hermeneutics. Moreover, this is what we might call a progressive hermeneutics – a hermeneutics which, unlike the hermeneutics that is psychoanalysis, increases the stock of understanding not just of the subject, but also of the whole of humanity. This is because the field of the symbolic is, for Ricoeur, unbounded. It is not circumscribed by the privileged signifiers of the Oedipal relation, nor is it an obstacle to its own understanding, and it mediates between the subject and reality, not between reality and some ineffable Real.

Thus it is that Ricoeur (1969: 18) explains what he means by 'symbols' at the beginning of *The Symbolism of Evil*:

> I shall always understand by symbol ... analogical meanings which are spontaneously formed and immediately significant, such as defilement, analogue of stain; sin, analogue of deviation; guilt, analogue of accusation. These symbols are on the same level as, for example, the meaning of water as threat and as renewal in the flood and in baptism, and finally on the same level as the most primitive hierophanies.

What is impressive about this list is that it is, in principle, expandable; implicitly, it is not closed. It is not a reductive list in the way that the set of symbols of the Freudian topography is. Moreover, the items it contains are as 'primitive', in a cultural sense, as the privileged symbols of the Freudian myth: Freudian psychoanalysis does not have a monopoly on those symbols which are irreducible, or held to be foundational. Thus it is that Ricoeur (1969: 348) explains the 'gift' part of the formula 'the symbol gives rise to thought': 'The symbol gives: a philosophy instructed by myths arises at a certain moment in reflection, it wishes to answer to a certain situation of modern culture.' The giving of the symbol is the antithesis of concealment. The 'certain situation' of which Ricoeur (1969: 349) writes is our very modernity: 'we moderns are the heirs of philology, of exegesis, of the phenomenology of religion, of the psychoanalysis of language'. Psychoanalysis takes its place among the other great discourses which have shaped our modernity, and which must colour our view of myths, and the way in which we interpret the symbols of which they are composed. But psychoanalysis does not have a monopolistic propriety over those symbols.

6

The Law of the Subject and the Law of the Other

Thus far, we have examined the place of desire in the constitution of the self (in Ricoeur's terminology) or the subject (in Lacan's). We have also tested the limits of psychoanalysis as forming the basis of a philosophy of desire and tested the limits of a philosophy of desire as an adequate philosophy of the self or subject in its totality. We have seen that, whether one takes the phenomenological or the psychoanalytic route, the hermeneutics of the self or subject has at its origin a certain intersubjectivity, whether that be the analogous recognition of other selves *qua* selves in phenomenology, or the loquacious *méconnaissance* of the Other in psychoanalysis. Each of these intersubjective origins represents an opening into the field of ethics, which is to say, they invite consideration of the movement from intersubjectivity as subjective origin, to intersubjective *relations*. It is to this consideration that we now turn in this chapter.

What is at stake may be found once again in Freud, remembering that for him the work of *Wo Es war, soll Ich werden* is 'a work of civilisation'. In *Civilisation and its Discontents*, Freud (1961b: 144) elaborates his theory that 'the development of civilisation has ... a far-reaching similarity to the development of the individual[,] and ... it employs the same methods'. Within this theoretical parameter, Freud (1961b: 143) makes 'objections' to 'the ethical demands of the cultural super-ego', to the effect that it 'does not trouble itself enough about the facts of the mental constitution of human beings. It issues a command and does not ask whether it is possible for people to obey it'. The command to which Freud (1961b: 143) refers here is 'Love thy neighbour as thyself', which Freud calls 'a mistake', since it is 'impossible to fulfil'. The failure of the attempt to fulfil the commandment leads, thinks Freud, to revolt, neurosis or unhappiness on the part of the subject. Freud (1961b: 143) then becomes dismissive of those who would try to follow this precept, and of the civilisation that produces it, and on three grounds: (i) 'anyone who follows such a precept ... only puts himself at a disadvantage *vis à vis* the person who disregards it'; (ii) the follower of the precept only gains 'the narcissistic satisfaction of being able to think oneself better than others'; and (iii) the afterlife promised by religion as a reward for following the precept is 'preach[ed] in vain'.

The first of these objections cannot be regarded as a genuine objection as such, since it merely repeats the point of the precept: to love one's neighbour as oneself is to do so in the very knowledge that this might not, and probably will not, be reciprocated: of course, this 'disadvantage' puts the subject in the position of being 'taken advantage of'. But Freud's incomprehension of why a subject should voluntarily submit to this is grounded in his assumption that people only do things for reward, which explains his second and third objections. Indeed, the notion of *voluntary* submission to the precepts of ethics is alien to Freud's thinking, which, in this respect, as in others, has a behaviouristic flavour: the subject's 'altruism' is nothing other than an inverted manifestation of his drives, which emanate from the id and over which he has no real control. Conformity to the ethical demand is nothing other than the re-presentation of the satisfaction of desire in another, more acceptable, form: thwarted in its desire to attain immediate gratification, the id attains the gratification of (moral) superiority over the other, or delayed satisfaction in the to-come of the afterlife, through the detour of ethical acts, this being analogous to the operation of the dream-work's secondary revision in making unconscious processes acceptable, or at least comprehensible, to the waking mind.

In short, Freud has a dim view of human nature, which leads to a rather defeatist view of ethics and social relations generally, colouring, for example, his political views:

> I too think it quite certain that a real change in the relations of human beings to possessions would be of more help in this direction than any ethical commands; but the recognition of this fact among socialists has been obscured and made useless for practical purposes by a fresh idealistic misconception of human nature. (Freud 1961b: 143)

So, for Freud socialism is 'useless' because it transfers the Pauline attitude towards others over to property: socialism is a secular version of Christianity.[1] Hence, Freud is just as defeatist in politics as he is in ethics: socialism, as the political expression of the ethical demand to love one's neighbour, is, because of human nature, impossible, and so neither loving one's neighbour nor socialism are worth attempting – any attempt in these directions is merely a neurotic, narcissistic attempt at personal reward disguising itself as altruism.[2] Presumably at least capitalism is less self-deluded.

And there Freud ends his book. Having dismissed ethics and politics (or at least, socialist politics) as shams, Freud (1961b: 144) 'hasten[s] to come to a close', rather than offer a positive ethical or political programme of his own. This must be because his own argument allows him no intellectual space in which to do so: Freud, he thinks, has understood human nature aright, and it is bad, and since this is human *nature* we are talking about, nothing can be done about it. This suspicion is confirmed if we turn to Freud's earlier, lengthy analysis of 'Love thy neighbour as thyself' in Chapter V of *Civilisation and its Discontents*. Here Freud (1961b: 109) remarks that if we were to adopt a 'naïve' view of this edict, 'as though we were hearing it for the first time[,] we shall be unable then to suppress a feeling of surprise and bewilderment'. Questions crowd themselves upon the naïve observer, such as 'Why should we do it? What good will it do us? But, above all, how shall we achieve it? How can it be possible?' (Freud 1961b: 109) The naïve questioner might observe that his love is valuable, and should not be thrown away 'without reflection'; that 'if I love someone, he must deserve it in some way' (109). That someone might be held to deserve it 'if he is so like me in important ways that I can love myself in him' (109). This places Freud's naïve subject's attitude to the stranger in conformity with Lacan's *Schema R*, which is to say, the subject is seen in relation to the Other dialectically: the *I* is situated in a point in the real corresponding to the *me* (that which I see of myself in the Other), while the ideal ego (that which I want to be) is situated in a point corresponding to the ego ideal (the ideal me that I see in the Other). The reality of the subject is stretched across the plane defined by these four points: *I* and my ideal ego on the side of the imaginary, and *me* and the ego ideal on the side of the symbolic. Hence, which is to be expected, Freud's theory of love is confirmed by Lacan. And this might well be a perfectly cogent psychological explanation of the subject's psychological relation to the Other. But the neighbour is not the Other in the Lacanian sense (of the privileged locus from which truth is spoken); as a stranger, the neighbour is just any old other, and this is why the neighbour lies beyond the limits of Freud's (and Lacan's, in his schema) explanation.

Of difficulty is Freud's use of the term 'deserve', which replicates the problems we noted above with his usage of the first-person 'I'. When he writes that the Other 'deserves' my love according to certain conditions, does this mean that this is a calculation made by the naïve subject, consciously or unconsciously? Whatever, the point is one not dissimilar to Benjamin Constant's in reply to Kant:[3] just as Constant maintained that I have a duty to tell the truth, but only to those who have a right to the truth, so Freud (or his putative subject) maintains that I have a duty to love, but only to love those who deserve it. The real problem here lies in the justification of this by reason or, more particularly, in the conflation of reason with the psychological which this justification entails. On the one hand, Freud's would be an entirely psychological account, which is to say, it *explains* the subject's motives in loving the Other and in not loving the stranger (Freud assumes that neighbours are strangers). On the other hand, it is through the 'judgement of my reason' that 'I am entitled to retain for myself' more love than I would show towards earthworms, say. The rational response to this is that neighbours, whether they are strangers or not, are not earthworms, but people, and that the injunction to 'love thy neighbour as oneself' is not an injunction to universal love in the sense of loving everything that inhabits the earth. But this response rather misses the mark, which is that the injunction to love does not pretend to be a rational precept. Of course, it is not rational to love one's neighbour as oneself – the Christian tradition, for example, has never claimed that it is. Freud enlists reason in support of the subject's self-interest, to the point of turning it into the same thing.

However, if, writes Freud (1961b: 109–10), the neighbour

> is a stranger to me and if he cannot attract me by any worth of his own or any significance that he might already have acquired for my emotional life, it will be hard for me to love him. Indeed, I should be wrong to do so, for my love is valued by all my own people as a sign of my preferring them, and it is an injustice to them if I put a stranger on a par with them.

Freud goes on to write that 'on closer inspection' he finds 'still further difficulties'. Because the stranger 'seems not to have the least trace of love for me and shows me not the slightest consideration', indeed, because the stranger is likely to insult me, slander me, injure me, and generally attempt to exercise his power over me, 'he has more claim to my hostility and even my hatred' (Freud 1961b: 110). What makes Freud's position scandalous is that, far from disavowing the 'naïve' view of the injunction, and the 'closer inspection' to which it leads, Freud goes on to adopt it as his own view. Or, at least, when admonished by 'a dignified voice' who says, 'It is precisely because your neighbour is not worthy of your love, and is on the contrary your enemy, that you should love him as yourself', he replies: 'I then understand that the case is one like that of *Credo quia absurdum*' (Freud 1961b: 111).

Once again, Freud's objection is that this is an offence against reason. But the reply to Freud need not consist of a defence of either reason in the face of this alleged assault, nor of irrationality, just as the reply to Freud need not consist of a defence of the goodness of human nature against his claim – to which the whole of his attack on the golden rule is leading – that human nature is characterised by an 'inclination to aggression', so that the neighbour is 'someone who tempts [people] to ... exploit his capacity for work without compensation, to use him sexually without his consent, to seize his possessions, to humiliate him, to cause him pain, to torture and to kill him' (Freud 1961b: 111).[4]

So confident is Freud in this analysis of human nature that he asks, rhetorically, 'Who, in the face of all his experience of life and of history, will have the courage to dispute this assertion?' (Freud 1961b: 111), and a few pages later, he complains of himself that 'in none of my previous writings have I had so strong a feeling as now that what I am describing is common knowledge and that I am using up paper and ink ... in order to expound things which are, in fact, self-evident' (Freud 1961b: 117). To some extent here Freud is a victim of his time, writing as he is between the wars and in the shadow of Nazism and Stalinism: it is not, he writes, 'unaccountable chance that the dream of a Germanic world-dominion called for anti-Semitism and its complement; and it is intelligible that the attempt to establish a new, communist civilisation in Russia should find its psychological support in the persecution of the bourgeois' (Freud 1961b: 114–15). This was not a time at which the states of Europe were being good neighbours. But, notwithstanding this, Freud is probably right at a certain level in his assertion that human nature is aggressive. *At a certain level*: that level is, precisely, that of the drive, or of instinct – in other words, of the animal. Insofar as humans are animals, such is human nature, and it appears to have been correctly analysed by Freud. But it would be a mistake to call this *human nature* as such, since it is more correctly the operation of animal nature within the human. Rather than oppose Freud with a counter-assertion that human nature is good, we want to say: there is no such thing as human nature; what it means to be human is to have the ability to transcend the animal nature that is within us. My neighbour is not an earthworm, but a fellow human being.

Lacan is ambivalent in his attitude towards Freud's *Civilisation and its Discontents*. On the one hand, writing of the passage in which Freud claims that he (Freud or the subject) will only give his love to whomever deserves it, Lacan writes that 'the whole Aristotelian conception of the good is alive in this man who is a true man; he tells us the most sensitive and reasonable things about what is worth sharing the good that is our love with'; on the other hand, however, 'what escapes him is perhaps the fact that precisely because we take that path we miss the opening onto *jouissance*' (1992: 186). What 'Freud makes us feel ... without articulating fully' is that while it is the nature of the good to be altruistic, love of one's neighbour is something different. Here Lacan articulates the point that Freud runs up against constantly in *Civilisation and its Discontents*: whenever he 'stops short in horror at the consequences of the commandment to love one's neighbour, we see evoked the presence of that fundamental evil which dwells within this neighbour' (Lacan 1992: 186). If this is the case, points out Lacan, then this evil 'also dwells within me'. Perhaps now we are in a position to explain Freud's slippage in his use of 'I' when articulating the views of the subject who attempts to love his neighbour – is this 'I' 'I, Freud', or is it 'I, the subject'? The subject's recoil in horror at the attempt practically to apply the edict 'love thy neighbour' is indistinguishable from Freud's recoil in horror at the *concept* of loving one's neighbour, the very neighbour whom Freud is only ever capable of seeing as a stranger. We might characterise this recoil as pathological.[5]

Freud's approach remains resolutely analytical. We might expect his critique of 'Love thy neighbour as thyself' to lead to an alternative ethics, but instead, it leads to an analysis of human nature. *Civilisation and its Discontents* consists in nothing other than a refusal of ethics, just as it is a refusal of politics. In politics, the communist system is psychologically untenable, but what Freud (1961b: 116) calls the 'American' system is equally damaging to civilisation, and Freud does not want to employ its methods. Freud has no positive political programme. Neither does he have an ethical programme in the face of the aggression he sees in human nature: human nature for him simply means the defeat of any positive ethics. Lacan, however, sees psychoanalysis as an ethical project, and the precise nature of that ethics may be discerned through an examination of Lacan's complex relation to Kant.

In his *Critique of Practical Reason*, Kant (1883: 118–19) provides the following well-known anecdote to illustrate the operation of the moral law:

> Suppose some one asserts of his lustful appetite that, when the desired object and the opportunity are present, it is quite irresistible. Ask him – if a gallows were erected before the house where he finds this opportunity, in order that he should be hanged thereon immediately after the gratification of his lust, whether he could not then control his passion; we need not be long in doubt what he would reply. Ask him, however – if his sovereign ordered him, on pain of the same immediate execution, to bear false witness against an honourable man, whom the prince might wish to destroy under a plausible pretext, would he consider it possible in that case to overcome his love of life, however great it may be. He would perhaps not venture to affirm whether he would do so or not, but he must unhesitatingly admit that it is possible to do so. He judges, therefore, that he can do a certain thing because he is conscious that he ought, and he recognises that he is free, a fact which but for the moral law he would never have known.

What is striking from this example is the personality Kant attributes to the hero of it. He is impetuous in thinking, but also likely through this impetuosity not to follow the Socratic maxim, 'know thyself', which can afford Kant the satisfaction of knowing him better: you *thought* the desired object was irresistible, but *now* see just how resistible it is. Kant asserts that 'we need not be long in doubt what he would reply', without actually telling us what the subject *would* reply – presumably his words are so self-evident that they need not be cited. Meanwhile, just as Kant has 'no doubt' that the subject would choose life over the satisfaction of desire, so also the subject, when the alternative situation is presented to him, 'unhesitatingly admit[s]' that 'it is possible' to forego life rather than bear false witness. Hence love of life is categorically ('no doubt') superior to desire, but love of truth is *possibly* superior to love of life.

The subject's consciousness of this possibility constitutes the recognition of his freedom. But we should pause here to note the order of Kant's argument. First, the subject recognises that he ought to do a certain thing (tell the truth); consequently, he recognises that he is able to do that thing; consequently, he recognises that he is free, 'a fact which but for the moral law he would never have known'. This sounds as if the great advantage of the moral law is that it shows people that they are free. If an alternative statement of the moral law is 'never to treat people as a means, but only as ends in themselves', it nevertheless appears that the moral law itself can be treated as a means to an end, that end being freedom. Hence, freedom is covertly more important to Kant even than truth itself, by which we might characterise him as a 'bourgeois' philosopher. Indeed, it appears that the subject need only recognise that he *can* obey the moral law to be free. (Lacan points out that freedom here in Kant's apologue is just like Hegel's – it is freedom to die.) Of course, by definition, to be free he must also be free to disobey it, which brings us to the paradox at the heart of Kant's categorical imperative: to be both *categorical* and *imperative*, the categorical imperative must carry with itself the possibility of the subject not obeying it, or, the subject is free to choose, but *must* choose to obey the categorical imperative, since it is categorical, and imperative.

This is, of course, a well-known criticism of Kant's position, and one which Kant himself spends some time addressing. But, for our purposes, we might examine why this parable is of interest to Lacan, and the answer is because it is a parable of desire. Kant is in 'no doubt' that what he calls 'lust' and 'passion' is a weaker force than love of life. But everyday life shows us otherwise, for example in the case of people with addictive personalities. This is Lacan's point in *The Ethics of Psychoanalysis*: 'Our philosopher from Königsberg was a nice person, and I don't want to imply that he was someone of limited stature or feeble passions, but he doesn't seem to have considered that under certain conditions . . . it is conceivable for such a step to be taken' (Lacan 1992: 108–9). And Lacan goes on to suggest two conditions whereby 'a man [might] sleep with a woman knowing full well that he is to be bumped off on the way out', namely, Freudian sublimation (the overvaluation of the object), and perversion ('the pleasure of cutting up the lady concerned in small pieces, for example').

Lacan points out that Kant allows the real behaviour of the individual in his example to bear the burden of proof within it – his is, after all, a discourse of 'practical reason' – and that Kant assumes that the reality of the individual and the weight of duty are the same thing. But Lacan's conclusion, that excessive object sublimation and perversion are two factors which might cause the subject to choose death over life in order to satisfy his desire, 'attracts our attention to the possibility of formulating . . . a different criterion of another, or even of the same, morality, in opposition to the reality principle' (Lacan 1992: 109). For Lacan, the motivation behind sleeping with the woman is of quite another order from the motivation behind hesitating before bearing false witness: it is of the order of desire, rather than the order of reality.

However, when returning to the same Kantian parable later in *The Ethics of Psychoanalysis*, Lacan points out that the theory of sublimation does not even need to be invoked for Kant's example to be ruined. 'The striking significance of the first example', he says 'resides in the fact that the night spent with the lady is paradoxically presented to us as a pleasure that is weighed against a punishment to be undergone; it is an opposition which homogenises them. There is in terms of pleasure a plus and a minus' (Lacan 1992: 189). He then goes on to cite Kant's example (in his *Essay on Negative Greatness*) of the Spartan Mother, who learns of the death of her son in the war: her first question is, But who won? Lacan (1992: 189) somewhat sarcastically notes that 'the little mathematical calculation Kant makes concerning the pleasure the family derives from the glory, from which one has to deduct the pain felt at the boy's loss, is quite touching'.[6] But Lacan wishes to substitute for Kant's concept of pleasure, his own concept of *jouissance* (sexual joy), which is at least partly defined by the very fact that it entails an acceptance of death as one of the possibilities of its attainment. Moreover, *jouissance* can be a form of evil, such as the evil of taking pleasure in doing the wrong thing. If this were the case, the moral law would become 'a support for the *jouissance*': in other words, the subject could claim that he accepted his punishment because it was in conformity with the moral law, whereas in reality it was merely in order to gain the gratification of doing the wrong thing. This would be an example, Lacan (1992: 189) says, of sin becoming 'what Saint Paul calls inordinately sinful' (in 2 Thessalonians 2:12, to have 'pleasure in unrighteousness'; and Romans 7:13, sin 'working death in me by that which is good'), and which Lacan accuses Kant of ignoring on this occasion.

Moreover, Lacan (1992: 190) also takes issue with Kant's second example and provides his own alternative: 'Let's talk about true witness, about a case of conscience which is raised if I am summoned to inform on my neighbour or my brother for activities which are prejudicial to the security of the state'. Lacan somewhat obscurely says that an example such as this 'shifts the emphasis placed on the universal rule'. In 2005, the British police arrested four terrorists who attempted to bomb London: when their photographs were shown on television, the parents of two of the suspects informed the police of their names. Presumably, those parents would have faced the same moral dilemma that Lacan describes and chose in favour of bearing true witness. Lacan's problem here is in his conception of the state, which he assumes to be a separate entity from the body of the people. But, for Kant, we recall, the sovereign will of the state is derived from the will and consent of the people, whose representative it is – the state is not a wholly autonomous *other* entity from the subject, but rather the subject is *part of* the state. The case of the arrested would-be bombers is pertinent here, since they conform precisely to Lacan's model of *jouissance* in this situation, being as they are would-be suicide bombers, who, by definition, are prepared to pay the price of death in order to accomplish their desires. Indeed, if the would-be bombers are betrayed by their parents and subsequently caught, they are saved from the death they would wish upon themselves, whereas both Kant's and Lacan's examples presuppose that the result of the betrayal will be the death of the 'neighbour or brother'. Like Sade, the modern liberal state 'refuses the death penalty'. Although the case of suicide bombers weakens Lacan's case against Kant's second example, paradoxically it strengthens his overall position on ethics, since it presents subjects who not only are prepared to sacrifice life in order to attain their desire, but they positively desire to die – the desire and its relationship to death are conflated into a singular desire-for-death. This is Kantian pathological perversion taken to the extreme.

But let us set aside for a moment the contingent fact that the state in which the would-be bombers were caught (the UK in 2005) does not have the death penalty.[7] If we are to assume that the state will execute the neighbour betrayed, and that the neighbour is not suicidal, the force of the dilemma facing the subject in Lacan's example is restored. Lacan (1992: 190) explicates it in these terms:

> Must I go toward my duty of truth insofar as it preserves the authentic place of my *jouissance*, even if it is empty? Or must I resign myself to this lie which, by making me substitute forcefully the good for the principle of *jouissance*, commands me to blow alternately hot and cold?

In her recent book *The Ethics of the Real*, which aims at a 'radical' restoration of Kantian ethics through the mediation of Lacanian theory, Alenka Zupančič (2000: 55), in commenting on this passage, explains:

> Once the good comes on stage, the question necessarily arises: *Whose good?* This is what Lacan has in mind with 'blow alternately hot and cold': if I do not betray my brother or my neighbour, I may betray my other countrymen. Who is to decide whose good is more valuable?

The answer, of course, is 'the subject'. But by what criteria are they to decide? In the case of the would-be suicide bombers, the decision is a utilitarian one: more lives will be saved if the bombers are betrayed than if they are not. This is the calculation advocated, for example, by Godwin's *Political Justice* (Godwin 1993), and presumably this is one of the calculations made by the bombers' parents, although doubtless it is tempered by the fact that the betrayal will save the lives of their offspring, too. But the standard objection to utilitarianism (eloquently voiced, for example, by Ricoeur) is that it makes of the minority a sacrificial victim, and so is not, properly speaking, ethical with regard to individuals.

Be this as it may, as Zupančič (2000: 56) points out, 'Kant actually does answer Lacan' while replying to Benjamin Constant in 'On a Supposed Right to Tell Lies'. Here, Kant (1883: 362) declares that

> Truth in utterances that cannot be avoided is the formal duty of a man to every one, however great the disadvantage that may arise from it to him or any other; and although I do no wrong to him who unjustly compels me to speak, yet I do wrong to men in general in the most essential point of duty.

In a parody of those who would reduce the thought of philosophers to single sentences, it has been claimed that Kant's moral philosophy can be summarised in the words 'never tell a lie', and yet Kant himself seems to find in this doctrine the summation of his entire moral theory. It may be the Other who compels our hero to speak, but it is the moral law which compels him to speak the truth, which he will do if he is a man of reason. Hence, 'never tell a lie' is a practical formulation of the analytic of the categorical imperative, which, we remember, is formulated thus in the *Groundwork of the Metaphysics of Morals*: 'Act only in accordance with that maxim through which you can at the same time will that it become a universal law' (Kant 1998: 31). Indeed, Kant (1893: 363) himself affirms as much when he writes: 'To be *truthful* (honest) in all declarations is therefore a sacred unconditional command of reason, and not to be limited by any expediency'.

The occasion for this declaration is a remark by Constant that 'no man has a right to a truth that injures others', and this remark in turn is made in response to a comment apocryphally attributed to Kant, to the effect that 'to tell a falsehood to a murderer who asked us whether our friend, of whom he was in pursuit, had not taken refuge in our house, would be a crime'. Kant's (1883: 362–3) justification for his response is a contractual one:

> If you have by a lie hindered a man who is even now planning a murder, you are legally responsible for all of the consequences. But if you have strictly adhered to the truth, public justice can find no fault with you, be the unforeseen consequence what it may. It may be that whilst you have honestly answered Yes to the murderer's question, whether his intended victim is in the house, the latter may have gone out unobserved, and so not have come in the way of the murderer, and the deed therefore not have been done; whereas, if you lied and said that he was not in the house, and he had really gone out (though unknown to you) so that the murderer met him as he went, and executed his purpose on him, then you might with justice be accused as the cause of his death. For, if you had spoken the truth as well as you knew it, perhaps the murderer while seeking for his enemy in the house might have been caught by neighbours coming up and the deed been prevented. Whoever then *tells a lie*, however good his intentions may be, must answer for the consequences of it . . . .

Kant's illustrative example is again taken from the realm of practical reason; the hero of his narrative follows it purely. But the realm of the practical has the consequence, fortunate for Kant's argument, of allowing in a temporal contingency. It just so happens that there is a delay between the murderer's questioning and his opportunity to execute the deed, a delay into which Kant is able to insert various ifs and buts: if you lie and the intended victim leaves early, you are responsible for his death, but if you tell the truth, the neighbours might apprehend the murderer. But we can easily imagine a variation on the story, whereby the temporal contingencies are removed. Suppose the murderer wants to avenge the death of his wife, but he is not sure whether or not his intended victim had killed her. He holds a gun against the head of the intended victim (who is bound and helpless), and asks you, Did this man kill my wife? If you answer (truthfully) Yes, then he shoots the victim; if you answer (falsely) No, then the victim lives. The advantage of such a version of the story is that it removes the temporal delay: there is no possibility of something contingent happening between your answer and the execution of the murderer's deed. What would Kant's answer here be? Presumably Yes, since according to his doctrine to be truthful admits of no exceptions on the grounds of expediency.

But we should pause here to note that Kant's introduction of a temporal delay is in one sense a red herring. It allows him to speculate on what might or might not happen in the intervening time, but this in order only to illustrate how the law might apportion blame in practice. The fact that telling a lie might do more harm than good, or that conversely, telling the truth might not in the event do the harm anticipated, does not alter the principle of pure reason which lies behind the story, which is consistent with the moral law. That civil law should coincide with the moral law is a happy coincidence in this case, albeit one that illustrates Kant's faith in the civil contract. In an earlier footnote, Kant (1883: 362 n. 1) remarks that 'I do not wish here to press this principle [i.e., never to lie] so far as to say that "falsehood is a violation of duty to oneself". For this principle belongs to Ethics, and here we are speaking only of a duty of justice'. However, justice in Kant's philosophy is subordinated to ethics, and we might easily perform the manoeuvre Kant refuses and examine the case ethically. If the victim is killed by the murderer (whether in Kant's original story or in our modification of it), the ethical implication of Kant's jury's decision to acquit the truth-teller – and, therefore, Kant's own ethical position – is that the murderer is wholly responsible for the victim's death and that the truth-teller, therefore, bears no responsibility.

Intuitively, this seems false, which is doubtless why Kant's rigour in his insistence on always telling the truth in this particular essay is what makes it the most scandalous of all of his works.[8] We can press this point further by modifying the example again: suppose the murderer is a madman, or an infant, or otherwise not responsible for his actions – not morally responsible, *de facto* or *de jure.* Kant's principle overrides not only the circumstances in which one might be faced with speaking the truth or lying but also the 'to whom' one might tell the truth or lie. Kant's ethics has no conception of 'the Other' – I do not speak the truth because I have a responsibility or duty to my interlocutor, but because I have a general duty to speak the truth, for the sake of conformity to the universal principle (the moral law), the constancy of which guarantees the fidelity of the social bond of truth in any situation whatever. Indeed, Kant's subject is one who betrays the third party, 'the Other of the Other' (whom Lacan does not believe to exist); Kant illustrates how it is possible to have a morality of truthfulness without an ethics of fidelity. Against Constant's argument that 'it is a duty to speak the truth, but only to him who has the right to the truth', Kant asserts that speaking the truth 'is an *unconditional duty* which holds in all circumstances'.

Kant's example seems perverse, in the technical psychoanalytic sense of being deflected from the true object, in this case, of duty. Kant's subject, in showing fidelity to the moral law, does not show fidelity to his friend – indeed, the murderer is *preferred over* the friend. Doubtless, Kant could dismiss such fidelity as a-rational or unenlightened 'sentiment' of the eighteenth-century sort that his *Critique of Practical Reason* was reacting against.[9] But his example also reveals an asymmetry in his position, and this is one acutely perceived by Zupančič (2000: 60): 'Kant', she says, 'goes so far as to claim that the subject who tells the murderer the truth is not responsible for the consequences of this action, whereas the subject who tells a lie is fully responsible for the outcome of the situation'. Zupančič (2000: 60) draws an illuminating consequence from this:

> Instead of illustrating the fact that duty is founded only in itself, and that it is precisely this point which allows for the freedom and responsibility of the moral subject, this notorious example, rather, illustrates the case of a pervert who hides the enjoyment he derives from betrayal behind a supposed respect for the Law.[10]

Zupančič is engaging in a certain loaded hermeneutic here: nowhere does Kant mention 'enjoyment', and Kant's subject's respect for the Law appears genuine, if misguided. But, nevertheless, Kant's example in this light does appear to be an illustration of his own concept, developed elsewhere, of 'radical evil' (cf. Kant 1934: 32).[11] This is not, however, 'what makes Kant's position unbearable' for Zupančič, which is, rather, the example's 'other aspect', namely, that while

> it is *possible* that someone would make it his duty to tell the murderer the truth [–] paradoxical as it may sound, this *could be an ethical act* [–] what is inadmissible is that the subject claims that his duty was imposed on him, that he could not act otherwise, that he only followed the commandment of the Law. . . .[12] Kant takes, in this case, the duty to tell the truth as a ready-made duty which has passed, once and for all, the test of the categorical imperative, and can thus be written on some master list of commandments valid for all future generations. (Zupančič 2000: 60)

Well, we might ask, what is wrong with that? This is, after all, what happens on Sinai. Zupančič's answer is not that it entails neglecting the circumstances of a particular situation, or the fact that each situation is different from any other (which would be Constant's objection): after all, Kant's own position is precisely that the particulars of each individual circumstance *should* be so neglected, in favour of considerations of the universal – the appeal to the universal verily *constitutes* the moral law. And it is this constitutional problem, of the moral law but equally of the ethical subject, which forms the basis of Zupančič's 'radical' objection. Zupančič's radical move is to reverse Kant's relation between the subject and the universal:

> The ethical subject is not an *agent* of the universal, he does not act in the name of the universal or with its authorisation – if this were the case, the

> subject would be an unnecessary, dispensable 'element' of ethics. The subject is not the agent of the universal, but its *agens.* This ... does not point towards a certain definition of the universal but, rather, towards a definition of the subject: it means that the subject is nothing other than this moment of universalisation, of the constitution or determination of the Law. The ethical subject is ... a subject who is ... born of this situation, who only emerges from it. The ethical subject is the point where the universal comes to itself and achieves its determination. (Zupančič 2000: 61–2)

Whatever the merits of this position, Zupančič employs an odd line of argument to arrive at it. The reason 'why it inadmissible to fulfil, once and for all, the enigmatic enunciation of the categorical imperative with a statement (i.e., "Tell the truth!"), which reduces the Law to a list of pre-established commandments' is not because to do this neglects 'all the particular circumstances which may occur in a concrete situation' (Zupančič 2000: 60–1), but rather, *because* the universal in its constitution or determination is dependent on the subject, and not vice versa. This does not explain *why* the universal is dependent on the subject; rather, it is asserted as an a priori which can be used as evidence that Kant's position is mistaken. In short, Zupančič's reversal of Kant is asserted, rather than argued.

Be this as it may, this does not necessarily entail that Zupančič's assertion is wrong, just as a rejection of Kant's position does not necessarily entail that Zupančič is right. We see from Zupančič's reading of Kant two essential, competing positions: either, the subject is derived from the universal, or, the universal is derived from the subject. But must we choose in this way, from only these alternatives?

In order to comprehend the significance of this question for Lacan's ethics, we must turn to where Lacan treats of the same Kantian parable yet again, in 'Kant with Sade'. Here Lacan repeats his point that 'no occasion precipitates certain people more surely toward their goal than one that involves defiance of or even contempt for the gallows'. 'Desire', he writes, 'suffices to make life meaningless if it turns someone into a coward': the subject of desire recognises the maxim *et non propter vitam vivendi perdere causas* ('do not lose the reasons for living for the sake of life itself'). Lacan's radical insight here, however, is that 'in a moral being..., precisely because he is moral' this maxim can rise 'to the rank of a categorical imperative' (Lacan 2006: 660).

But Lacan goes further and also analyses the second half of Kant's apologue, in which the subject unhesitatingly admits that it would be possible for him to overcome his love of life for the sake of telling the truth. Of this, Lacan (2006: 661) says that 'it no more proves [Kant's] point than the first stage did', since a question can be posed as a counter-example: would it be the subject's 'duty to bear true witness were this the means by which the tyrant could satisfy his desire' (Lacan 2006: 661)? Hence, 'we could make the maxim that one must counter a tyrant's desire into a duty, if a tyrant is someone who appropriates the power to enslave the Other's desire' (Lacan 2006: 662). Lacan's conclusion is that 'desire can have not only the same success but can obtain it more legitimately' than the Law in putting into balance everything pathological. (For Kant, a 'pathological' decision is one made from feeling only, or by following the appeal of one's own desires, without the application of reason, and, hence, without appeal to the moral law. Crucially, a pathological decision is made by appeal to self-interest, and is, therefore, inimicable to the dutiful. Indeed, Kant defines the dutiful in dialectical opposition to the pathological: duty is born of the rejection, by reason, of pathological self-interest.)

It is at this point that we realise why Lacan should be interested in Sade in relation to Kant. 'The man who cares only for the enjoyment of life', says Kant (1893: 110), 'does not ask whether the ideas are of the understanding or the senses, but only *how much* and *how great pleasure* they will give for the longest time'. As is well known, it is Lacan's contention that Sade's *Philosophy in the Bedroom* not only 'accords with' Kant's *Critique of Practical Reason*, but also 'completes it' and gives it its truth. The defence of calumny in *Philosophy in the Bedroom* is a counterpart to Kant's example of the sovereign who requires his subject to lie on pain of death. Indeed, as Lacan points out, Sade

> proceeds in like manner to justify point by point the fundamental imperatives of the moral law, extolling incest, adultery, theft, and everything else you can think of. If you adopt the opposite of all the laws of the Decalogue, you will end up with the coherent exposition of something which in the last instance may be articulated as follows: 'Let us take as the universal maxim of our conduct the right to enjoy any other person whatsoever as the instrument of our pleasure'. (Lacan 1992: 78–9)

One of the effects of Sade's reversal of the Decalogue, and of Lacan's reading of him doing so, is to unpick the link between Kant's two formulations of the moral law as they are presented in the *Groundwork of the Metaphysics of Morals*: 'act only in accordance with that maxim through which you can at the same time will that it become a universal law', and 'so act that you use humanity, whether in your own person or in the person of any other, always at the same time as an end, never merely as a means' (Kant 1998: 31 and 38). Sade (or at least his character Dolmancé) takes the opposite of the second formulation as his maxim, and yet it still does not contradict the moral law as expressed in the first version. This shows that (i) the first expression of the moral law in Kant does not necessarily entail the second, and that (ii) *any* maxim can be applied universally – even maxims directly opposed to the 'good' – so long as the subject applying the maxim is exercising free will. Bad maxims serve the function of universal applicability just as well as good ones.

If this is so, then a potential contradiction is to be found in Kant's ethics. If Sade proves Kant, then it is no accident that, as is well known, Sade's *Philosophy in the Bedroom* is riddled with contradictions. One of the most glaring is that the pamphlet 'One more effort ...' simultaneously advocates universal emancipation ('Never may an act of possession be exercised upon a free being; the exclusive possession of a woman is no less unjust than the possession of slaves; all men are born free, all have equal rights: never should we lose sight of these principles; according to which never may there be granted to one sex the right to lay monopolising hands upon the other, and never may one of these sexes, or classes, arbitrarily possess the other' [Sade 1965: 318]) and the universal right of any being to enjoy another, even against their will ('it is legitimate to force the woman's will in this connection' [Sade 1965: 320]), a contradiction that is an internal repetition of that made in the main dialogue (when Mme de St. Ange tells Eugenie that 'your body is your own, yours alone; in all the world there is but yourself who has the right to enjoy it as you see fit' (Sade 1965: 221), which contradicts Dolmancé's doctrine of cruelty generally, and particularly the violation of Eugenie's mother which all of the other principal characters participate in.

At this point, the question of how to read Sade's text intrudes itself. For one recent commentator, *Philosophy in the Bedroom* 'is strongly satirical in character and conception', and contains 'parodic and satirical elements[,] and [a] strong plea for women's sexual freedom' (Phillips 2001: 63); moreover, 'in defence of Sade, one might argue that the notion of compulsory prostitution for men and women is not so much a serious project as an ironic comment on the ultimate impossibility of total satisfaction' (Phillips 2001: 75). Another commentator, meanwhile, is quoted approvingly thus: 'that Sade truly felt an enthusiasm for murder among the stench of blood and the procession of the condemned seems as likely as that Swift, after his *Modest Proposal*, felt an appetite for infant flesh' (Phillips 2001: 74). Now, the problem with this 'ironic' or 'Swiftian' reading of Sade is precisely the contradictory content of Sade's text. Swift, by contrast, is nothing if not consistent. It is true that at no point does Swift's *A Modest Proposal* step outside itself and announce 'this is a satire', but its internal consistency allows it to be read as the diametrical opposite, or inversion, of the author's true intent, so long as the reader brings to the text the *one* piece of extratextual information, that the rationality of the 'modest proposal' of the title is itself incompatible with moral sentiment. When we turn to Sade, the case is entirely different, and not least because Sade is writing post-Kant, or at least, as Lacan points out, because he proves Kant's thesis, a thesis which is precisely one based on the appeal to reason. If we are to be charitable to Sade and treat his work as satire or irony, then the contradictions within it demand *which* pieces of it, or which halves of the dichotomies of the contradictions, we are to accept as real, and which as satirical. And this (moral) choice is not guided by an appeal to the author, as it is with Swift, since Sade himself is as ambiguous a character as those he presents in his novels.

Thus, if we are to defend Sade as ironic satirist, the only recourse is to our own subjective moral principles's and it is this procedure which informs, for example, John Phillips' reading. For Phillips, whatever in Sade 'seems in tune with the liberal-mindedness of modern Western culture' (Phillips 2001: 74–5) or 'liberal if not feminist doctrine' (Phillips 2001: 76) (for example, 'the woman's right to choose' in the case of abortion, or the according to women the same sexual rights as men), is read as Sade's real position, whereas anything that Phillips cannot stomach is held to be ironic or satirical. One can see the critic's problem, since, as with Swift, there is no clue internal to the text as to what is intended ironically and what is not. But to pick and choose which parts of the text to treat ironically does not accord with the central tenet of Sade's text, which is that the moral law collapses as soon as we realise that any action whatever can be made to conform to it. Hence, when Phillips (2001: 76) writes that 'at its logical extreme . . . this doctrine of individual licence is seen to justify the most horrific "crimes" of rape and even of murder, which in Sade's terms are not crimes because they belong to the natural order', the status of the phrase 'in Sade's terms' is not clear: is this Sade the man, or Sade the ironist? Is Sade (either *tout court*, or according to Phillips) really saying that rape and murder are not crimes, or is he saying that, if the logic of the appeal to nature here ironically presented is pursued, we would be left in the unacceptable position of rape and murder not being crimes? The unanswerability of this question is replicated in the hesitation revealed by the scare quotes around 'crimes': does Phillips put 'crimes' in quotation marks to indicate that rape and murder are not really crimes according to Sade's actual thinking, or that they are not really crimes according to the logic of Sade's satirical irony (I am discounting the possibility that the scare quotes indicate that Phillips does not consider rape and murder to be crimes)?

As we can see, the possibilities afforded interpretation by seeing *Philosophy in the Bedroom* as *partially* ironic soon multiply to the point of confusion, which might have been Sade's intention, or which might indicate to us Sade's insanity, 'moral' or otherwise, or which, more likely, might indicate that such a reading is taking the wrong tack. This brings us to the vexed question of the ending to *Philosophy in the Bedroom*, whereby, egged on by Eugenie, the participants have Eugenie's mother raped by a syphilitic footman and then sew up her orifices, 'so that the virulent humour, more concentrated, less subject to evaporation and not to leakage, will more promptly cinder [her] bones' (Sade 1965: 363). Phillips reads this scene as one of *cartoon* violence 'from which the victim always recovers': 'though utterly repulsive if read on a realistic level, Eugenie's actions imply a fantastic use of the mother as object that is funny, in part precisely *because* it is so unthinkable' (Phillips 2001: 77), and 'the victim lives to recover from an abuse which, though painful and shocking, is, we assume, not irreversible' (Phillips 2001:78). This is surely to read in diametric opposition to what the text explicitly says: Mme de Mistival is sewn up in order to prevent the syphilitic sperm from escaping, in other words, precisely in order to make the violence done her irreversible. Indeed, as Phillips rightly goes on to show, *Philosophy in the Bedroom* is presented in the form of a drama that the actions might be *staged*, at least in the reader's imagination, which has the effect of heightening their 'thinkability' to the reader. Sade's crimes, such as those perpetrated against Mme de Mistival, are not literally 'unthinkable' in the same way as a square circle is, and so long as this is the case, Sade will force us to think them. Sade's great achievement (in Kant's sense of 'negative greatness') is to make the unthinkable thinkable: the dramatic form forces the action before our imaginative gaze. For Sade, nothing is unthinkable. He is truly 'obscene', in Baudrillard's sense of the word, that nothing is hidden, not even, or especially not, from the mind's eye.

Again, then, we must agree with Lacan, who sees the final scene not as a joke, but as 'a tragic experience, insofar as it projects its condition ... in a light from beyond all fear and pity' (Lacan 2006: 666). But Lacan also reminds us that Sade refuses the death penalty:[13] as Mme de Mistival is prepared to be inseminated, she cries out, 'What a hideous damnation!', to which Eugenie replies, 'Better that than to die, Mamma' (Sade 1965: 363). Many commentators assume Lacan's comment to be a reference to the final scene of *Philosophy in the Bedroom,* but we might also turn to the passage in 'One more effort ...', which makes a distinction between the death *penalty* (imposed by the law) and murder, committed by the individual subject. It is the latter that is permissible in Sade's ethics, not the former,[14] and Sade's justification for this position is one of appeal to Nature.

We remember, too, that for Kant the moral law is a natural law. Hence, says Lacan (2006: 667), Sade stopped 'at the point where desire and the law become bound up with each other'. But in so doing, he shows 'what a natural society is like' (Lacan 1992: 79). If Sade's categorical imperative is 'Let us take as the universal maxim of our conduct the right to enjoy any other person whatsoever as the instrument of our pleasure',[15] then 'this conception opens wide the flood gates that in imagination he proposes as the horizon of our desire; everyone is invited to pursue to the limits the demands of his lust, and to realise them' (Lacan 1992: 79).

Perhaps somewhat surprisingly, Lacan's 'repugnance' at this leads him to a defence of (moral) sentiment, the elimination of which, of course, forms the impetus behind the entirety of Kant's moral philosophy:

> If one eliminates from morality every element of sentiment, if one removes or invalidates all guidance to be found in sentiments, then in the final analysis the Sadian world is conceivable – even if it is its inversion, its caricature – as one of the possible forms of the world governed by a radical ethics, by the Kantian ethics as elaborated in 1788. (Lacan 1992: 79)

Lacan is equally dismissive of both Kantian and Sadian ethics: each, in historical reality, has had 'no social consequence at all' (because no one actually, explicitly performs the mental 'gymnastics' of the categorical imperative, and society has not, in fact, become a Sadian free-for-all). Lacan's own response, meanwhile, to the truth that he has discovered, namely that Sade demonstrates Kant, is a return to a pre-Kantian ethics of sentiment, although Lacan does not elaborate as to what this would consist of. Just as Sade ultimately stops short of abandoning the Law altogether (since to do so would be inherently contradictory: 'I take as my maxim always to oppose the Law' would itself become a new Law), so Lacan ultimately stops short of articulating his own theory of moral sentiments.

This stopping short is a result of the limitations of psychoanalysis as such. At the end of the series of seminars entitled *The Ethics of Psychoanalysis*, Lacan proposes that, 'from an analytical point of view, the only thing of which one can be guilty is of having given ground relative to one's desire' (Lacan 1992: 319). This is so, says Lacan, 'regardless of whether it is admissible or not in a given ethics'. The crucial point here is that Lacan writes *from an analytical point of view*: psychoanalysis, as any analysis, does not pretend to synthesis. The claim about giving ground relative to one's desire returns Lacan to the impasse arrived at in Freud's *Civilisation and its Discontents*: that psychoanalysis merely observes what is the case for any given subject and is incapable, so long as it is analysis, of arriving at a positive ethics of its own. This is why *The Ethics of Psychoanalysis* does not pretend to give moral instruction on how psychoanalysis should be conducted (such practical issues as patient confidentiality, the level of fees to be charged, etc.), nor does it set out an ethical programme to be compared to the ethical programmes of philosophy. Since it is grounded in the practical reason of the subject's behaviour, psychoanalysis must content itself with being limited to discussion of what that behaviour reveals about the existing claims of the philosophers' ethical systems when they, too, venture to ground their theories in examples drawn from reality.

In this respect, Lacan's critique of Kant finds him instructive but wanting: Kant requires the completion that his inverse, Sade, brings. There are two essential insights here. The first is that Kant unwittingly grounds the freedom entailed by the choice to follow the moral law in a denial of desire. The second, which follows from the first, is that the possibility of acting so as always to make another a means to an end rather than an end in himself is just as consistent with the first principle of the moral law (always to act as though the individual action were conformable to a general law) as is its opposite: Sade shows that evil may be one's guiding principle determining the categorical imperative just as much as good may be. But the result of this tempering of Kant by Sade is to leave the Kantian moral framework in place: the subject still faces the Law, whether that be Kant's moral law, or Sade's (and Freud's) law of Nature. Psychoanalysis cannot answer the question, 'What should I do, faced with the Law?', nor does it pretend to: it merely analyses what happens to the subject when this question is posed.

After its encounter with psychoanalysis, then, but still in the wake of Kant, there are two possibilities for the development of an ethics. The first is to attempt an 'ethics after Lacan', meaning both an ethics which takes up where Lacan left off and an ethics that attempts to remain faithful to the Lacanian project – an ethics that leaves analysis behind to synthesise a project, notwithstanding that Lacan did not attempt this himself. Such is the path taken by, for example, Slavoj Žižek (we have already touched on this in the work of one of his disciples, Zupančič, above), and this we will examine in the penultimate chapter. The second is to remain faithful to philosophy and to attempt to synthesise an ethics notwithstanding the blow served to Kant by Freudianism. Such is the path taken by Ricoeur, and this will be the subject of the next chapter.

7

Ethics Following Ricoeur

In the last chapter, we saw how, for Freud (1961b: 143), the commandment to 'love thy neighbour as thyself' is 'impossible to fulfil; such an enormous inflation of love can only lower its value, not get rid of the difficulty'. 'The difficulty' is what the current chapter addresses: in so doing, we will follow a line through Ricoeur's later ethics – a line determined by the place, precisely, of the commandment to 'love thy neighbour as thyself' in human relations. Of course, this presupposes a faith on the part of Ricoeur in the New Commandment's being possible, but this is not merely an intuitive a priori on Ricoeur's part (as a belief in 'nature' appears to be on Freud's), but, as we shall see, the culmination of a developed philosophical position.

We have seen in the last chapter, too, how Lacan uses Sade to modify Kant's categorical imperative. The second formulation of the imperative, never to use another human being as a means but always as an end in itself is shown through the Sadean economics of desire to be reversible and, once reversed, as equally applicable to the first formulation of the categorical imperative – to act always as if your behaviour could be adopted as a general rule – as the original. In other words, Lacan's critique of Kant demonstrates, first, that evil is just as capable of being generalisable as a rule of behaviour as good, and, second, that, if I recognise evil in another person – the other person who is hostile and would cheat, insult and injure me, according to Freud – then I must recognise also the capacity for that evil residing in me, too. If, for Lacan, Sade completes Kant, it is because Sade and Freud agree: nature is too strong a force to be truly overcome by civilisation, which is a mere veneer over our still-intact base desires, which are to accrue to ourselves the objects of our lust, and, en route to this, to gain power and dominance over others. The Sadean abandonment of conventional morality may thus be seen as an ongoing Freudian catharsis. Sade's characters act out the hidden fantasies of us all; Sade achieves in writing what the psychoanalyst hopes to achieve in the patient, an exposition of a fantasy that reflects what Lacan would call the 'real' of the subject, a real that is incompatible with and unliveable in external reality. Sade, in this interpretation, becomes the philosopher of *jouissance*; as well as demonstrating the truth of Kant, he also demonstrates the truth of Freud's equation of civilisation at the societal level with repression at the level of the individual. Civilisation is collective repression.

This effectively reverses the received view of Sade: far from being mad, he becomes the sanest person alive in the France of the 1790s. And there is a certain attraction to this view: against the background of the Terror, Sade seems a harmless fantasist – his fantasies never killed anyone, and, if this is your civilisation, his writings are an impressive articulation of discontentment with it, being as they are an only slightly distorted mirror of the society that enabled him to produce them. Lacan's reading of Kant through Freud and Sade is equally impressive. It gives both Sade and Freud philosophical weight; they are shown to expose serious flaws in Kant's thinking and to demonstrate that, once Kant starts to illustrate his principles of 'pure practical reason' drawing on examples taken from 'practical reason', which is to say, behaviour in an imagined real world, his philosophy is covertly a philosophy of desire. But impressive though it may be, Lacan's reading of Kant is not itself an ethics, whatever his claims, and this is because he still does not overcome Freud's defeatism in the face of human nature. Demonstrating that Kant's subject might accept death as the price to pay for the satisfaction of desire, or that desire might be as powerful a motive for action as the moral law, may deal a blow to Kantian moral philosophy, but it still leaves unanswered the question, What am I to do?

If the blow dealt by psychoanalysis to Kantian ethics leads to a moral impasse, then perhaps Ricoeur's treatment of Kant can lead us out of it. Pamela Sue Anderson (Anderson 1993) argues a strong case for a 'critical restoration' of Kantianism in Ricoeur's *Philosophy of the Will*. The task remains to examine how Ricoeur's 'post-Kantianism' leads to a positive ethics in his later works, written after his encounter with psychoanalysis, bearing in mind that Ricoeur describes himself as a 'post-Hegelian Kantian'. Ricoeur's 'Hegelian moment' is an acceptance of *Sittlichkeit*, 'the network of axiological beliefs governing the distribution of permission and prohibition in a given community' (Ricoeur 1991: 200), as an opening into what Hegel calls 'concrete ethical life', which Ricoeur roughly equates with Kantian 'practical reason'. Indeed, *Sittlichkeit* is the concept underlying the formation of the liberal state, and Ricoeur is very much in favour of the liberal state, not least because it acts as an 'institutional mediation of freedom' between people's desires and the disastrous consequences for practical reason if these desires were unfettered. One is reminded of the different careers of Lacan and Ricoeur in the 1960s: Ricoeur, as *doyen* of Nanterre, attempted in real life – in the domain of practical reason – to be representative of an institution that mediated the freedom of the individual in precisely such a way, whereas Lacan revelled in his position of exclusion from all institutions (other than the ones he founded himself). Instructive here, perhaps, is the respective attitudes displayed by the people – in this case the students – to these figures: Ricoeur vilified by them as 'old clown'[1] while being forced to acquiesce to the power of the State between which and them he was attempting to mediate, and Lacan invited to address the students as a 'right' to which they were entitled and which they had been denied by the instruments of the State.[2] In this respect, Ricoeur and Lacan were acting out their own, albeit diminutive, form of the Terror, and the differences between them in evaluating Hegel's remarks on the Terror is illuminating. Lacan, we recall, based the entire dialectic of desire and demand – we are thinking here especially of the 'highwayman's demand' in the *Four Fundamental Concepts of Psychoanalysis* – on the asymmetrical choice, *Freedom or death!* This, for Lacan, is the existential choice that governs any subject whatever in his subjectivity. Ricoeur (1991: 203), meanwhile, writes:

> Our contemporaries are increasingly tempted by the idea of an unfettered freedom, outside of institutions, while every institution appears to them to be essentially constraining and repressive. Only they forget the terrible equation established by Hegel in his chapter on the Terror in the *Phenomenology of Mind* – the equation between freedom and death, when no institution mediates freedom. The divorce between freedom and institution, if it were to last, would mark the greatest repudiation of the idea of practical reason.

Far from being for Ricoeur, then, an inevitable constituting factor of the human subject, the false choice between freedom and death is something 'terrible' to be fought against – precisely through the invocation of institutions, which 'Freudian Marxists' such as Althusser would doubtless see as 'repressive' in the psychoanalytic sense.

This, however, marks the limit of Ricoeur's Hegelianism. Ricoeur stops short of the *Aufhebung* of 'objective mind', which he sees as the *Aufhebung* of the State itself in Hegel. Such an *Aufhebung* is dangerous, both theoretically and practically. Theoretically, it reintroduces a dichotomy between intention and action at the level of the State that Ricoeur finds unacceptable at the level of the individual in Kant. This is a recurring theme in Ricoeur's work; a particularly clear example may be found in *Memory, History, Forgetting,* where he agrees with Derrida that 'separating the guilty person from his act, in other words, forgiving the guilty person while condemning his action, would be to forgive a subject other than the one who committed the act' (Ricoeur 2004: 490). Likewise, 'the Hegelian State is a State in intention, and the conceptual analysis provides no way to bridge the gap between this State in intention and the real State' (Ricoeur 1991: 205). From a practical point of view, meanwhile,

> all the post-Hegelian fanaticisms are contained *in nuce* in the idea that the individual knows himself in the State that itself knows itself in the objective Mind. For if a man or a group of men, a party, assume for themselves the monopoly of the knowledge of practice, they will also assume the right to act for the good of others in spite of them. It is in this way that a knowledge of the objective Mind engenders a tyranny. (Ricoeur 1991: 205)

In this way, Ricoeur's thinking is consistent from his very earliest political writings (such as the essays 'State and Violence' and 'The Political Paradox' collected in *History and Truth* (Ricoeur 1965: 234–46 and 247–70), to his very last. For Ricoeur, the alternative to the *Aufhebung* of 'objective mind' is 'to generate all the higher-level communities, such as the State, solely on the basis of the constitution of others in an intersubjective relation' (Ricoeur 1991: 204) – in other words, on the basis of the hypothesis developed in Husserl's Fifth *Cartesian Meditation*. Hence, Husserl's thesis of constitution becomes not only an opening into ethics, but also into politics.

The trajectory of Ricoeur's thinking, therefore, is this: Kantian ethics require the modification of Hegelian *Sittlichkeit*, a community founded in a constitution, that guards against the unbridled individualism to which Kant's philosophy would otherwise lead. But, unlike in Hegel, *Sittlichkeit* need not entail 'universal mind', which is to be rejected since it is an invitation to totalitarianism. Rather, institutions are to be founded on the intersubjectivity described by Husserl. This is what it means for Ricoeur to be a 'post-Hegelian Kantian'. But if we return to Ricoeur's treatment of Kant, we see that Husserl's intersubjectivity is implicit in what lies in the gap between the first and second formulations of Kant's categorical imperative ('act only in accordance with that maxim through which you can at the same time will that it become a universal law'; and 'so act that you use humanity, whether in your person or the person of any other, always at the same time as an end, never as a means') (Kant 1998: 31).

The transition between these two formulations seems abrupt; in order to bridge it, Ricoeur invokes the golden rule, expressed in the Talmud as 'Do not do unto your neighbour what you would hate him to do to you', and in Luke as 'Treat others as you would like them to treat you'. Of these two formulae, Ricoeur (1992: 219) writes:

> The respective merits of the negative formula (do not ...) and the positive formula (do such and such) balance one another; the

> interdiction leaves open the range of things that are not forbidden and in this way makes room for moral invention in the order of what is permitted; on its part, the positive commandment designates more clearly the motive of benevolence that prompts us to do something on behalf of our neighbour.

We must return to this 'motive of benevolence': clearly, for Ricoeur, it exists, whereas in Freud it is merely the displacement of a baser motive. But, meanwhile, what is impressive about both of these formulations is that they enunciate 'a *norm of reciprocity*'. This norm of reciprocity is established against what Ricoeur claims to be a background presupposition of dissymmetry between the parties involved in the golden rule: 'I do to you' implies an agent and a patient (and, Ricoeur claims, 'suffering or submission'), which is reversed in 'you do to me', the 'reciprocity' restoring the balance between the parties that the (grammatical) agent–patient relation had initially disrupted.

Now, according to Ricoeur (1992: 219), the golden rule 'represents the simplest formula that can serve as a transition between solicitude and the second Kantian imperative', and 'by placing the golden rule in this intermediary position, we allow ourselves the possibility of treating the Kantian imperative as the formalisation of the golden rule'. This is notwithstanding the fact that Kant distanced himself from the golden rule and was disdainful of it. But what is the purpose of assimilating the second imperative to the golden rule? It is in order to resolve a tension between the terms 'humanity' and 'person' in the formulation of the second imperative: 'so act that you use humanity, whether in your person or the person of any other, always at the same time as an end, never as a means'. As Ricoeur (1992: 222) points out, in Kant 'the idea of humanity as a singular term is introduced in the context of an abstract universality that governs the principle of autonomy, without the consideration of persons', whereas 'the idea of persons as ends in themselves ... demands that one take into account the plurality of persons, without allowing one to take this idea as far as the conception of otherness'.

If in *Oneself as Another* Ricoeur works hard to make the golden rule assimilable to (the second formulation of) the Kantian moral imperative, in his essay 'Ethical and Theological Considerations on the Golden Rule', which slightly pre-dates *Oneself as Another*, he emphasises the difference between the two rules, in order to prefer the golden rule over Kant: 'We might think [Kant's] second formulation [of the moral law] equivalent to the golden rule. But this is not entirely true' (Ricoeur 1995b: 294). This represents a different strategy from that adopted in *Oneself as Another*, but the same point lies at the heart of it: 'The second formulation of the imperative is addressed to the humanity that is identical in each person, not to persons as in fact multiple and different'; whereas 'the golden rule sets the relation between persons in the first rank' (Ricoeur 1995b: 294). So, in *Oneself as Another* the strategy is to repair the defect in Kant's categorical imperative by assimilating the golden rule into it, whereas in 'Considerations on the Golden Rule' the strategy is to emphasise the superiority of the golden rule over the categorical imperative. But the central critical point remains the same: what is valuable about both the golden rule and the categorical imperative is the reciprocity they establish between parties; the categorical imperative requires the caveat that the personhood of individual persons has priority over the common humanity which those persons share. This latter point addresses the question of why bother with Kant at all – why not simply stick with the golden rule? Kant's autonomy of persons – founded on a freedom not necessarily implied by the golden rule – allows Ricoeur to retain a sense of Hegelian *Sittlichkeit* within his ethics, without signing up to the Hegelian 'universal mind'.

This shared critical point notwithstanding, 'Considerations on the Golden Rule' is much harsher towards Kant than is *Oneself as Another*. In the former, Ricoeur (1995b: 294) emphasises what the golden rule emphasises: 'the fundamental asymmetry between what someone *does* and what *is done* to another'. Ricoeur (1995b: 294) articulates this asymmetry rather more forcefully and clearly here than he does in *Oneself as Another*: the 'other' is not necessarily, or not only, an adversary, but is also 'potentially the victim of my action'. This is important in that it introduces the notion of violence into moral philosophy, but 'the potential aggressor to whom the golden rule is addressed is me' (Ricoeur 1995b: 295). While Kant did not ignore this problem, Kant is wrong, says Ricoeur, to have condemned the golden rule for its lack of formalism: not only is the golden rule 'just as formal as the Kantian categorical imperative', it is also 'formal without being empty' (1995b: 295). The 'emptiness' of Kant's categorical imperative derives from his refusal to include any empirical content within it: rather gnomically, Ricoeur says that this is owing 'to the tie between such contents and the sphere of desire and pleasure, which threatened to corrupt the principle of autonomy through a return to heteronomy' (1995b: 295). To each his own regarding desire and pleasure, but to be categorical, the categorical imperative must be applicable regardless of the predispositions of any one individual, and, as we have seen in Chapter 6, Kant bases the ability to follow the moral law (in its first formulation) on the freedom of the autonomous subject. For Kant, it follows that one cannot prove a *categorical* imperative through an empirical example. His example of an example's inadequacy is the following:

> When it is said 'you ought not to promise anything deceitfully', and one assumes that the necessity for this omission is not giving counsel for

> avoiding some other ill – in which case what is said would be 'you ought not to make a lying promise lest if it comes to light you destroy your credit' – but that an action of this kind must be regarded as in itself evil and that the imperative of prohibition is therefore categorical: one still cannot show with certainty in any example that the will is here determined merely through the law, without another incentive, although it seems to be so; for it is always possible that covert fear of disgrace, perhaps also obscure apprehension of other dangers, may have had an influence on the will. ... In such a case ... the so-called moral imperative, which as such appears to be categorical and unconditional, would in fact be only a pragmatic precept that makes us attentive to our advantage and merely teaches us to take this into consideration. (Kant 1998: 29–30)

Hence, for Kant, the universal applicability of the categorical imperative is dependent on its being free of any empirical content: formalism is by definition empty, if 'empty' means 'independent of empirical circumstance'.

It is in this very respect that the golden rule differs from the Kantian categorical imperative:

> By setting violence in the very same place that Kant put desire, the golden rule incorporates a fundamental aspect of human action, the *power* exercised *on* or *over* another, and therefore refuses to draw a line between the a priori and the empirical. The golden rule takes into account the whole of action and interaction, of acting and suffering. It is addressed to acting and suffering human beings, with all the fragility and vulnerability included in this action. (Ricoeur 1995b: 296)

Thus it is that the golden rule becomes the thread tying Ricoeur's late work to the analysis of the fault to be found in *Philosophy of the Will* and, especially, in *The Voluntary and the Involuntary*. Thus it is, also, that 'Considerations on the Golden Rule', although contemporary with *Oneself as Another*, goes beyond it. *Oneself as Another* is content to use the golden rule to bring out the 'subtle discordance' in the Kantian moral imperative between, on the one hand, the plurality that is entailed by the notion of a person as an end in himself and, on the other hand, the idea of 'humanity' in Kant, which, like Hegel's 'universal mind', is an obstacle to a notion of otherness. In *Oneself as Another*, the Kantian imperative is a formalisation of the golden rule, and behind the golden rule is 'the voice which asked that the plurality of persons and their otherness not be obliterated by the globalising idea of humanity' (Ricoeur 1992: 227). In 'Considerations on the Golden Rule', meanwhile, the golden rule needs no formalisation, since it is already formalised, and, moreover, it does the extra work of reintroducing the empirical into the categorical imperative.

Where is all this leading? To love. In *Oneself as Another*, Ricoeur simply 'likens' the golden rule to the New Commandment, to 'Love thy neighbour as thyself'. It was this specific commandment, we recall, that caused Freud so much anguish. In both 'Considerations on the Golden Rule' and a slightly later essay, 'Love and Justice', however, the New Commandment becomes a 'corrective' to the golden rule: while it does not abolish it, nevertheless, a difference is recognised between the two imperatives; the former 'reinterprets' the latter 'in terms of generosity' (Ricoeur 1996b: 35). Thus, we see a progressive development in Ricoeur's thought from the moral imperative to the golden rule to the New Commandment, each correcting the previous. Roughly, we may characterise this as a movement from the Law, to justice, to love.

To each of the two commandments, the golden rule and the New Commandment, there corresponds two respective logics and economies: to the former, the logic of equivalence and the economy of exchange; to the latter, the logic of superabundance and the economy of the gift. The logic of equivalence and economy of exchange are ethical insofar as they do justice to each of the parties: what I do for you is reciprocated in what you do for me. But the logic of superabundance and economy of the gift are hyperethical: in doing to or for you, I expect nothing in return. Such is the commandment to love; we might say that it is a commandment to love unconditionally. The New Commandment, Ricoeur reminds us, finds its most extreme expression in the variant that reads: love thine enemies as thyself. Effectively, this abolishes the distinction between friends and enemies.

We must not think, however, that the New Commandment simply replaces the golden rule: rather, Ricoeur aims at their 'reconciliation'. This is partly because the abolition of the golden rule would entail the abolition of justice in everyday ethics, and partly because the hyperethical quality of the New Commandment leaves it open to 'perverse' interpretations, such as failing to act at all out of cowardice. Hence, the commandment of love should not replace the golden rule but reinterpret it. Asking 'what distribution of tasks, of roles, or of advantages and obligations could be established, in the spirit of distributive justice, if the maxim of lending while expecting nothing in return were set up as a universal rule?' (Ricoeur 1996b: 35), Ricoeur answers that the New Commandment 'has to pass through the rule of morality, summed up in the golden rule and formalised by the rule of justice'. 'Yet', he says, 'the opposite is no less true'. Just as the New Commandment must be informed by the golden rule, so too must the rule of justice be informed by the rule of love:

> Without the corrective of the commandment to love, the golden rule would be constantly drawn in the direction of a utilitarian maxim whose formula is *Do ut des*: I give *so that* you will give. The rule 'Give *because* it has been given you' corrects the 'in order that' of the utilitarian maxim and saves the golden rule from an always possible perverse interpretation. (Ricoeur 1996b: 35–6)

Hence, justice is 'the necessary medium of love; precisely because love is hypermoral, it enters the practical and ethical sphere only under the aegis of justice' (Ricoeur 1996b: 36–7). As is his way with so many philosophical problems, once again Ricoeur does not simply oppose one logic or concept against another, but 'reorients' them 'by disorientating'. The Kantian moral imperative, in its insistence on the autonomy of the individual, acts as a corrective to the Hegelian notion of the 'universal mind', while Hegelian *Sittlichkeit* corrects Kant's absolute autonomy of the individual. The golden rule, as a rule of justice, gives the Kantian moral imperative an ethical dimension by allowing into it the necessity of accounting for individuals acting within the practical sphere and indicates that the moral imperative entails reciprocity, while the Kantian moral imperative establishes the golden rule as a formal rule. The New Commandment protects this 'reciprocity' of the golden rule from a perverse utilitarian interpretation, while the golden rule returns love to the ethical sphere by ensuring that it is enacted through the medium of justice.

Thus it is that in the late 1980s and early 1990s, some quarter of a century after his encounter with Freud, Ricoeur develops an ethics based on the commandment to 'Love thy neighbour as thyself'. But for all that, has he countered Freud's (1961b: 143) claim in *Civilisation and its Discontents* that 'the commandment is impossible to fulfil'? In the previous chapter, we criticised Freud for his defeatism and, by extension, Lacan for not having a positive ethical programme. Ricoeur, on the contrary, does have a positive ethical programme of the kind we have just outlined. At a basic level, this is to be expected: it is a matter of the distinction between the respective tasks of the psychoanalytic theorist and the philosopher. In this respect, the question of whether it is *possible* to fulfil the commandment to love would be for Ricoeur a non-question, since his is an analysis of the philosophical implications of its call to action, and is, moreover, rooted in the tradition of philosophical ethics which traces a trajectory from Aristotle through Kant to Rawls and beyond. Freud, meanwhile, though he had read Kant and other philosophers, was no philosopher himself.

But, in other respects, dismissing the question of whether it is possible to love one's neighbour as oneself as a non-question avoids confronting the issue. Ricoeur (1996b: 26) hints at this himself when he writes of the 'disturbing' aspect to the commandment to love, that it is 'ordering a feeling': clearly the commandment would, in that case, be impossible to fulfil, and in any case, as Kant points out, 'pathological love' 'has no place in the sphere of ethics' (Ricoeur 1996b: 26). Moreover, Ricoeur (1996b: 26) anticipates Freud's objection: 'If so-called spiritual love is just a sublimated erotic love, the commandment to love can only be the expression of the tyranny of the superego over the affective sphere'.[3] The entire Ricoeurean programme of tempering the golden rule with the New Commandment, and of tempering the Kantian moral imperative with the golden rule, will fail if the New Commandment is impossible to obey.

What rescues Ricoeur's argument from this difficulty is the fact that it is one not based on a claim about nature. Kant (1998: 31), we recall, writes that

> Since the universality of law in accordance with which effects take place constitutes what is properly called *nature* in the most general sense (as regards its form) – that is, the existence of things insofar as it is determined in accordance with universal laws – the universal imperative of duty can also go as follows: *act as if the maxim of your action were to become by your will a* **universal law of nature**.

Freud, equally, is convinced that he has discovered a law of nature in the fundamental aggressivity of mankind. From this point of view, Freud and Kant are merely inversions of one another: Kant has a positive view of human nature as one guided by the altruism consequent upon duty, whereas Freud has a negative view of human nature based on his analysis of the aggressivity of instinct (and, in this, he is influenced by Darwin).

In contrast, we may see that Ricoeur's ethics is not dependent on a view of nature at all, or at least, a view of nature that is androcentric or anthropomorphic. We could say that hermeneutics takes the place of nature. As early as *The Symbolism of Evil,* Ricoeur had written of the symbol as a gift: 'The symbol gives: a philosophy instructed by myths arises at a certain moment in reflection' (1969: 348). The command to love thy neighbour as thyself, meanwhile, is also determined by a logic of superabundance, an economy of the gift. Thus, there is what Ricoeur himself in other contexts would call a 'secret communion' between his early work on symbolism and his late work on ethics. The common tie is what Jaspers would call the givenness of a situation, the situation of what Heidegger would characterise as man being always already an interpreting animal. The fact that man originarily interprets creates a distance between man and nature: the gift of thought, mediated through the symbols he interprets, becomes nothing other than the gift of love. The religious dimension to this is the superabundance of man being a created being, and in his biblical exegeses Ricoeur duly finds the symbols which signify the superabundance of the gift of creation. But from a strictly philosophical point of view, signification as such can be read the same way: as a gift ('the gift of speech') which is *excessive* (Levinas would call it 'hyperbolic') in relation to the nature it describes.

This gives Ricoeur's philosophy an openness and optimism absent from Freud's psychoanalysis. Freud reduces ethics (or the impulse to ethics) to conscience, and conscience to an internalisation, in the form of the superego, of the external structure that is civilisation. (In *Totem and Taboo,* Freud explains that, conversely, civilisation arises when man learns to turn his inhibitions into prohibitions, a process of externalisation.) Conscience, for Freud, is always a guilty conscience, since it is always an agent of repression. But has Ricoeur, meanwhile, succeeded where Freud (and Lacan) failed: in answering the question, What am I to do? Ricoeur not so much answers this question, as replaces it by another, How am I to live the good life? The answer is through maintaining self-constancy:

> Self-constancy is for each person that manner of conducting himself or herself so that others can *count on* that person. Because someone is counting on me, I am *accountable for* my actions before another. The term 'responsibility' unites both meanings: 'counting on' and 'being accountable for'. (Ricoeur 1992: 165)

Such self-constancy is consistent with *agape,* which Freud (1961b: 102) himself defines (in disdain) as 'a state of evenly suspended, steadfast, affectionate feeling'. But Ricoeur bases his *agape* not on 'genital eroticism', as does Freud, but on discourse, or, more particularly, on a specific capacity for discourse unique to humans (and, thus, again distanced from Freudian 'nature'), namely, to promise. It is the promise, the keeping of one's word, that cements self-constancy over time. Such is the nature of responsibility: in promising, I place myself in a position of solicitude in relation to another, and I am doing disservice to both myself and this other if I claim, at a later date, that I am 'not the same person' as I was when I made the promise. The promise thus constitutes the verbal insertion of an ethics into intersubjectivity, as well as maintaining the intersubjective relation identified in Husserl's Fifth *Cartesian Meditation* over time. If 'I owe myself to others', this is a debt repaid over time; the promise entails a truly reciprocal relation, in that it both guarantees that I will be there for the other through my self-constancy and guarantees my self-constancy in the obligation I place on myself to fulfil the promise.

Thus, we see that Ricoeur's ethics, in arriving at a concept of responsibility, finally 'goes beyond' Freud. If Freudianism, as an archaeology of the subject, finds the explanations of human vicissitudes in childhood, then Ricoeur's forward-looking ethics grounds the subject in adulthood: the adulthood of a *responsible* individual, who nevertheless carries within him the child that he was – but a child 'corrected', in the same way that love corrects justice and justice corrects the moral imperative. Ricoeur points out that the concept of justice has its origins – historically, conceptually, and where the two meet, at the level of the history of the individual subject – in indignation, manifested in the cry 'It is unjust!' 'We initially enter the problem of justice', says Ricoeur (1998: 120), 'through the feeling of *in*justice' – and, we might add, this is a childish feeling. This is not to say that, in seeking justice, we abandon the childish indignation at injustice: but it is tempered by the adult notion of responsibility. The sense of responsibility can only be accrued through time, since it is over time that constancy is demonstrated. Hence, once again we might say of Ricoeur's later writings what he himself said of his reading of Oedipus: just as there the tragedy was 'not the tragedy of Oedipus the child, but of Oedipus Rex', so likewise the ethical life is lived not by the irresponsible child, but by the responsible adult. It is as an adult that I am accountable for my actions, and am thus responsible to and for others, as well as them having responsibilities towards me. Freudian psychoanalysis, in eclipsing responsibility by the unconscious, treats 'the subject' as a child. The counterpart to responsibility, of course, is freedom, and the determinist flavour of psychoanalysis is of one piece with its regression to childish irresponsibility.

Of the cry of indignation, the 'That's not fair!', Ricoeur (2000: x) writes that 'its perspicacity is sometimes confusing when measured against the yardstick of our adult hesitations when summoned to pronounce in positive terms upon the justice and fairness of something'. This confusion is owing to the obstacle to true justice that the cry of injustice throws up: that of vengeance. 'The great conquest, in this respect,' says Ricoeur (2000: xi), 'consists in separating vengeance and justice.' Vengeance adds 'violence to violence, suffering to suffering': what is it, then, other than a manifestation of Freudian 'aggressivity', the notion that I will harm my neighbour if he dare harm me, as expressed in the dictum, 'An eye for an eye, a tooth for a tooth'? But justice is not merely the inversion of injustice, just as Ricoeur does not replace Freud's view of 'nature' by one of his own. Rather, justice requires impartiality, which is guaranteed by the addition of a third party, he who judges. Ricoeur (2000: 127–32) analyses the role of the third party in his short essay 'The Act of Judging': what we may add to that analysis is that the addition of a third party implies a surrendering of something of the function of the dispensing of justice from myself to another. With the presence of the third party, I must surrender something of myself – my desire for vengeance, and, hence, the aggressivity that is its foundation.

The New Commandment, to 'love thy neighbour as thyself', thus becomes the guiding principle of Ricoeur's ethics. Ultimately, it does not matter whether Freud's objection that it is 'impossible to fulfil' is answered. The movement towards its fulfilment, the striving after its possibility, is a hope and a promise for Ricoeur. This positive outlook gives hope, too, for civilisation, represented in Ricoeur in the building of 'just institutions'. It serves as an antidote to the Freudian 'discontent' with civilisation.

8

Ethics After Lacan

The previous chapter explored the ethics developed by Ricoeur subsequent to his encounter with Freud. In the present chapter, we will examine the kind of ethics that follows from Lacanian theory. The word 'after', as opposed to 'following', in the title, however, signals that Lacan himself did not develop these ideas in the years leading up to his death in 1981. As an exemplar of a developed Lacanian ethics, therefore, we turn to the work of Slavoj Žižek, who is probably the most prominent Lacanian writing today.

On the face of it it, would appear that the differences between Ricoeur and Žižek are insurmountable. In ethics, Ricoeur is what Žižek characterises as a 'universalist' in the sphere of political justice, grounding as he does his politics in a procedural distributive theory of justice. It is true that Ricoeur adds an important twist to Rawls' theory of justice: in his paper 'Is a Procedural Theory of Justice Possible?', he answers that question by asserting that 'it is our preunderstanding of the just and the unjust that assures the deontological intention of the self-proclaimed argument, including the maximin rule' (Ricoeur 2000: 56). Ricoeur thus finds something prior even to Rawls' 'original position': this is the golden rule, and, without being informed by it, Rawls' maximin principle would lapse into the utilitarianism which it hints at. But Rawls' proceduralism is saved from utilitarianism by *phronēsis*, the application of the maximin principle not in Rawls' imaginary world of the original position, but in real life, in which the maximin principle may carry with it the *Bildung* of ethics in the Judaeo-Christian tradition. It is this *Bildung* that gives the maximin principle its ethical dimension, and thus saves it from utilitarianism. But if we accept that this happens, that is, if we believe in the efficacy of the Judaeo-Christian ethical *Bildung*, then it is because we 'have confidence in the capacity of ordinary citizens as regards their rationality, that is, their aptitude for putting themselves in the place of another, or, better, transcending their place' (Ricoeur 2000: 57). Ricoeur does have this faith in 'the capacity of ordinary citizens', a capacity for 'surpassing prejudices' (bearing in mind that the point of Rawls adopting the 'original position' in an imaginary world was that such a world was one without prejudice); 'without this act of confidence', he writes, 'the philosophical fable of the original position would be only an unbelievable and irrelevant hypothesis' (Ricoeur 2000: 57). Žižek, meanwhile, holds, at least implicitly, that Rawls' 'original position' is an unbelievable and irrelevant hypothesis, since it is based on a principle of exclusion – the exclusion, precisely, of reality. Notwithstanding the twist Ricoeur adds to Rawls' theory, he still would remain, for Žižek, confined within a realm of 'pre-political' ethics, as if the tradition of ethics of which Ricoeur speaks were not itself also always already political as well as ethical. As soon as we enter the real world, rather than the world of Rawls' thought experiment, the world populated by Ricoeur's ethical individuals, we are also, by definition, in the political world. The difference here comes down to this: Ricoeur founds his politics on a prior ethics to which politics is reducible, whereas Žižek founds his ethics on a prior politics, to which ethics is reducible.

For all the differences between Žižek and Ricoeur, however, it is the question of the *cogito* that forms the starting point of Žižek's ethical investigations, just as it is in Ricoeur. In his Introduction to *Cogito and the Unconscious,* Žižek (1998: 6) claims that 'Lacan pleads for a psychoanalytic *return to cogito*'. This would appear to fly in the face of the position we have elaborated throughout this book: that, in Žižek's own words, there is an '*antagonism* between *cogito* (the transparent subject of self-consciousness) and the unconscious, its opaque Other that subverts the certitudes of consciousness' (Žižek 1998: 6). How can the claim that Lacan pleads for a 'return to the *cogito*' be reconciled with the mortal blow psychoanalysis, through Freud's formula *Wo Es war, soll Ich werden* and Lacan's interpretation of it, appears to deal the *cogito*?

The answer lies in the relationship between psychoanalysis and philosophy, as Žižek sees it. His project is neither to psychoanalyse philosophy – 'discern pathological psychic motivations beneath fundamental philosophical attitudes' – nor to critique the conceptual presuppositions of psychoanalysis – those 'that psychoanalysis itself does not render thematic' (Žižek 1998: 1) – from a philosophical point of view. Rather, Žižek takes seriously the claim that 'psychoanalysis renders visible something that the modern philosophy of subjectivity accomplishes without knowing it, its own grounding gesture, which philosophy has to disavow if it is to assume its place within academic knowledge' (Žižek 1998: 1–2). This is not the same, he insists, as 'psychoanalysing philosophy', but is, rather, 'to bring to light the philosophical implications of psychoanalysis, that is, to retranslate, to transpose psychoanalytic propositions back into philosophy, to "elevate them to the dignity of philosophical propositions"' (Žižek 1998: 2). In the course of this, Žižek also elevates Lacan to the dignity of philosopher: Lacan 'was doing [this] all the time', and we should 'appreciate' his 'paradoxical achievement': that 'on the very behalf of psychoanalysis, he returns to the modern rationalist notion of subject' (Žižek 1998: 2–3).

In practice, however, this tends to look a little like psychoanalysing philosophy, as when Žižek (1998: 2) claims that Lacan reads 'the obsessional compulsion to think – "if I stop thinking, I will cease to exist" – as the truth of the Cartesian *cogito ergo sum*'. This appears a somewhat reductive way of interpreting Lacan's relationship with the *cogito*: as we saw in Chapters 3 and 4 above, Lacan's position is rather more complex than this. Really, it is *Žižek's* position that the truth of the *cogito* is 'the obsessional compulsion to think'. But if this is a swipe at phenomenology in the wake of Husserl, then it misses its mark. The claim that the *cogito* must be constantly reasserted, that it is an ongoing process rather than a unique event, is a claim about phenomenological consciousness and its relation to (the passage of) time. The phenomenologist is not obsessed by this in the clinical sense: it is a philosophical position arrived at through the development of a philosophy of time in conjunction with a meditative examination of the experience of the *cogito*. To say that the phenomenologist is *compelled* to think already presupposes that he is compelled by a something, and yet the existence of that something (Nietzsche's and Freud's *Es*) is precisely what the phenomenological exploration of the *cogito* in relation to time seeks to challenge. The phenomenologist does not claim (or even privately presuppose) that 'if I stop thinking, I will cease to exist' – he claims merely that only through the *maintenance* (the prolonging of the 'now') of thinking can the truth of the *cogito* be apodictic. While it is true that Husserl pointed out that 'apodicticity and adequacy of evidence are not the same thing', his search for adequacy is not motivated by paranoia that he might cease to exist: he does not have a fear of what Lacan calls 'aphanisis'. This is the whole point of *epochē*: it brackets off any such existential angst.

But what of the claim that Lacan 'returns to the modern rationalist notion of the subject'? Here Žižek says that 'Lacan's underlying thesis . . . is even more radical than with the unconscious: not only has the Freudian subject nothing to do with the self-transparent, unified self-consciousness, it is the Cartesian subject itself . . . that is already a shibboleth within the domain of philosophy itself' (1998: 3). The point of a shibboleth, Žižek explains, is that 'the difference is visible only from one side, that is, only the people of Gilead perceive the difference in the pronunciation of the word "shibboleth" – the unfortunate people of Ephraim are unaware of any difference and, consequently, cannot grasp at all what they have said wrong, why they have to die' (3). Now, for Žižek, 'the supreme case of shibboleth in psychoanalytic theory is the very notion of the unconscious: when Freud proposes his thesis on the unconscious psychic processes, philosophers immediately react to it by saying "Of course! We knew this for a long time . . ."' (3). Where is the analogy here? Presumably Žižek means us to take Freud as corresponding to the people of Ephraim, condemned by the Gilead philosophers. From this perspective, shibboleth = unconscious, and the Freudian unconscious becomes nothing other than the unconscious of philosophy as such. But the analogy is imperfect: in the original story, the people of Ephraim are condemned for an erroneous pronunciation of the word 'shibboleth', as compared to the true pronunciation of the people of Gilead. But Žižek wants to claim that Freud has the unique, true 'pronunciation' of the unconscious, while he himself condemns philosophy's multifarious variations on this theme as erroneous:

> all of a sudden, the place swarms with hermeneutical and other recuperations that endeavour to (re)integrate psychoanalysis into the standard philosophical problematic (by providing its "philosophical foundation": unconscious is grounded in the opacity of the life-world context, in the latent, nonfulfilled subjective intention, etc.), while the surplus that resists this integration is rejected .... (Žižek 1998: 3)

This effectively reproduces the complaint made by Lacan against Ricoeur in 1964: that Ricoeur (or, in Žižek's account, unnamed philosophers) retains something of the dimension of the unconscious, monopolises it for himself and calls it hermeneutics. But if this is true – and we hope that our reading of Ricoeur up to this point has demonstrated that it is not – then psychoanalysis cannot be the shibboleth of (hermeneutic) philosophy, since the people of Gilead performed an act of absolute exclusion towards the people of Ephraim by condemning them to death (reflecting the rule of absolute exteriority of prohibition that is the 'shibboleth rule'), whereas Žižek accuses philosophy of 'recuperating' the unconscious.

What, then, does Žižek's endorsement of Lacan's 'psychoanalytic return to *cogito*' mean? It entails an odd kind of reversal of both philosophical received opinion and its postmodern variant: transcendental philosophy has a nostalgia for the *cogito* on the grounds that it rescues the subject, in the self-certainty of pure consciousness, from the threat posed by the unconscious, while postmodernism searches for 'the diverse forms of asserting one's subjectivity' rather than asserting the transcendental subject as such. Žižek, on the other hand, endeavours 'to think *a subject bereft of subjectivity*'. The 'kind of monster [that] remains when we subtract from the subject the wealth of self-experience that constitutes subjectivity' (Žižek 1998: 7) is the Cartesian subject. Far from restoring the subject to full subjectivity, then, for Žižek the *cogito* deprives the subject of an essential part of its subjectivity, what he calls 'all the wealth of the "human person"'(7). By implication, the 'wealth of the "human person"' is contained in the unconscious. This represents something of a radicalisation of Freud, for whom 'the id stands for the untamed passions' (Freud

1973: 109). Žižek is what may be called a passionate philosopher: if 'Lacan asserts that the subject of psychoanalysis is none other than the Cartesian *cogito*', then 'the Freudian unconscious emerges through the very reduction of the "person's" substantial content to the evanescent punctuality of the *cogito*' (Žižek 1998: 4); the unconscious completes the person.

If this is the theory, then *The Ticklish Subject* is Žižek's most sustained attempt to put it into practice. In the Introduction to that book, he explains that his aim is 'to reassert the Cartesian subject' in the face of the attacks on it which characterise, he thinks, 'today's academia' (Žižek 1999a: 2). However, as we might guess from the theoretical exposition in *Cogito and the Unconscious*, this does not mean reasserting the Cartesian subject as a transcendental subject in the tradition of Kant, the German Idealists, Husserl and Descartes himself; rather, it is to reassert the Cartesian subject as reclaimed by Lacanian psychoanalysis:

> The point, of course, is not to return to the *cogito* in the guise in which this notion has dominated modern thought (the self-transparent thinking subject), but to bring to light its forgotten obverse, the excessive, unacknowledged kernel of the *cogito*, which is far from the pacifying image of the transparent Self. (Žižek 1999a: 2).

Hence, the obverse of the *cogito*, the unconscious, is actually its kernel (surely some mixing of metaphors here!), and the *cogito* has implied or entailed the unconscious all along, without philosophy realising it.

Žižek's project is informed by a Lacanian notion of negation or *lack* as constituting the subject. Responding to Daniel Dennett's (1991) 'heterophenomenological' theory (elaborated in *Consciousness Explained*) that subjective experience is the symbolic fiction, or supposition, of the theorist of the subject, rather than the domain of phenomena directly accessible to the subject, Žižek concedes a point to both Dennett and Kant: namely, the so-called 'reflexivity thesis'. Self-consciousness, according to this view, is not Husserlian apperception (as described in *Ideas I*: the subject perceives that he is perceiving and, when applied to consciousness, is conscious that he is conscious), since that would lead to an infinite regress. Rather, 'self-consciousness is not an additional reflexive turn of the gaze from the object one is conscious of upon oneself, but is constitutive of "direct" consciousness itself: "to be conscious of X" *means that* I "take myself" to be related to X ...'. This has consequences in the sphere of ethics: 'spontaneity', for example, when viewed from the perspective of such a 'reflexivity', 'means precisely that this very passive succumbing to a temptation already involves a previous active acceptance of such a passive position toward the temptation'; likewise, 'when I directly immerse myself in an activity, this immersion is always grounded in an implicit act of immersing oneself; when I follow my most brutal instincts and "behave like an animal", I still remain the one who *decided* to behave in that way . . .', etc. As Žižek succinctly puts it, 'every immediacy is always already mediated' (Žižek 1998: 261).

This concession to Dennett and Kant enables Žižek audaciously to solve (or to claim to have solved) the 'hard question' of consciousness: what *is* 'consciousness'? This is the Holy Grail of cognitive science, but we do not need cognitive science when we have Žižek to show us that the truth lay in Lacan all along:

> Consciousness (or self-awareness) occurs only insofar as it appears to itself as an inexplicable emergence, that is, only insofar as it misrecognises its own causes, the network that generates it. . . . The ultimate paradox of consciousness is that consciousness – the very organ of 'awareness' – can only occur insofar as it is *unaware* of its own conditions. (Žižek 1998: 269)

Moreover, '(Self-)consciousness (the "thick moment" of consciousness, the awareness that I am now-here-alive) is originally passive. . .: what originally I am "aware of" is that I am *not* in control, that my design misfired, that things just drift by' (Žižek 1998: 269). As Lacan (1972: 190) puts it in 'Of Structure as an Inmixing . . .': 'Life is something which goes, as we say in French, *à la dérive*. Life goes down the river, from time to time touching a bank, staying for a while here and there, without understanding anything . . .'.

This has the extraordinary effect of making Dennett another discoverer of the unconscious, without his knowing it. Dennett introduces the hypothesis of the 'objectively subjective' to describe this category of true phenomenal self-experience that is never given to us in direct experience. But while Dennett introduces the hypothesis merely to dismiss it as a self-defeating paradox, Žižek (1998: 267) claims that the 'objectively subjective' is 'the very locus of the unconscious: does the Freudian unconscious not designate precisely the way things appear to us without our ever being directly aware of them?'

Manque à être, Lacanian lack in being, is, thus, the Other of the reflexive self-consciousness; it is the 'not knowing' of 'not knowing that I knew that'. Again there is an ethical dimension to this, one which leads back to the second formulation of the Kantian categorical imperative, always to treat a person as an end in themselves, never as a means. Respect, for Žižek (1999b: 292), becomes respect for the Other's lack:

> When we respect another subject, we do not do it on account of some outstanding property of this subject, but, on the contrary, on account of

> some fundamental lack that defines its very being – 'respect' means that we ... do not approach the other ... so closely that we dissolve the semblance that conceals/envelops the lack and thus render this lack fully visible.

Žižek (1999b: 292–3) explains that, for example, 'for the respected person, the elementary gesture of undermining the respect others have is to expose their lack: for a cripple to show his deformed crippled leg, etc.'.

The maintenance of 'proper distance' from the Other Žižek calls Lacanian 'ex-timacy'. Once this Lacanian ethical framework of existential lack has been established, it becomes the master trope of Žižek's entire discourse. It governs, for example, his examples. David Lynch, for example:

> The nightmare sequence of *The Elephant Man* ... is accompanied by a strange vibrating noise that seems to transgress the border separating interior from exterior: it is as if, in this noise, the extreme *externality* of a machine coincides with the utmost *intimacy* of the bodily interior, with the rhythm of the palpitating heart. Does not this coincidence of the very core of the subject's being, of his/her life-substance, with the externality of a machine, offer a perfect illustration of the Lacanian notion of *ex-timacy*? (Žižek 1999a: 57)

And so it goes on. 'Lacanian terms' become the medium through which culture is read. But this is too easy! Fourteen books in nine years, and yet all curiously in some ways one and the same book. ... And why all the ellipses? Are they signifiers too of a lack, a gap to be filled ... by what? Lacanian truth that only Žižek's readers, as his big Other, can provide? Žižek replaces Lacan's notoriously 'difficult' style by one that is uncomfortably easy: fast to write, fast to read. But one cannot help wondering whether something is lost in translation, that Žižek creates a lack of his own.

At the risk of being disrespectful by drawing attention to this lack, we might start by noticing that in Lacan's discourse, the style is indistinguishable from the substance. It is Socratic and, as such, has a heuristic function. This is consistent with Lacan's praise of the *agalma,* the buried treasure, which Socrates possesses and which Alcibiades thinks he can attain merely by sitting next to Socrates, as if knowledge can be poured into the subject like pouring wine from a bottle. Finding the truth of Lacanian discourse requires a dialectical, and dialogic, engagement with him on the part of the reader: it *should be* difficult, just as crossing the bar of repression is difficult. It becomes easier, however, when one hears Lacan speak,[1] when the dramatic pauses in the performance lend the discourse a structure of strophe and antistrophe (the pause being the gap filled by the incomprehension of the Other, which the antistrophe displaces). All of this is accompanied by a mischievous smile: there is a level at which Lacanian discourse, when witnessed as a performance, is funny.

Žižek takes Lacan too seriously. In taking Lacan seriously as a philosopher, or at least as someone who has something serious to say (regarding the *cogito*, regarding ethics) to the philosopher, Žižek forgets that there is an element of charlatanism attaching to Lacan in which his audience must be to an extent complicit if it is to derive a sense of *jouissance* from the performance.

It is not just, though, that Žižek takes Lacan too seriously: he also takes him too literally and too reductively. This may be seen if we examine the Lynch example quoted above. 'Does not this coincidence of the very core of the subject's being, of his/her life-substance, with the externality of a machine, offer a perfect illustration of the Lacanian notion of *ex-timacy*?', Žižek asks. Perhaps the illustration is too perfect. Never does Žižek question the status of the 'example', the symbolic efficacy of the 'illustration', in his own work. The Lacanian paradigm, he wants to argue, is descriptive of life as it really is in the modern world. Life as it really is in the modern world is illustrated through examples of popular culture, which, in turn, illustrate the Lacanian paradigm. But all of this depends on the mimetic veracity of the illustration, if not at the level that connects it with the Lacanian paradigm, then at least on the level that connects it with reality. To claim that the films of David Lynch illustrate something fundamental about real life is fair enough, but *what* do they illustrate about real life? Clearly they are (mostly) not mimetic of life in the realist sense. No, the sense in which they illustrate real life is through being illustrative of the Lacanian paradigm that describes real life. But this is merely a circular argument.

This brings us to the way in which Žižek translates Lacanian concepts. In the Lynch example, the 'externality of the machine', we are told, 'coincides' with 'the very core of the subject's being'. Hence, 'the very core of the subject's being' is his heart. But this is so only in this example: elsewhere, it is the cripple's crippled leg (since this is what defines him as 'cripple'), but 'on closer analysis, one would have to link the notion of respect to that of castration: *respect is ultimately always respect for (Other's) castration*'. Hence, ultimately, the 'core of the subject's being' is not the heart, or the leg, but the penis, or lack of it. Does Žižek really mean this? The Freudian echo of *Kern unseres Wesen* in 'core of the subject's being' might lead us to think so, but that would mean that, just as the post-Cartesian phenomenologist is (allegedly) compulsively obsessed with thinking the *cogito*, so Žižek would be compulsively obsessed with the penis.

But such would be an unfair reading of Žižek. What governs his ethical economy is not the lack of a heart, leg, penis, or anything else specific, but lack as such: it is lack as such that is constitutive of the subject who must borrow his self-awareness from the discourse of the Other. Why, then, does he define respect as respect for the Other's castration, specifically, and not as respect for the Other's lack, generally? Why equate lack with one of its synecdoches, castration? The answer may be found in an essay published in 1994 on Otto Weininger, where he explains that when he speaks of 'castration', it is of 'symbolic castration': in other words, we are not thinking of the penis, but of the 'phallus' in the Lacanian sense:

> What Lacan designates as the 'phallic function' is [the] very splitting between the domain of phallic enjoyment and the desexualised 'public' field that eludes it. . . . In this precise sense the phallus is the signifier of castration: 'symbolic castration' is ultimately another name for the paradox of 'states that are essentially by-products': *if we are to achieve fulfilment through phallic enjoyment, we must renounce it as our explicit goal.* (Žižek 1999b: 141)

However, it is not 'ethical economy', but 'political economy', that is Žižek's principal concern (insofar as the two may be distinguished).[2] What is the lack in public life today, that which frustrates the attainment of our goal of collective enjoyment? The answer is what Žižek calls 'the demise of symbolic efficiency'. Everything is going to pot, he thinks, and the reason for this is that the 'big Other' no longer exists. For Žižek (1999a: 322), 'the big Other is the symbolic order'; in one sense, it has never *existed* as such, precisely because it is symbolic. But his complaint against contemporary society is that nowadays not only does the big Other not exist in reality; it no longer exists as an *order*. It does not command the respect of people. The *order* of the symbolic is a fiction; its 'efficiency' lies in the willingness of people to believe it. The malaise of modern society is a form of cynicism: paradoxically, for Žižek (and again he attributes this view to Lacan), the cynic errs more in 'believing his eyes' than in believing the fictional discourse that constitutes the symbolic order, the big Other.

Again, Žižek provides a multitude of examples to illustrate this point, which cumulatively show how this decline in the efficiency of the symbolic order – our faith in it, or its capacity for convincing us of its truth – becomes the underlying sadness of the subject in late capitalism. Sadness rather than tragedy: it is a marker of this kind of cynicism that it divests the subject of the dignity of being persecuted for holding a belief. Hence, the American Communists of the 1950s had a 'sublime beauty' in their belief in the Soviet Union, even though what they believed in was of itself appalling; likewise, Anne Frank had a 'sublime beauty' in her belief in the ultimate goodness of mankind, even though the evidence all around her was to the contrary. 'Symbolic efficiency' is defined as the minimum of reification required whereby 'it is not enough for us ... to know some fact in order for it to be operative, [but] the symbolic institution must also know/"register" this fact' (Žižek 1999a: 326). Hence, if a professional person who is awarded a promotion but does not see the result on their salary slip goes to a minor bureaucrat in the institution where they work and shows them the decree awarding them promotion, and the bureaucrat replies 'Sorry, I haven't been informed of this yet, so I can't help you', the bureaucrat is demonstrating a faith in the symbolic order. Likewise, if a citizen wants the number of their house changed because they think it is bringing them bad luck, and when asked 'Why don't you do it yourself?', replies 'It has to be done properly, by the relevant state institution', they too are demonstrating a faith in the symbolic order. Both the bureaucrat and the citizen are like the American Communists and Anne Frank: they believe the word of the Other over the evidence of their own eyes. As Žižek (1999a: 327) writes, symbolic efficiency 'concerns the point at which, when the Other of the symbolic institution confronts me with the choice of "Whom do you believe, my word or your eyes?", I choose the Other's word without hesitation, dismissing the factual testimony of my eyes'.

What may strike one as odd about Žižek's position is that it reverses the tendency of Freud's imperative, *Wo Es war, soll Ich werden.* What Žižek has a nostalgia for is, if not the unconscious as such, at least the authority of the symbolic order. Even though the symbolic order is a fiction, even though he, Žižek, cannot by definition believe in it himself (otherwise he would not be in a position to define and describe it), he laments the passing of its 'efficiency'. The 'efficiency' of the symbolic order is its performative power: for Žižek (1999a: 330), the overwhelming problem with global society today is that 'the big Other no longer exists', by which he means that 'the symbolic fiction which confers a performative status on one level of my identity, determining which of my acts will display "symbolic efficiency", is no longer fully operative'. Consequently, 'what is increasingly undermined is the symbolic *trust* which persists against all sceptical data' (Žižek 1999a: 332). So, today we witness a proliferation of committees to decide on the ethical questions raised by new developments in technology (in medicine, biogenetics, etc.), because we now 'need to invent the basic rules of proper ethical conduct, since we lack any form of big Other, any symbolic point of reference that would serve as a safe and unproblematic moral anchor': a 'universally accepted point of reference ... is missing' (Žižek 1999a: 333).

But what is that cause of the death of the big Other? It is, says Žižek (1999a: 342), 'universalised reflexivity': 'Notions like "trust" all rely on a minimum of *non-reflected* acceptance of the symbolic Institution –

ultimately, trust always involves a leap of faith: when I trust somebody, I trust him because I simply take him at his word, not for rational reasons which tell me to trust him.'

Reflexivity, on the other hand, leads to the 'disintegration of symbolic Trust': hence, for example, fathers (in Lacanian terms) are no longer looked upon as Ego Ideals (role models), but as ideal egos (competitors). The respective roles of childhood and adulthood are reversed, so that, on the one hand, children are accorded adult rights and are treated as free-choosing consumers with access to the judicial system, etc., whereas, on the other hand, institutions such as universities, which were designed to replace the family, are becoming more familial, providing counselling and 'emotional support' as well as an education, so that childhood dependency is prolonged into adulthood. All of this is symptomatic of what Žižek calls a 'post-Oedipal' society, in which there is no longer any prohibitive Law. Psychoanalytically, we are no longer dealing (as Freud was) 'with the severe authoritarian father who forbids you to enjoy, but with the obscene father who enjoins you to enjoy, and thus renders you impotent or frigid much more effectively' (Žižek 1999a: 345).

In Žižek's analysis, the reflexive disavowal of the big Other thus becomes responsible for all the sundry malaises of modern life, such as the disintegration of the family, political correctness, the infantilisation of adulthood as represented by the proliferation of emotional counselling, etc. If, on the face of it, this is reactionary, it is the reactionism of a revolutionary. Take, for example, Žižek's (1999a: 361) complaint against the culture of complaint:

> Is not the culture of complaint ... today's version of hysteria, of the hysterical impossible demand addressed to the Other, a demand that actually *wants to be rejected*, since the subject grounds his/her existence in his/her complaint: 'I am insofar as I make the Other responsible for and/or guilty of my misery'? Instead of undermining the position of the Other, the complaining underprivileged address themselves to it: by translating their demand into the terms of legalistic complaint, they *confirm the Other in its position in the very gesture of attacking it.*

This symbolic inefficiency leads Žižek to rail against contemporary responses to the 'risk society' (a term he owes to Beck and Giddens) in which we live: technology has given rise to a plethora of 'low probability–high consequence' risks, such as food additives, nuclear power, genetic engineering, etc.: while the risk of something going wrong with any of these is small, the consequences of something going wrong would be catastrophic. The risk of the human race becoming infertile through chemical food additives is very small, but the consequence would be the annihilation of the human race. What is odd about these kinds of risks are that they make the strategy of avoiding both extremes impossible: it is impossible *not* either to scaremonger on the one hand, or to downplay the dangers on the other. The result is a deadlock, resulting from a 'gap between knowledge and decision': we are forced to make decisions, but no one knows the global outcomes of those decisions. According to Žižek (1999a: 337), this reverses Lacan's 'forced choice' ('Your money or your life!', or 'Freedom or death!'): 'in the contemporary risk society . . . the choice is really "free" and is, for this very reason, experienced as even more frustrating – we find ourselves constantly in the position of having to decide about matters that will fundamentally affect our lives, but without a proper foundation in knowledge'.

And this is not the only reversal. In today's late capitalist society (which is liberal and permissive – not repressive, as it was in Freud's day), the relative positions of unconscious and super-ego are also reversed. In the previous chapter, we saw how Lacan demonstrates the existence of a gap between the formalism of Kant's moral law and the autonomy of the agent who obeys it (a gap replicated in the difference between the first and second formulations of the categorical imperative). Reading Sade shows how the injunction to enjoy can be taken as a universal rule just as easily – rationally and logically – as the injunction to do one's duty. It is Žižek's contention that in contemporary liberal permissive society, this substitution has actually taken place. 'The basic lesson of psychoanalysis', he says, 'is that the Unconscious is, at its most radical, not the wealth of illicit "repressed" desires but *the fundamental law itself*' (Žižek 1999a: 366). When, however, the symbolic order is drained of its efficiency, 'the place of the law itself must remain empty'. Moreover, the injunction of the super-ego is no longer 'Thou shalt not', but 'You may'. Instead of 'Do your duty!' we have 'Enjoy!'. This new injunction Žižek calls 'totalitarian', since it permits everything – nothing is prohibited – so long as everything is done in obedience to the call of the new Master, which is consumer capitalism. (The phenomenon of Viagra, for example, becomes a solution to a particularly late consumer capitalist problem: male impotence is no longer caused by the repressive injunction of a prohibiting super-ego, but by its opposite, a permissive super-ego. When the subject cannot live up to this ego ideal, he can submit to the law of the master by buying a 'cure', albeit one which bypasses the underlying psychological problem rather than addressing it.)

Žižek is, therefore, a 'post-psychoanalytic' psychoanalytic theorist. Freudian psychoanalysis of the sort that tells the subject that, no matter what the dictates of contemporary society (internalised as the super-ego), his unconscious desires are acceptable, is no longer adequate, since the super-ego itself has absorbed psychoanalysis and dictates precisely the sort of thing that was formerly, in Freud's time, kept repressed in the unconscious.

But what is Žižek's positive programme to address this situation? The answer is obscure, couched in the language of avoiding traps and rejecting games:

> What psychoanalytic ethics opposes to this totalitarian *You may!* is not some basic *You mustn't!*, some fundamental prohibition or limitation to be unconditionally respected. . . . The ethical stance of self-limitation . . . is ultimately incompatible with psychoanalysis. One should reject the usual liberal-conservative game of fighting 'totalitarianism' with a reference to some firm set of ethical standards whose abandonment is supposed to lead to catastrophe. . . . The choice is between bad and worse; what Freudian ethics opposes to the 'bad' superego version of *You may!* is another, even more radical *You may!*, a *Scilicet* ('You are allowed to . . .') . . . no longer vouched for by any figure of the Master. Lacan's maxim 'Do not compromise your desire!' fully endorses the pragmatic paradox of ordering you to be free: it exhorts you to dare. (Žižek 1999a: 391–2)

And, thus, Žižek's book ends, leaving unanswered the question, 'Dare to do what?' Žižek's post-psychoanalysis seems as incapable of addressing the question 'What should I do?' as Freudian–Lacanian psychoanalysis. Of course, Žižek could retort that if you need to ask, you still haven't thrown off the shackles of the master, or have transferred the figure of mastery on to Žižek himself: why should he tell you what to do? But, nevertheless, there are hints in Žižek's text as to what we might dare: dare to follow our own desires or passions. For example, Žižek 'dares' (in the face of a liberal-conservative condemnatory consensus) to admire the 'dignity' of Mary Kay Letourneau, jailed for her passionate love affair with a fourteen-year-old schoolboy. A significant absence from Žižek's account of Letourneau, however, is an address to the thoughts, feelings and desires of the boy (unnamed for legal reasons) in the affair – a trait of exclusion which Žižek shares with the liberals and conservatives whom he condemns.

So, then, what about the boy? What about the other? This is a question of responsibility, and it is a trait of Žižek's work that it treads a line between not being responsible and being irresponsible. *Responsibility* is the great unsaid of Žižek's work and, however persuasive it might otherwise be, it is this absence that leads us, if not to prefer Ricoeur over Žižek, then at least to supplement the latter by the former. The notion of responsibility depends on a different conception of the Other from that found in (Lancanian or Žižekian) psychoanalysis: instead of conceiving of the Other as a linguistic projection of the unconscious, we should conceive of the Other as an other person who calls us to responsibility. To be sure, there is something in common between these two conceptions, and that is the notion of the Other as master. For Ricoeur (1992: 190), following

Lévinas, the Other is the 'master of justice'.[3] The task of the self thus becomes to accept the mastery of the Other, rather than to overcome it as psychoanalysis would have us do. This is truly daring, since it requires, as Lacan rightly points out in his reinterpretation of the master–slave dialectic, that I sacrifice something of myself. The dare lies in acceding to this demand, through what Ricoeur calls solicitude.

In order to understand solicitude, Ricoeur returns to the place where he started, to Gabriel Marcel. For Ricoeur, the rule of fidelity is assimilable to the rule of justice. And the rule of fidelity enjoins me to be true to myself. I maintain my self-constancy through keeping my promises. However, 'the obligation to maintain one's self in keeping one's promises is in danger of solidifying into the Stoic rigidity of simple constancy, if it is not permeated by the desire to respond to an expectation, even to a request coming from another' (Ricoeur 1992: 267). Ricoeur accepts Marcel's response to this 'double bind': 'It is to the other that I wish to be faithful. To this fidelity, Gabriel Marcel gives the beautiful name of *disponsibilité* (availability, disposability)' (Ricoeur 1992: 268).

Now, since the golden rule 'establishes the other in the position of someone to whom an obligation is owed',[4] this availability 'is the key that opens self-constancy' to this dialogic structure (Ricoeur 1992: 268):

> 'From you', says the other, 'I expect that you will keep your word'; to you, I reply: 'You can count on me'. This *counting on* connects self-constancy, in its moral tenor, to the principle of reciprocity founded in solicitude. The principle of keeping one's word as it is given is thus no more than the application of the rule of reciprocity to the class of actions in which language itself is involved as the institution governing all the forms of community. Not keeping one's promise is betraying both the other's expectation and the institution that mediates the trust of speaking subjects.

Ricoeur's desire, then, is a 'deontological desire', 'the desire to live well with and for others in just institutions' (Ricoeur 1992: 239). Of course, this desire is open to psychoanalytic critique, but one can dare to pursue its fulfillment notwithstanding. This 'notwithstanding' is articulated by the communality of Ricoeur's desire: through the mutual reciprocity of the plurality of others organised in a social community, Ricoeur's deontological desire is no longer 'pathological' in Kant's sense. Neither, says Žižek, is Lacan's desire. But the crucial difference is one of faith, as opposed to the scepticism of a psychoanalysis that dares to be more sceptical than Descartes. Faith in the institution of language and fidelity to the Other is a desire in which we can all participate. It is the desire which sustains resistance to the cynicism generated by the loss of efficiency of the symbolic order.

9

Conclusion

In *The Voluntary and the Involuntary*, Ricoeur remarks that to conceive of the unconscious as thinking is a mark of cowardice, the opposite of generosity. The notion that the unconscious should think is a species of determinism – the opposite of freedom – and, as such, relieves the subject of responsibility for his actions. That *it thinks* is at once an internalisation – the 'it' is part of myself, but a part which is inaccessible to me – and concomitantly a turning away from the other as a meaningful being. It is Husserl's great insight that the Cartesian *cogito* presupposes all intentionality, and, in so doing, presupposes an ethics insofar as meaning can only be intended to an other. The unconscious as something that thinks deals the *cogito* a fatal wound, insofar as the intentionality that accompanies it is always in danger of being reflexive, of turning in on itself. Husserl's Fifth Meditation, in its theory of analogy, shows how others must each be *cogitationes* in relation to me. A thinking unconscious leads not so much to philosophical solipsism (a charge levelled against pre-*Ideas II* Husserl) but to a radical scepticism. The doubt with which Descartes clears the philosophical decks as a preliminary move would become permanent and universal: the subject would no longer be able to trust himself, and, hence, trust his fidelity towards others, even in its most intimate intentional speech acts such as 'I love you'. And this 'intentional scepticism' is very much a characteristic of post-Freudian psychoanalytic theory, at least as it is popularly understood: each intentional act, especially those of the most intimate kind, becomes open to suspicious questioning: everything is held to have an ulterior motive, which is reducible to an interiorisation – the 'Oedipus Complex'.

Nevertheless, after psychoanalysis, phenomenology can never be the same again. We cannot simply say, as Husserl comes close to doing, that the unconscious does not exist. As Ricoeur (1989: 102) writes in 'Consciousness and the Unconscious', 'Husserl's phenomenology is incapable of taking the failure of consciousness all the way. It remains within the circle of correlations between noesis and noema and can make room for the notion of the unconscious only by way of the theme of "passive genesis"'. As he goes on to write, 'Freudian realism is the necessary stage to bring the failure of reflective consciousness to its completion.' 'This failure', he continues, 'begins a process of converting consciousness in such a way as to understand the necessity of letting go all avarice with regard to itself, including that subtle self-concupiscence which may be what is narcissistic in the immediate consciousness of life' (Ricoeur 1989: 103). The Freudian unconscious demonstrates that Cartesian certainty is mere presumption; understanding the unconscious is the route to overcoming this presumption and arriving at full thought.

But there is a second route to understanding consciousness in its relation to the unconscious that is equally worth pursuing, and that is to explore the Freudian concept of the unconscious divested of its realism. Whether the 'realism of the unconscious' is, in fact, posited by Freud himself (as the early Ricoeur claims) or is 'traversed' by Freud (as the later Ricoeur claims) is, to some extent, a moot point. What is more pertinent is that an unconscious divested of, or traversing, its 'realism', is an unconscious which escapes interiorisation. In fact, such an anti-realist unconscious also enables phenomenology to traverse the interiorisation (narcissism) to which the self-certainty of the *cogito* leaves it similarly prone. In less abstract terms, an anti-realist conception of the unconscious is one that recognises that the unconscious is not *my* unconscious in the sense of a collection of meanings which I 'have' in my psyche but which are hidden from me. Rather, it is an unconscious dependent on the other; 'my' unconscious only has meaning to another person. The traversal of the realism of the unconscious in Freud, then, is the psychoanalytic counterpart to the Husserlian discovery of 'analogy' in his *Ideas II* and *Cartesian Meditations*: the problem of what Husserl calls 'constitution' can only be solved by recourse to an other that is external to the self-reflexivity of the Cartesian subject. As Merleau-Ponty (1962: 159) famously remarks, 'I borrow myself from others', and a Freudian unconscious which traverses the realism that Freud at one stage ascribes to it is likewise a mode of borrowing myself from an other.

Is this saying anything different from Lacan? Lacan's linguisticisation of Freud has the effect of transposing the realism of the unconscious into the realm of language (as a result of Lacan's doctrine of 'the materiality of the signifier'). There are two issues at stake here: first, of whether Lacan's is a cogent theory of language as such, and, second, of whether the claim that 'the unconscious is structured as a language' is true. On the first point, we have seen that Lacan at once adheres to a structuralist model of language following Roman Jakobson and engages in a creative misreading of Jakobson's theory. In general terms, we may say that Lacan's implicit theory of language suffers from the same shortcoming as any structuralist theory: it fails to account for what Chomsky calls 'creativity' in language. This is a result of structuralism's focus on the minimal unit of signification in language (variously identified as the morpheme or the semanteme, but in practice equating to the word), at the expense of grammar. The distinction between a theory of language that sees the potential for meaning being unbounded, as opposed to one which conceives of language as a very large, but finite, set of significations, is one which leaves Lacanian psychoanalysis lacking. More specifically, Lacan accepts Jakobson's theory of metaphor and metonymy, on the one hand, and misreads it, on the other. By misreading it, what Jakobson calls 'metaphor' becomes 'metonymy' in Lacan, and vice versa. This misreading is creative, however, in that it exposes the fact that what Jakobson calls 'metaphor' and 'metonymy' collapse anyway into a zero-point of signification, which is a point of tautology or pure repetition (to paraphrase both Popeye and Gloria Gaynor, 'I am what I am'). By accepting Jakobson's theory, Lacan is still caught within the paradigm of the word, as opposed to larger significatory units such as the sentence, text, or discourse, as the fundamental carrier of meaning. Indeed, Lacan's theory of language collapses meaning into signification.

This brings us to Lacan's claim that 'the unconscious is structured as a language'. As Ricoeur (1970: 400) writes in *De l'interprétation*, 'the problem is to assign an appropriate meaning to the word "like"'. In giving an 'economic' explanation of the unconscious, Freud appears to be proposing a model that is 'like' language insofar as the mechanisms of the unconscious incorporate infra- and supralinguistic phenomena. This is not the same as saying that the mechanisms of the unconscious lend themselves to the same kind of explanation and analysis as do the phenomena of language. Here Lacan wants to have his cake and eat it: both to say (in agreement with Ricoeur) that the word 'like' indicates that the unconscious is not language as such, and, through the doctrine of the materiality of the signifier, to claim that the unconscious 'is the discourse of the Other'. There is a double misconception here on Lacan's part. First, it is only true that 'structured' and 'as a language' mean the same thing if one collapses all semiotic into language (Lacan's own example of von Frisch's bees should have made him wary of this), and, second, Lacan equates 'language' with 'discourse'.

In terms of language, then, we might say that Round One goes to Ricoeur, although we should note, with appropriate emphasis on the word 'like', the utility of the formula 'the unconscious is structured like a language'. Ricoeur's most general criticism of Freud in *De l'interprétation*, meanwhile, is that, while Freud's is a heuristic hermeneutics of desire, he takes desire to be the universal governing trait of humanity. We might say something similar of Lacan, especially in the sphere of ethics: while Lacan makes a valuable contribution to an ethics of desire, he mistakenly assumes ethics to be governed by desire. The heuristic moment here lies between Kant and Hegel as read by Lacan. Kantian ethics is both the fullest statement of an ethics available philosophically and in need of the corrective of Sade. The two modes of the categorical imperative – to act always so that I can will that my action can become a universal law and to treat humanity always as an end in itself, never as a means – exhaust ethical possibility. However, Kant is mistaken in assuming that either of these modes can be assimilated to the other, as the case of Sade shows. Sade makes a universal law of treating humanity as a means towards the satisfaction of his desire. This fact, for which we are indebted to Lacan for its explication, can be interpreted in two ways. The first is Lacan's way, which is strictly Kantian insofar as it follows Kant's own logic to a conclusion that Kant himself would have abhorred: 'pathological' desire can itself be incorporated into an ethical act; the pathological is not what is excluded from the ethical but that which is its ultimate foundation. This seems unsatisfactory: Lacanian psychoanalysis thus formalises what was always latent in Freud, namely, the doctrine that there is no such thing as true altruism; the 'altruistic' act is always secretly motivated by (a) desire. Incorporating pathological desire into ethics ultimately dissolves the true meaning of ethics. This is the lesson of the twentieth century: the Nazis were Sadists in the deep meaning of the word.

The alternative way of interpreting Lacan's Sadean discovery is to acknowledge that acting on pathological desire can be made a universal rule but then to resist it. Resisting here means both resisting the universalisation, and resisting the desire. (Psychoanalysis always assumes that resistance is a bad thing; perhaps this is why Lacan did not resist the Nazis.[1]) The positing of the 'universal law' is a moment in Kant where he prefigures Hegel; or, to put it another way, Hegel's 'universal' is a formalisation of the Kantian universal through the mechanism of the State. Here, once again, we prefer Ricoeur's move to Lacan's. For Ricoeur, it is the constitutionality of the State – *Sittlichkeit* – which is to be admired, but the notion that the State is the reflection of a collective will that sublates the will of the individual is what is to be resisted – again, such is the lesson of twentieth-century totalitarianism. Seen in this way, the master–slave dialectic may be construed as a movement of *Geist* in mutual recognition which does not necessarily lead, as Hegel himself thought, to an *Aufhebung* of consciousness specifically manifested in the universal. Lacan, meanwhile, reads the master–slave dialectic as a moment of terror: *Freedom or death!* places the subject in an impossible situation whereby he can only survive at the price of a surrender, of succumbing to a lack. Again, the difference between Lacan and Ricoeur is slim, but significant. As in Ricoeur, Lacan's mapping of Hegelianism onto Freudianism allows the construal of desire as dialectical in the Hegelian sense: desire is the desire of the Other. This formula has a grammar of double articulation: desire is desire for the Other, and desire is perceived by the subject to come from the position of the Other. In other words, as with Ricoeur, we are led through Hegel into a position of mutual recognition. However, the difference between Ricoeur and Lacan on this point is this: for Lacan, all recognition is a misrecognition (*méconnaissance*), whereas Ricoeur has faith in – is not suspicious of – the reciprocity of the recognition of the Other.

This leads Lacan and Ricoeur to two differing approaches to the problematic of the 'desire to be'. In some ways, we have come full circle here, since the desire to be is what motivates the Cartesian in his constant work of reaffirming the 'I think ...'. For Lacan, the desire to be has a counterpart in *manque à être*, the lack at the *Kern unseres wesens*. This is where 'the signification of the phallus' is of fundamental importance to Lacanian theory, in grounding the being-in-the-world of the gendered subject. Woman is defined as a desire-to-have that which she lacks, and man as a desire-to-be that which he is not. In both cases, it is the phallus as master signifier that determines the relation of the subject to being through desire. Thus it is that, through the intercession of Hegel, Freud's biologistic theory of 'penis envy' becomes rewritten in the symbolic dimension, the phallus being understood here as a signifier, not as a material object. Nevertheless, we once again run up against the unanswerable problem in Lacan of the materiality of the signifier: why *this* signifier, rather than any other?

What is unsatisfying about this dimension of Lacanian theory from an ethical point of view is that it sees the dialectic of desire, or of desire and demand, from the position of the subject. 'What does the other want of me?' is the Lacanian question – that is why Lacan's Hegelian moment is a moment of terror. Ricoeur, meanwhile, inverts Lacan's question: 'What can I do for the Other?' When Lacan writes that a woman's love is the gift of that which she does not have, he is assuming love to be sexual love – indeed, in Lacanian theory as in psychoanalysis generally, there is no other kind of love than the sexual, this being both cause and effect of psychoanalysis' refusal to countenance altruism.[2] But Ricoeur's mutual tempering of Kantian individualism by Hegelian *Sittlichkeit* and Hegelian universalism by Kantian individualism leads him to the opposite position from Lacan. While Lacan (in common with Freud) cannot countenance loving one's neighbour,[3] for Ricoeur, the New Commandment, to love thy neighbour as thyself, becomes the ethical norm that rewrites the categorical imperative just as it is implied by it. If Lacan subsumes *agape* into *eros*, so Ricoeur subsumes *eros* into *agape*. Ricoeur's Hegelian moment is not one of terror but of love – love is the opposite of terror. This entails seeing the reciprocal relation between the subject and the Other not from the point of view of the subject but from the point of view of the Other. It is in this way that the question, 'What does the Other want of me?' is reversed into 'What may I do for the Other?'. The desexualisation of love in Ricoeur means that love itself can be universal: love is a gift, yes, but no longer the gift of the woman, but of anyone. Such is the logic of its superabundance.

The irony is that this notion of *disponsibility* (of putting myself at an Other's disposal) is in one way implied by psychoanalysis itself, in that, as Ricoeur points out very early in his career, the unconscious only exists for an other. Just as (to paraphrase Wittgenstein) there can be no private language, so there can, in a certain sense, be no private unconscious, if by 'private' we mean something wholly internalised to the thinking subject. In fact, this is another way in which the unconscious is (structured) *like* a language. I am dependent on the Other as my unconscious interlocutor. In psychoanalysis, when the Other is the analyst, transference takes place – in psychoanalytic parlance, transference is a form of love. From a Lacanian perspective, in analysis, transference places the analyst in the position of the *sujet supposer savoir*, the subject who is supposed to know, the subject who is the repository of the *agalma*, or hidden treasure, or knowledge (whereas in fact, the subject already knows, but does not know what he knows, or that he knows it). In *The Voluntary and the Involuntary*, Ricoeur's response to the phenomenon of transference (indeed, to the phenomenon of analysis) is that it cedes too much power to the analyst, as if the analyst is the only one capable of curing the patient. In this early work, Ricoeur sees no reason why a patient might not cure themselves through going through the analytic process as a sort of internal dialogue – Ricoeur is apparently sceptical of psychoanalysis as an institutional practice.

In his later works, Ricoeur never returns to this question directly. But from a theoretical perspective, his late works on love and justice may be seen as providing the intellectual lever whereby the power relation between analyst and analysand might be dissolved. This is, of course, not really, or is no longer, a question of the relationship between analyst and patient as such – after all, psychoanalysis as a practice is only of interest to, or available to, a small number of rich neurotics. It is, rather, a question of social organisation. If the subject's love of the Other is no longer pathological, but an instantiation of universal *agape*, then a new concept of desire is called for. Deontological desire is 'the desire to live well with and for others in just institutions' (Ricoeur 1992: 239). The 'with and for others' is accounted for by love of the neighbour, governed by love's superabundance whereby, regardless of the vicissitudes of the neighbour, I maintain an attitude of solicitude. But there is a certain truth in Freud's claim that such love is an impossible ideal. Rather than succumb to Freudian defeatism, however, the deontological desiring subject turns to the third party, to the judge who mediates between the self and the Other, the subject and his neighbour. Justice, which is harsher than love, makes the sacrifice of something of myself bearable, and at the societal level this is achieved through the operation of the institutional third party (the courts, the university, etc.). In 'Of Structure as an Inmixing ...' Lacan (1972: 190) boasts that 'after fifteen years I have taught my pupils to count at most up to five which is difficult (four is easier) and they have understood that much'. But maybe three is enough: the subject, the Other, and the institutional third party that, through justice, makes the Other's demand of the subject bearable and the subject's love of the Other possible.

Notes

1. Introduction

[1] Roudinesco (1997: 260) describes Lacan's performances at the Hôpital Sainte-Anne thus:

> He spoke in fits and starts, with now and then a sigh or a roar. He always brought with him a few sheets of paper covered with notes and sketches; these served to maintain the suspense created by his intermittent delivery. Sometimes he muttered, like Oedipus at Colonus trying by ominous silence to suspend the course of time; sometimes he raised his voice like Hamlet facing death, as if to contradict the slowness of impending thought. At once sombre and tumultuous, he could bring forth from broken speech or imperfect memory the rigorous logic of an unconscious whose ebb and flow he seemed to echo. His seminars used to produce a collective catharsis; everyone present felt that Lacan was speaking to him alone.

Everyone, that is, except Paul Ricoeur (1998: 70):

> I lived through those meetings as a sort of obligation, terrible drudgery and frustration, which I assiduously imposed on myself, because I always had the impression that he was *going to* say something important that had not yet been said, that this would be said the next time and so on; he had a consummate art of suspense, which I had found absolutely intolerable. For me it was really an ordeal to go back time after time, feeling a kind of obligation but also an incredible disappointment. ... The atmosphere of veneration that reigned at the seminar was stupefying! It was unimaginable that someone could stand up and say that he had not understood or that it was absurd....

[2] For a full account see Reagan 1996: 33–9.

[3] Cf. Ricoeur 1998: 68–9.

[4] Lacan (1979: 153) signalled his reassessment of Ricoeur's paper, and, hence, his break with Ricoeur, as early as 1964, in *The Four Fundamental Concepts of Psychoanalysis*:

> I was recently rereading, in the context of an address I gave to a congress that took place in 1960, what someone else said about the unconscious. This person – it was M. Ricoeur in fact – was trying to remove himself as far as possible from his own position in order to conceptualise our domain. He had certainly gone a long way to reach what, for a philosopher, is the area most difficult of access, namely, the reality of the unconscious – that the

> unconscious is not an ambiguity of acts, future knowledge that is already known not to be known, but lacuna, cut, rupture inscribed in a certain lack. M. Ricoeur concedes that there is something of this dimension to be retained. But, philosopher that he is, he monopolises it for himself. He calls it hermeneutics.

The reason Lacan was 'recently rereading' Ricoeur's paper was that it was in 1964 that he was asked to edit his own paper ready for the publication of the proceedings in 1966. Presumably, it is as a result of this rereading that Lacan asks for the discussion following Ricoeur's paper to be cut. Not wishing Ricoeur to 'monopolise' the unconscious, Lacan succeeds in monopolising it for *him*self (he calls it psychoanalysis). Ricoeur (1998: 69) calls this 'an incredible lack of intellectual integrity' on Lacan's part.

[5] According to S. H. Clark (1990: 81), 'Lacan's attempt to equate the role of the dynamics in Freud's thought, its force, life energy, to the ancillary effects of the functioning of an autonomous linguistic system ... is refuted by his own formula' *S'/S x S/s.*

[6] The other being where Ricoeur (1970: 395) examines Lacan's claim that 'the unconscious is structured like a language'.

[7] This is the centrepiece of Clark's (1990: 76–82) comparison of Ricoeur and Lacan, which occupies some six pages of his *Paul Ricoeur.*

> The argumentative convenience of [Jakobson's] schema is achieved only at the cost of restricting the entire linguistic field to two tropes. It is posited, according to the fallacious principle of a hierarchical organisation, that these are equally dominant at every level. ... Rather than attempt to remedy the fundamental shortcomings of his model, Lacan accentuates its extreme restrictiveness; and consequently his transposition of tropic structures onto psychic processes invites dismissal as both crude and misleading. (Clark 1990: 80)

[8] Ricoeur (1995b: 21) makes a similar point in his 'Intellectual Autobiography':

> It was ... insinuated that the difference in treating the unconscious in *The Voluntary and the Involuntary,* which had been very much influenced by Roland Dalbiez, and in *On Interpretation,* was due to the unavowed influence of Lacan. This was to forget *The Symbolism of Evil* and my teaching at the Sorbonne, where I had focussed, before attending Lacan's seminars, on the conflict in Freud between the economic model and the linguistic model.

2. The *Cogito* and its Detractors

[1] Cf. Husserl 1991, and Heidegger 1962: 464–86.

[2] Cf. 'fig. 1', reproduced in Freud 1961a: 24.

[3] One Angus Fletcher in opening the discussion which followed Lacan's presentation of 'Of Structure as an Inmixing'. See Lacan 1972: 195.

[4] Lacan had already visited Freud's *Wo Es war, soll Ich werden* in the seminars presented in the two years immediately preceding 'The Freudian Thing'. In the Seminar of 1953–4, *Freud's Papers on Technique,* he asks, 'When Freud writes *Wo Es*

war, soll Ich werden, must we take it to mean that the task is to enlarge the field of consciousness? Or is it a matter of displacement?' (Lacan 1988a: 194). In answer, we might say that this is a false dichotomy, that the two possibilities are not mutually exclusive: the ego, for Freud, enlarges itself by displacing the id. Again Lacan identifies the *Es* with the subject here, at least provisionally. In the Seminar of 1954–5 (*The Ego in Freud's Theory and in the Technique of Psychoanalysis*), meanwhile, Lacan (1988b: 246) remarks that

> There are two meanings to be given to Freud's phrase – *Wo Es war, soll Ich werden.* This *Es*, take it as the letter *S*. It is there, it is always there. It is the subject. He knows himself or he doesn't know himself. That isn't even the most important thing – he speaks or he doesn't speak. At the end of the analysis, it is him who must be called on to speak, and to enter into relation with the real Others. Where the *S* was, there the *Ich* should be.

[5] Nevertheless, Lacan and Ey were good friends, and otherwise in broad agreement. It was Ey who was to invite Lacan to Bonneval in 1960.

[6] This manoeuvre is adopted by Slavoj Žižek (1999a) in *The Ticklish Subject*, the implications of which we explore in Chapter 8 below.

[7] Lacan's reminder that Descartes' *cogito* is initially uttered in the historical context of determining what constitutes a science becomes important in a later seminar, 'Science and Truth', in Lacan's answer to the question of whether psychoanalysis is itself a science. This is a question to be distinguished, says Lacan (2006: 733), from 'the fact that its praxis implies no other subject than that of science', by which Lacan means truth. Lacan insists on the distinction between truth and knowledge, and again returns to *Wo Es war, soll Ich werden*, which, he claims, is a 'call' by Freud to consider this question. Once again, Lacan 'retranslates' this as 'Where it was, there I must come to be as a subject'. 'An inscription does not etch into the same side of the parchment when it comes from the printing-plate of truth and when it comes from that of knowledge', says Lacan (2006: 734).

[8] Of course, this position is dependent on the quasi-existential position that *there is faith*, or *I have faith*, which in turn rests on the argument developed in the earlier *Metaphysical Journal* (Marcel 1952), that atheism is self-contradictory, since it depends upon a denial of the possibility of something which lies beyond all possible perception – since this something is posited, precisely, as beyond all possible perception, its 'existence' (in inverted commas – we speak of existence only of what is in the world) can be neither empirically verified nor falsified.

[9] All translations of Ricoeur's *Gabriel Marcel et Karl Jaspers* are my own.

3. From the *Cogito* to the Unconscious

[1] As reflected in the main title of the English translation, *Freedom and Nature.*

[2] Cf. Ricoeur's (1967a: 136) 'Husserl's Fifth Cartesian Meditation':

> On the one hand, one must say that the sense of the Other, of the psychophysical man, hence also of me insofar as I am an Other among Others, is constituted 'purely in me, the mediating ego'. . .; this latter is against any

hypostasis of society into an absolute being. On the other hand, it is legitimate to profess a realism of reciprocity which at its limit makes me an Other among Others.

[3] Slavoj Žižek laments the loss of authority of the analyst in the analytic situation in contemporary society, in which everyone knows about psychoanalysis. In a movement of what he calls 'reflexivisation of interpretation', people are not so much having symptoms that can be interpreted in a Jungian, Kleinian, Lacanian, etc., way, but are having symptoms which are *already* Jungian, Kleinian, Lacanian, etc. The result of this is an abnegation of responsibility on the part of the analysand, losing as he does the moral compass provided by the analyst, what Žižek (1999: 346) calls his 'symbolic efficiency':

> What happens in psychoanalytic treatment is similar to the paradox . . . of the neo-Nazi skinhead who, when really pressed to give the reasons for his violence, suddenly starts to talk like social workers, sociologists and social psychologists, quoting diminished social mobility, rising insecurity, the disintegration of paternal authority, lack of maternal love in his early childhood. . . .

Whether the analyst is worthy of the status of moral compass (implicit in Lacan's theory of the *sujet supposer savoir*), and whether 'symbolic efficiency' is an adequate term to describe such a phenomenon, is a question to which we shall return in Chapter 8.

[4] Some years later, Ricoeur was to return to this question of the distinction between plausibility and truth in Freud, Freud's claim to truth being, of course, that on which rests psychoanalysis's claim to be a scientific discipline. Cf. 'The Question of Proof in Freud's Psychoanalytic Writings', in Ricoeur 1981: 247–73.

[5] If, to paraphrase Saussure, it is one of the tasks of a science to delimit itself as a discipline, psychoanalysis is unable to do this so long as doctrine and method are intertwined within it. The methods of the hard sciences are (or should be) free of doctrine (unless we take belief in the efficacy of experimental empiricism to be a 'doctrine').

[6] In Freud 1976: 182–99.

4. The Unconscious and Language

[1] This seems a point lost on Lacan, who in 'Of Structure as an Inmixing . . .' rejects the notion of the mind being a totality in itself, an 'intentional unity', and ascribes this view to 'the so-called phenomenological movement' (Lacan 1972: 190). For Lacan in this lecture, phenomenology is clearly in direct opposition to the psychoanalytic project.

[2] Ricoeur (1970: 379) goes on to remark that 'Husserl and Freud are seen to be the heirs of Brentano, who had both of them as students'.

[3] In Chapter VI of *The Interpretation of Dreams*: cf. Freud 1976: 381–651.

[4] Jakobson finds justification for this view in the work of Peirce. Cf. the former's short essay 'Visual and Auditory Signs', in Jakobson 1971: 334–7.

[5] Cf. 'On Linguistic Aspects of Translation', in Jakobson 1971: 260–6.

[6] Thus Saussure (1983: 67): 'The ... terms [*signified* and *signifier*] have the advantage of indicating the distinction which separates each from the other and both from the whole of which they are part.'

[7] Lacan 2006: 445–88.

[8] William Godwin, *Caleb Williams*, 'Postscript'.

[9] From Victor Hugo, *Booz endormi.*

[10] In *Paul Ricoeur* (Simms 2003: 72), I gave the following as an example of metaphor: Fred Bloggs is a table. Since this is a newly coined metaphor (requiring the explanation that Fred is a square, with a wooden personality, in order to be understood), it does not, in fact, quite fit with Jakobson's examples of metaphors, all of which are neither dead nor fully alive in the sense of being newly coined. All of Jakobson's examples are of recognised metaphors: both terms, substitute and substituted, are pre-known, just as it is pre-known that the President of the USA has his official residence in Washington in the metonymy 'Washington condemned Iraqi aggression'. I remarked there on the difficulty of the epistemology of the subject associated with 'Washington condemned ...': someone who did not know that the US President resides in Washington would not get the metonymy. But the same epistemological difficulty also lies on the side of metaphor in Jakobson's schema, as we have seen with the *ginger pop* example. Indeed, the only metaphors that can work as metaphors in Jakobson are these received, half-alive and half-dead ones. While Ricoeur chides Jakobson for failing to account for newly coined metaphors, the same is true of dead metaphors in the latter's limited schema.

5. From the Symbolic to the Ethical

[1] In any case, 'neither one nor the other' is not the negation of 'either one or the other or both'; 'neither one nor the other' is the negation of *aut*, rendered '$\sim P \wedge \sim Q$', whereas the negation of *vel* would be 'neither one nor the other nor both', rendered '$\sim P \wedge \sim Q \wedge \sim(P \wedge Q)$'.

[2] Cf. Merleau-Ponty 1968.

[3] 'The Hermeneutics of Symbols and Philosophical Reflection: II', in Ricoeur 1989: 315–34.

[4] Ricoeur distinguishes between philosophical and psychoanalytic hermeneutics as two distinct types. His position regarding the 'archaeological' nature of the latter and the 'teleological' mature of the former is summarised as follows:

> The opposition between *the unconscious* and *Spirit* is expressed in the very duality of these interpretations. The two sciences of interpretation represent two contrary movements: an analytical and regressive movement toward the unconscious and a synthetic and progressive movement toward Spirit. On the one hand, in Hegelian phenomenology, every figure receives its meaning from the one that follows it: Stoicism is the truth of the mutual recognition of master and slave, but scepticism, which destroys the distinction between master and slave, is the truth of the Stoic position, etc. The truth of one moment resides in the subsequent moment; intelligibility always proceeds from the end to the beginning. This is the reason why we

> can say that consciousness is a task, that it is ultimately complete and secure only when it comes to an end. On the other hand, the concept of the unconscious signifies that understanding always proceeds from figures that are prior to it; man is the only being who is always drawn back to his own infancy. The unconscious is thus the principle of all regression and all stagnation. (Ricoeur 1989: 325–6)

[5] Lacan 2006: 197–268.

[6] Cf. von Frisch 1994.

[7] Cf. Peirce 1932: 134–73, and Burks 1949.

[8] P. B. Shelley, *Prometheus Unbound,* III, iv. 116.

6. The Law of the Subject and the Law of the Other

[1] People have often said the same of psychoanalysis, of course, not least in its emphasis on the 'talking cure', which might be read as a form of secular confession. The essential difference in this respect, however, is that in religious confession the priest makes a moral judgement, which the analyst withholds.

[2] Freud is yet more explicit on this point in Chapter V of *Civilisation and its Discontents*:

> I have no concern with any economic criticisms of the communist system; I cannot enquire into whether the abolition of private property is expedient or advantageous. But I am able to recognise that the psychological premisses on which the system is based are an untenable illusion. In abolishing private property we deprive the human love of aggression of one of its instruments. . .; but we have in no way altered the differences in power and influence which are misused by aggressiveness, nor have we altered anything in its nature. (Freud 1961b: 113)

And in a footnote Freud's attitude towards nature is revealed to be even more defeatist: 'Nature, by endowing individuals with extremely unequal physical attributes and mental capacities, has introduced injustices against which there is no remedy' (Freud 1961b: 113).

[3] Cf. Kant, 'On a Supposed Right to Tell Lies from Benevolent Motives', in Kant 1883: 361–6.

[4] Lacan (1992: 185) says of this passage that 'If I hadn't told you the title of the work from which this passage comes, I could have pretended it was from Sade'. Conversely, when Lacan (2006: 667) writes of Sade,

> Listen to him praise his technique of immediately implementing whatever comes into his head, thinking too that by replacing repentance with reiteration he can be done with the law within. To encourage us to follow his example, he comes up with nothing better than the promise that nature, woman that she is, will magically give us ever more,

we could pretend that he is writing of Freud.

[5] Certainly, one is struck by the failure of imagination it manifests: that loving one's neighbour is unimaginable for Freud shows nothing more than that: that it is unimaginable *for Freud.* Freud conceives of love as being held in a pint pot: he has a

finite amount which he shares out amongst his friends according to their worth. But Paul and the Scriptures argue that love is superabundant. If one has a child and then a second child one loves (or should love) each of them equally, but this does not mean that when the second child is born, the love afforded the first child is cut by half, in order to give the second child an equal share. Rather, *more* love is produced, even though the first child is loved to the fullest extent possible. Of course, children themselves often do not grasp this, and psychoanalysis is good at identifying the vicissitudes of childhood jealousies, and using them, archaeologically, as an explanation of adult life. But in *Civilisation and its Discontents* the elderly Freud, looking backwards over his entire career as a psychoanalytic theorist, adopts precisely the 'naïve' theory of ethics – we might call it 'the child's theory' – as his own, just as, analogously, the child's theory of castration becomes the psychoanalytic theory of the 'castration complex'. *Civilisation and its Discontents*, like psychoanalysis generally, sometimes slips from being an archaeology of the 'naïve', or of the child, to being naïve as such, or childish.

[6] Kant gives two further instances of this kind of calculation in his *Anthropology*, as examples of what he calls 'bitter joy':

> A person who is in precarious circumstances and then inherits the estate of his parents or other worthy and generous relatives, cannot avoid rejoicing over their death, though he cannot keep from reproaching himself for his joy. This is exactly what takes place in the mind of a colleague who attends, with sincere sadness, the funeral of his honoured predecessor. (Kant 1978: 138–9)

What makes these examples disconcerting is the possibility that we could imagine a person of whom they were an accurate reflection. But for most 'normal' (which is to say, non-pathological) people, is the experience as Kant describes it? In the case of the death of the parents, one simply does not rejoice over the death – one might rejoice over the good fortune of the inherited wealth, but the notion of that inheritance being caused by the death, and that, therefore, the death is rejoiced at also, does not come into the calculation, if calculation it still be. Hence, the subject does not so much reproach himself for his joy at inheriting wealth, if indeed joy he has, but feel guilty that this feeling of joy should be co-present with the feeling of sorrow over the death. But what is more likely, however, is that the sorrow over the death eclipses any thought of joy entering the head of the subject – the cares of the world which the inheritance would absolve in any case pale into insignificance in the face of the absolute that is the death of a loved one. The same could also be said *mutatis mutandis* of Kant's second example, of the colleague succeeding his predecessor: we need only note in addition the bourgeois quality of this example, based as it is on the relative *professional* standings of its participants.

[7] Incidentally, the case of suicide bombers demonstrates the uselessness of the death penalty, either as punishment or deterrent, in certain situations.

[8] Zupančič (1998: 48) calls it 'the most "abjected" part of Kant's philosophy. But against those who would dismiss it as a 'temporary aberration', she writes that it

> brings into play nothing less than the basic principles of Kantian ethics. If the moral law is indeed unconditional, if it does not follow from any notion of the good, but is itself the ground for any possible definition of the good,

> then it is clear why Kant cannot accept that the good of our fellowman might serve us as an excuse for not doing our duty. Those who are not willing to accept this aspect of Kant's position in the discussed example but reject it, are also rejecting the entire edifice of Kantian ethics that hangs precisely upon this point (Zupančič 1998: 49).

[9] Cf. Adam Smith's *Theory of Moral Sentiments* (Smith 2002).

[10] Zupančič (1998: 49) makes a similar point in her essay 'The Subject of the Law', and in so doing, fleshes out somewhat her justification for characterising the motivation behind Kant's hero's action as one of enjoyment:

> If ... we accept Kant's position, there is yet another trap to be avoided, namely the 'Sadean trap'. The Kantian subject cannot escape the Real involved in the unconditional duty by hiding himself behind the image of his fellow man – but neither can this subject hide behind his duty and use the duty as an *excuse* for his actions.... The type of discourse where I use my duty as an excuse for my actions is perverse in the strictest sense of the word. Here, the subject attributes to the Other (to the duty or to the Law), the surplus enjoyment that he finds in his actions: 'I am sorry if my actions hurt you, but I only did what the Other wanted me to do, so go and see Him if you have any objections'. In this case, the subject hides behind the law.

[11] Radical evil occurs when we make the principle of self-love the condition of following the moral law. As Zupančič (1998: 53) explains,

> "radical evil" reverses the hierarchy of (pathological) incentives and the law: it makes the former the condition of the latter, whereas the latter (i.e. the law) ought to be the supreme condition or "criterion" for the satisfaction of the incentives. We obey the moral law only "by accident", when it suits us or when it is compatible with our pathological inclinations.

[12] Zupančič (1998: 51) makes the same point in 'The Subject of the Law'.

[13] This fact leads some commentators dangerously close to vindicating Sade. Emmancio Bencivenga (1996: 45), for example, writes that Sade's victims 'go through unimaginable torments, but they don't die. And that is just as it should be: their being what they are – that is, humans, that is, rational beings – is not denied by the torments but rather exalted by them'.

[14]

> The law which attempts a man's life is impractical, unjust, inadmissible. Not ... that we lack an infinite number of cases where, without offence to Nature ..., men have freely taken one another's lives, simply exercising a prerogative received from their common mother; but it is impossible for the law to obtain the same privileges, since the law, cold and impersonal, is a total stranger to the passions which are able to justify in man the cruel act of murder. Man receives his impressions from Nature, who is able to forgive him this act; the law, on the contrary, always opposed as it is to Nature and receiving nothing from her, cannot be authorised to permit itself the same extravagances: not having the same motives, the law cannot have the same rights. (Sade 1965: 310)

[15] It is worth remarking that both Kant and Sade share the same concept of pleasure, namely that it is determined dialectically in relation to pain. Here is Kant (1978: 133) on tobacco: 'Tobacco ... is initially linked with an unpleasant

sensation. But just because nature instantaneously does away with the pain (by secretion of mucus at the palate or in the nose), tobacco (especially when smoked) becomes a sort of companion who entertains and constantly stimulates sensations ...'). Dolmancé, meanwhile, says of being sodomised that 'the pangs ... are soon to change into pleasures' (Sade 1965: 231). Kant's smoking, then, and Sade's being sodomised, share the same formal structure of initial pain giving way to pleasure, the initial pain being a necessary *rite de passage* on which the subsequent pleasure is contingent. Hence, the incentive to persevere with the act of smoking or sodomy is derived from imagination, the imagined experience of the pleasures which are to come, and which are subsequently, but soon, realised.

7. Ethics Following Ricoeur

1 See the photograph reproduced in Reagan 1996.

2 Cf. Jacques Lacan, 'Impromptu at Vincennes', in Lacan 1987b: 116–27.

3 Ricoeur may be alluding to the following passage in Freud (1961b: 101–2):

> A small minority are enabled by their constitution to find happiness, in spite of everything, along the path of love. But far-reaching mental changes in the function of love are necessary before this can happen. These people make themselves independent of their object's acquiescence by displacing what they mainly value from being loved onto loving; they protect themselves against the loss of the object by directing their love, not to single objects but to all men alike; and they avoid the uncertainties and disappointments of genital love by turning away from its sexual aims and transforming the instinct into an impulse with an *inhibited aim*. What they bring about in themselves in this way is a state of evenly suspended, steadfast, affectionate feeling, which has little external resemblance any more to the stormy agitations of genital love, from which it is nevertheless derived. Perhaps St. Francis of Assisi went furthest in thus exploiting love for the benefit of an inner feeling of happiness.

We might note the blithe disregard for any explanation for a human motivation other than one which is, well, Freudian. Again we run up against the question of proof in Freud's theories: St. Francis of Assisi's motives can be explained, consistently, by Freudianism – but a *consistent* explanation need not be a *true* explanation, and concomitantly, it is not necessarily the case that St. Francis was self-deluded. More generally, Freud offers no evidence other than consistency with his own theory that 'evenly suspended, steadfast, affectionate feeling' is, or is always, 'derived' from 'genital love'. In short, Freud derives all *agape* from *eros*, but offers no argument against the counter-claim that the relationship could be the other way around.

8. Ethics After Lacan

[1] As in the television programmes transcribed in *Television* (Lacan 1987a). These were broadcast in the UK in the 1980s, when Channel 4 TV was a public service broadcaster, but have not been seen since.

[2] Žižek criticises Rawls (along with Taylor, Habermas and Lyotard) for reducing the political to a pre-political ethics; they criticise, he says, politics for being unifying, totalitarian, violent, etc., 'without engaging in an alternative political project' (Žižek 1999a: 171).

[3] Ricoeur (2000: 29) accepts, too, Lévinas' basic premise, that 'it is from others rather than from our inner conscience or heart of hearts that the moral injunction is said to proceed'. The psychoanalytic theory of Freud conflates this distinction in its notion of the super-ego being an interiorisation of this external injunction; the Lacan–Žižek notion of the symbolic order reifies this conflation.

[4] As Ricoeur (1996a: 17) puts it in his essay 'Fragility and Responsibility',

> The ability to designate oneself as author of one's acts is affirmed, or, better, attested, in the relation of self to self: I ... myself, you ... yourself, he ... himself, she ... herself. The appeal, the injunction, and also the trust which proceed from the fragile, result in its being always *another* who declares us responsible, or, as Lévinas says, calls us to responsibility. Another, by relying on me, renders me accountable for my acts.

9. Conclusion

[1] Cf. Roudinesco 1997: 158.

[2] In *On Feminine Sexuality* Lacan (1998: 75) explicitly denies a distinction between *agape* and *eros*, and implicitly describes Anders Nygren's book of that title as 'stupid'.

[3] Strictly speaking, Freud finds it impossible to love the neighbour, whereas Lacan, following Sade, finds it impossible to *be* a neighbour.

Bibliography

Anderson, Pamela Sue, 1993: *Ricoeur and Kant: Philosophy of the Will* (American Academy of Religion Studies in Religion 66). Atlanta, Ga: Scholars Press.

Bencivenga, Emmancio, 1996: 'Kant's Sadism', *Philosophy and Literature* 20, 39–46.

Burks, Arthur W., 1949: 'Icon, Index, and Symbol', *Philosophy and Phenomenological Research* 9:3, 673–89.

Chomsky, Noam, 1959: 'A Review of B. F. Skinner's *Verbal Behavior*', *Language* 35:1, 26–58.

Clark, S. H., 1990: *Paul Ricoeur*. London and New York: Routledge.

Dennett, Daniel, 1991: *Consciousness Explained*. London: Allen Lane.

Dosse, François, 1997: *Paul Ricoeur: Le sens d'une vie*. Paris: La Découverte.

Dufrenne, Mikel, and Paul Ricoeur, 1947: *Karl Jaspers et la philosophie de l'existence: Préface de Karl Jaspers*. Paris: Seuil.

Freud, Sigmund, 1961a: *The Ego and the Id*, trans. Joan Riviere, in *The Ego and the Id and Other Works*, ed. James Strachey et al. (Standard Edition of the Complete Psychological Works 19). London: Hogarth, pp. 1–66.

——, 1961b: *Civilisation and its Discontents*, trans. Joan Riviere, in *The Future of an Illusion, Civilisation and its Discontents, and Other Works*, ed. James Strachey et al. (Standard Edition of the Complete Psychological Works 21). London: Hogarth, pp. 64–145.

——, 1973: *New Introductory Lectures on Psychoanalysis*, trans. James Strachey, ed. James Strachey and Angela Richards (Pelican Freud Library 2). Harmondsworth: Penguin.

——, 1976: *The Interpretation of Dreams*, trans. James Strachey, ed. James Strachey, Alan Tyson and Angela Richards (Pelican Freud Library 4). Harmondsworth: Penguin.

Godwin, William, 1993: *An Enquiry Concerning Political Justice*, ed. Mark Philp (Political and Philosophical Writings of William Godwin 3). London: Pickering.

Groddeck, Georg, 1949: *The Book of the It*, trans. V. M. E. Collins. London: Vision.

Hegel, G. W. F., 1967: *The Phenomenology of Mind*, trans. J. B. Baillie. New York and Evanston: Harper.

——, 1991: *Elements of the Philosophy of Right*, ed. Allen W. Wood, trans. H. B. Nisbet. Cambridge: Cambridge University Press.

Heidegger, Martin, 1962: *Being and Time*, trans. John Macquarrie and Edward Robinson. Oxford: Blackwell.

Husserl Edmund, 1973: *Cartesian Meditations: An Introduction to Phenomenology*, trans. Dorion Cairns. The Hague: Nijhoff.

——, 1982: *Ideas Pertaining to a Pure Phenomenology and to a Phenomenological Philosophy, First Book: General Introduction to a Pure Phenomenology*, trans F. Kersten (Collected Works 2). The Hague: Nijhoff.

——, 1989: *Ideas Pertaining to a Pure Phenomenology and to a Phenomenological Philosophy, Second Book: Studies in the Phenomenology of Constitution*, trans. R. Rojcewicz and A. Schuwer (Collected Works 3). Dordrecht: Kluwer.

——, 1991: *On the Phenomenology of the Consciousness of Internal Time, 1893–1917*, trans. John Barnett Brough (Collected Works 4). Dordrecht: Kluwer.

Jakobson, Roman, 1971: *Selected Writings II: Word and Language*. The Hague and Paris: Mouton.

Jameson, Fredric, 1982: 'Imaginary and Symbolic in Lacan: Marxism, Psychoanalytic Criticism, and the Problem of the Subject', in Shoshana Felman (ed.), *Literature and Psychoanalysis: The Question of Reading: Otherwise*. Baltimore, Md. and London: Johns Hopkins University Press, pp. 338–95.

Jaspers, Karl, 1969: *Philosophy, Volume 1*, trans. E. B. Ashton. Chicago, Ill. and London: University of Chicago Press.

——, 1970: *Philosophy, Volume 2*, trans. E. B. Ashton. Chicago, Ill. and London: University of Chicago Press.

——, 1971: *Philosophy, Volume 3*, trans. E. B. Ashton. Chicago, Ill. and London: University of Chicago Press.

Kant, Immanuel, 1883: *Critique of Practical Reason and Other Works on the Theory of Ethics*, trans. Thomas Kingsmill Abbott. London: Longman, 3rd edn.

——, 1934: *Religion within the Limits of Reason Alone*, trans. Theodore M. Greene and Hoyt H. Hudson. Chicago, Ill. and London: Open Court.

——, 1978: *Anthropology from a Pragmatic Point of View*, trans. Victor Lyle Dowdell, ed. Hans H. Rudnick. Carbondale, Ill. and Edwardsville, Ill.: Southern Illinois University Press.

——, 1998: *Groundwork of the Metaphysics of Morals*, trans. and ed. Mary Gregor. Cambridge: Cambridge University Press.

Klossowski, Pierre, 1986: 'Sade, or the Philosopher-Villain', trans. Alphonso Lingis, *Substance* 50, 5–25.

Lacan, Jacques, 1966: *Écrits*, ed. Jacques-Alain Miller. Paris: Seuil.

——, 1972: 'Of Structure as an Inmixing of an Otherness Prerequisite to Any Subject Whatever', in Richard Macksey and Eugenio Donato (eds), *The Structuralist Controversy: The Languages of Criticism and the Sciences of*

Man. Baltimore, Md. and London: Johns Hopkins University Press, pp. 186–200.
——, 1979: *The Four Fundamental Concepts of Psycho-Analysis*, ed. Jacques-Alain Miller, trans. Alan Sheridan. Harmondsworth: Penguin.
——, 1982: 'Desire and the Interpretation of Desire in *Hamlet*', ed. Jacques-Alain Miller, trans. James Hulbert, in Shoshana Felman (ed.), *Literature and Psychoanalysis: The Question of Reading: Otherwise*. Baltimore, Md. and London: Johns Hopkins University Press, pp. 11–52.
——, 1987a: *Television*, trans. Denis Hollier, Rossalind Krauss and Annette Michelson, *October* 40, 1–50.
——, 1987b: *Dossier on the Institutional Debate*, trans. Jeffrey Mehlman, *October* 40, 51–133.
——, 1988a: *The Seminar of Jacques Lacan, Book I: Freud's Papers on Technique, 1953–1954*, ed. Jacques-Alain Miller, trans. John Forrester. Cambridge: Cambridge University Press.
——, 1988b: *The Seminar of Jacques Lacan, Book II: The Ego in Freud's Theory and in the Technique of Psychoanalysis, 1954–1955*, ed. Jacques-Alain Miller, trans. Sylvana Tomaselli. Cambridge: Cambridge University Press.
——, 1992: *The Ethics of Psychoanalysis, 1959–1960: The Seminar of Jacques Lacan, Book VII*, ed. Jacques-Alain Miller, trans. Dennis Porter. London: Routledge.
——, 1993: *The Psychoses: The Seminar of Jacques Lacan, Book III, 1955–1956*, ed. Jacques-Alain Miller, trans. Russell Grigg. London: Routledge.
——, 1998: *On Feminine Sexuality, The Limits of Love and Knowledge: Encore 1972–1973* (Seminar of Jacques Lacan 20), ed. Jacques-Alain Miller, trans. Bruce Fink. New York and London: Norton.
——, 2006: *Écrits: The First Complete Edition in English*, trans. Bruce Fink with Héloïse Fink and Russell Grigg. New York and London: Norton.
Lakoff, George, and Mark Johnson, 1980: *Metaphors We Live By*. Chicago, Ill. and London: University of Chicago Press.
Lyotard, Jean-François, 1989: 'The Dream-Work Does Not Think', trans. Mary Lydon, in Andrew Benjamin (ed.), *The Lyotard Reader*. Oxford and Cambridge, Mass.: Blackwell, pp. 19–55.
Marcel, Gabriel, 1948: 'On the Ontological Mystery', in *The Philosophy of Existence*, trans. Manya Harari (Changing World 3). London: Harvill, pp. 1–31.
——, 1949: 'A Metaphysical Diary', in *Being and Having*, trans. Katherine Farrer. Westminster: Dacre, pp. 9–153.
——, 1952: *Metaphysical Journal*, trans. Bernard Wall. London: Rockliff.
Nietzsche, Friedrich, 1966: *Beyond Good and Evil: Prelude to a Philosophy of the Future*, trans. Walter Kaufmann. New York: Vintage.
Merleau-Ponty, Maurice, 1962: *Phenomenology of Perception*, trans. Colin Smith. London: Routledge.
——, 1968: *The Visible and the Invisible*, ed. Claude Lefort, trans. Alphonso Lingis. Evanston, Ill.: Northwestern University Press.

Peirce, Charles Sanders, 1932: 'Speculative Grammar', in *Collected Papers of Charles Sanders Peirce II: Elements of Logic*, ed. Charles Hartshorne and Paul Weiss. Cambridge, Mass.: Harvard University Press, pp. 127–73.

Phillips, John, 2001: *Sade: The Libertine Novels*. London and Sterling: Pluto.

Plato, 1951: *The Symposium*, trans. Walter Hamilton. Harmondsworth: Penguin.

Reagan, Charles E., 1996: *Paul Ricoeur: His Life and Work*. Chicago, Ill. and London: University of Chicago Press.

Ricoeur, Paul, 1947: *Gabriel Marcel et Karl Jaspers: Philosophie du mystère et philosophie du paradoxe*. Paris: Temps Présent.

——, 1965: *History and Truth*, trans. Charles A. Kelbley. Evanston, Ill.: Northwestern University Press.

——, 1966: *Freedom and Nature: The Voluntary and the Involuntary*, trans. Erazim V. Kohák. Evanston, Ill.: Northwestern University Press.

——, 1967a: *Husserl: An Analysis of his Philosophy*, trans. Edward G. Ballard and Lester E. Embree. Evanston, Ill.: Northwestern University Press.

——, 1967b: *Fallible Man*, trans. Charles Kelbley. Chicago, Ill.: Regnery.

——, 1969: *The Symbolism of Evil*, trans. Emerson Buchanan. Boston, Mass.: Beacon.

——, 1970: *Freud and Philosophy: An Essay on Interpretation*, trans. Denis Savage. New Haven, Conn. and London: Yale University Press.

——, 1981: 'The Question of Proof in Freud's Psychoanalytic Writings', in *Hermeneutics and the Human Sciences*, trans. and ed. John B. Thompson. Cambridge: Cambridge University Press, pp. 247–73.

——, 1989: *The Conflict of Interpretations: Essays in Hermeneutics*, ed. Don Ihde. London: Athlone.

——, 1991: *From Text to Action: Essays in Hermeneutics II*, trans. Kathleen Blamey and John B. Thompson. London: Athlone.

——, 1992: *Oneself as Another*, trans. Kathleen Blamey. Chicago, Ill. and London: University of Chicago Press.

——, 1995a: 'Intellectual Autobiography', trans. Kathleen Blamey, in Lewis Edwin Hahn (ed.), *The Philosophy of Paul Ricoeur*. Chicago, Ill.: Open Court, pp. 3–51.

——, 1995b: 'Ethical and Theological Considerations on the Golden Rule', in *Figuring the Sacred: Religion, Narrative, and Imagination*, trans. David Pellauer, ed. Mark I. Wallace. Minneapolis, Minn.: Fortress.

——, 1996a: 'Fragility and Responsibility', trans. Elisabeth Iwanowski, in Richard Kearney (ed.), *Paul Ricoeur: The Hermeneutics of Action*. London: Sage, pp. 15–22.

——, 1996b: 'Love and Justice', trans. David Pellauer, in Richard Kearney (ed.), *Paul Ricoeur: The Hermeneutics of Action*. London: Sage, pp. 23–39.

——, 1998: *Critique and Conviction: Conversations with François Azouvi and Marc de Launay*, trans. Kathleen Blamey. Cambridge: Polity.

——, 2000: *The Just*, trans. David Pellauer. Chicago, Ill. and London: University of Chicago Press.
——, 2003: *The Rule of Metaphor: The Creation of Meaning in Language*, trans. Robert Czerny with Kathleen McLaughlin and John Costello. London and New York: Routledge.
——, 2004: *Memory, History, Forgetting*, trans. Kathleen Blamey and David Pellauer. Chicago, Ill. and London: University of Chicago Press.
Roudinesco, Elisabeth, 1990: *Jacques Lacan & Co.: A History of Psychoanalysis in France, 1925–1985*, trans. Jeffrey Mehlman. London: Free Association.
——, 1997: *Jacques Lacan: An Outline of a Life and a History of a System of Thought*, trans. Barbara Bray. Cambridge: Polity.
Sade, Donatien-Alphonse-François, Marquis de, 1965: *Philosophy in the Bedroom*, in *Justine, Philosophy in the Bedroom and Other Writings*, trans. Richard Seaver and Austryn Wainhouse. London: Arrow.
Saussure, F. de, 1983: *Course in General Linguistics*, ed. Charles Bally, Albert Sechehaye, and Albert Riedlinger, trans. Roy Harris. London: Duckworth.
Simms, Karl, 2003: *Paul Ricoeur*. London and New York: Routledge.
Smith, Adam, 2002: *The Theory of Moral Sentiments*, ed. Knud Haakonssen. Cambridge: Cambridge University Press.
Tort, Michel, 1966: '*De l'interprétation* ou la machine herméneutique', in *Les Temps Modernes* 237, 1461–93, and 238, 1629–52.
von Frisch, Karl, 1994: *The Dance Language and Orientation of Bees*, trans. Leigh E. Chadwick. Cambridge, Mass.: Harvard University Press.
Wittgenstein, Ludwig, 1966: 'Conversations on Freud', in *Lectures & Conversations on Aesthetics, Psychology and Religious Belief*, ed. Cyril Barrett. Oxford: Blackwell, pp. 41–52.
Žižek, Slavoj, 1989: *The Sublime Object of Ideology*. London and New York: Verso.
——, 1998a: 'Introduction: Cogito as a Shibboleth', in Slavoj Žižek (ed.), *Cogito and the Unconscious* (Sic 2). Durham and London: Duke University Press, 1–8.
——, 1998b: 'The Cartesian Subject versus the Cartesian Theatre', in Slavoj Žižek (ed.), *Cogito and the Unconscious* (Sic 2). Durham, NC and London: Duke University Press, pp. 247–74.
——, 1999a: *The Ticklish Subject: The Absent Centre of Political Ontology*. London and New York: Verso.
——, 1999b: 'Kant with (or against) Sade', in Elizabeth Wright and Edmond Wright (eds), *The Žižek Reader*. Oxford and Malden, Mass.: Blackwell, pp. 283–301.
Zupančič, Alenka, 1998: 'The Subject of the Law', in Slavoj Žižek (ed.), *Cogito and the Unconscious* (Sic 2). Durham, NC and London: Duke University Press, pp. 41–73.
——, 2000: *Ethics of the Real: Kant, Lacan*. London and New York: Verso.

Index